PRECIOUS MOTHER,

PRECIOUS CROWN

PRECIOUS MOTHER, PRECIOUS CROWN

The Life and Mission

of

Elizabeth Taylor Watkins

F. Calvin Parker

Library of Congress Catalog Card Number 96-71656

Parker, F. Calvin (Franklin Calvin), 1926-
    Precious mother, precious crown: the life and mission of
Elizabeth Taylor Watkins.

Includes bibliographical references and index.
1. Watkins, Elizabeth Taylor, 1900-1983. 2. Missionaries—Japan
—Biography. 3. Missionaries—United States—Biography

ISBN Number 1-57087-343-7

Professional Press
Chapel Hill, NC 27515-4371

Manufactured in the United States of America
01 00 99 98 97 96   10 9 8 7 6 5 4 3 2 1

Contents

Illustrations

Other illustrations

Front cover: Elizabeth in Japan in 1981. Southside Baptist Church,
Spartanburg, S.C.
Back cover: Scroll presented to Elizabeth by the Japanese
government. Southside Baptist Church, Spartanburg

Preface

ELIZABETH TAYLOR WATKINS (1900–1983) was one of my missionary colleagues in Japan until her mandatory retirement in 1970. We saw each other at more conferences and conventions than I could possibly recall, and at one of the annual meetings of our Southern Baptist Mission, the two of us, neither one musical, sang a giddy duet to indulge the stunt-night crowd. My wife and I stayed in Elizabeth's home a time or two, and she visited in ours. She sent us birthday cards faithfully, even in her declining years, and always with a thoughtful note attached.

But I knew very little about Elizabeth's earlier life until after her death, when I was writing *The Southern Baptist Mission in Japan, 1889–1989*. That assignment gave me access to missionary records and correspondence at the Foreign Mission Board (now the International Mission Board) in Richmond, Virginia, where I discovered that Elizabeth's files, highly revealing in themselves, were supplemented with an autobiography she had written at the Board's request. The 292-page manuscript, completed on her eightieth birthday, ushered me into the holy of holies of a life as fascinating as it was dedicated. For the first time I realized that Elizabeth's spiritual pilgrimage had led through incredibly jagged terrain.

Hers was a story that screamed to be told. I used bits of it in my centennial history but hoped someday to see the autobiography itself in print. "I'd like to have parts made into a book," Elizabeth had written. "but don't know how to go about it." That was challenge enough for me to undertake the necessary editing when time permitted.

The autobiography, as is typical of this genre, is a reconstruction of her life, a reinventing of herself for public display. It is a selective recollection and imaginative interpretation of past events. As editor, I set out to verify Elizabeth's statements and provide an objective frame of reference for understanding the work as a whole.

The project took me to Salt Lake City, where the subject had rounded out her years. There the Reverend Lavoid Robertson presented me with two pasteboard boxes filled with Elizabeth's personal correspondence and other papers that had been in his custody since her death. The material was helter-skelter. Many letters were undated, and the contents of those nestled in envelopes did not necessarily match the postmark date. Numerous leaves were scattered or missing. Sorting these papers was tedious work, but reading them lifted me into a state of ecstasy not unlike that of my Old Testament professor in the late 1940s who was working through the newly discovered Dead Sea Scrolls. The papers were a gold mine.

Among the letters Elizabeth preserved are more than two hundred addressed to her mother Lizzie. The earliest was written when she was eight and the latest when she was forty-one, four years before Lizzie's death. Besides the letters—often ten to twenty pages in length—there are journals (including Lizzie's), diary fragments, and New Year's resolutions, along with financial, medical, and educational records. These documents will be catalogued as the Elizabeth Watkins Papers at the Southern Baptist Historical Library and Archives, Nashville, Tennessee.

Rereading Elizabeth's autobiography in the light of these documents, I was pleased to learn that her late-in-life portrait of herself was consistent in essence with her earlier self-portraits. To whatever extent she reinvented herself, she did so not at seventy-nine but at twenty-nine, when she wrote out a testimony—a self-introduction—for her fellow missionaries in Japan. There is no observable change in the spiritual lens through which she observed her life at these two points fifty years apart.

While affirming the basic integrity of the autobiography, the earlier documents also indicate that it is not always accurate. There are places where time spans are altered, separate events confounded, and descriptions embellished—not intentionally, but because long-term recollections tend to blur. When it became evident that Elizabeth had written up her life without consulting the bulk of her own correspondence, I decided to scuttle the autobiography as the main conveyance of her story.

Thus the project turned into a biography, one that is based primarily on sources contemporary with the events they describe, on spontaneous writings as fresh as this morning's mail. I have also drawn from the autobiography, albeit cautiously and sparingly, because it offers some plausible data not available elsewhere.

The material on Elizabeth turned out to be far more voluminous than I had imagined, forcing me to be selective to the point of near despair. It has been my goal to be as fair and objective as is possible for one writing about an esteemed colleague. The book reveals her human frailties and failures, her character flaws and errors of judgment. But it accepts her motives as honest, her bedrock faith as sincere. I have striven for realism and balance within the constraints of an evangelical Christian milieu.

Elizabeth is to be commended for not trashing her personal papers. By storing them, even in a state of disorder, she made possible a reasonably full and accurate account of her life. Still, I wish I had been more inquisitive during the nineteen years we were colleagues in Japan. I wish I had begun this project while she was available for interviews. There are a thousand questions I could have asked.

Many of Elizabeth's relatives, coworkers, and friends helped fill this gap by kindly sharing their recollections of one who made an indelible mark on their lives. Some asked not to be quoted directly or identified with specific contributions, and I have honored their requests. I gladly acknowledge my indebtedness to the following:

†Nina Belle Alley
Curtis and Mary Lee Askew
Judy Dawn Barking
Lolita Hannah Bissell
†Horace L. Bomar
Melvin Bradshaw
Ralph and Gena Calcote
†Coleman D. Clarke
Mary Neal Clarke
Bea Conrad
Luther and Louise Copeland
Helen B. Davis

Harriet S. Downey
Mary Ellen Dozier
B. P. (Bill) and Rebekah Sue Emanuel
Wayne and Mary Lou Emanuel
Jean Brownell Falck
Elizabeth Garrott
Martha Hagood
Lenora Hudson
Emma Hyatt
Kakiwa Inui
Beryle and Elouise Lovelace
Ramona Mercer
Marion and Thelma Moorhead
†Toraji Murakami
Ichirō Odori
Toshio Odori
Lou S. Otts
Harriett Parker
Lavoid and Geneva Robertson
Robert C. and Helen Sherer
Frances Talley
James and Darleene Watters
Darwin and Anita Welsh
Don and Judy West.

Finally, I want to express appreciation to those who in other ways enabled this work. Bill Sumners of the Southern Baptist Historical Library and Archives rendered valuable service, as did staff personnel in many other libraries, courthouses, and administrative offices. At the Foreign (now International) Mission Board, Edith Jeter facilitated my research in the archives, and Victoria Bleich made available many of the photographs that enhance this book. Lolita Hannah Bissell, Fern Buchanan, Mikio Hirosawa, Lavoid Robertson, and Don and Judy West also provided illustrations (see list on page vii). Joe Chris Robertson helped me interpret some photographs. Pauline Binkley Cheek, Marion and Thelma Moorhead, and my wife Harriett reviewed the full manuscript. Bill and Rebekah Sue Emanuel, Ramona Mercer, Fred S.

and Jeannette Rolater, Robert C. and Helen Sherer, Frances Talley, and Patsy Wolfe kindly read portions. The contributions of the above are enormous, but I alone am responsible for the flaws that remain.

A brief explanation of some stylistic matters may be helpful. To reduce the number of endnotes, I occasionally have grouped in a single note all the citations within a paragraph. Direct quotations are cited first, in the order of their appearance in the paragraph. The endnotes only indicate sources; they do not amplify the discussion in the text.

As a hedge against ambiguity, I have capitalized the initial letter of three oft-used terms in order to convey a particular meaning. "Convention" refers to the Southern Baptist Convention or the Japan Baptist Convention as an organization and not a general meeting of delegates; "Board" refers to the Foreign (now International) Mission Board of the Southern Baptist Convention; and "Mission" refers to the Board's Japan Mission, the organization of Southern Baptist missionaries in Japan. I have made an exception in the compound "mission meeting," the common designation of an annual or other general session of the Mission.

Scripture quotations are taken from the King James Version, in keeping with Elizabeth's own practice.

Note on Japanese Terms

Japanese personal names are given in the Western order of surname last.

Japanese vowels and diphthongs are pronounced approximately as follows:

> *a* as in f*a*ther
> *e* as in r*e*d
> *i* as in pol*i*ce
> *o* as in b*o*ne
> *u* as in r*u*le
> *ai* as in *ai*sle
> *ei* as in *ei*ght

A macron over a vowel, as in Kōbe and Kyūshū, indicates that the vowel's pronunciation is prolonged. In the text I have omitted the macrons from the familiar name Tokyo (pronounced Tōkyō). Japanese consonants are generally pronounced as in English. The doubling of a consonant, as in Beppu, indicates a protraction of its sound.

Introduction

THE FOREIGN MISSION BOARD
of the Southern Baptist Convention

JAMES D. BELOTE
SECRETARY FOR EAST ASIA

BAKER J. CAUTHEN, EXECUTIVE SECRETARY
3806 MONUMENT AVENUE • P. O. BOX 6597 • RICHMOND, VIRGINIA 23230

April 16, 1970

Miss Elizabeth T. Watkins
Matsukage, Shogakko Mae, Hirose 6
Yawatahama Shi, Japan

Dear Miss Watkins:

At its semiannual meeting held yesterday in Richmond, Virginia, the Foreign Mission Board took the following action:

"That Miss Elizabeth T. Watkins (Japan Mission) be placed on emeritus status as of April 30, 1970, and that a letter of appreciation be sent to her for her many years of service in Japan."

IT WAS EARLY SPRING IN JAPAN, when pink and pinkish-white cherry blossoms liven up the countryside, relieve the uniform drabness of cities, and add a sparkle to millions of seal-brown, overworked eyes. For the score of Southern Baptist missionaries in the Central Japan Station, it was the week for their first station meeting of 1970. They converged on the city of Kōbe, arriving by ferry from Shikoku across the picturesque Inland Sea or by train from Hiroshima, Nagoya, and points between. Clean, compact taxis with automatic doors delivered them to a Western-style duplex east of downtown. This was the residence afterwards converted to Kōbe Friendship House, whose religious and social ministries would be appreciated most in the somber weeks following the Great Hanshin Earthquake of 1995 that left more than six thousand dead.

In their three-day meeting a quarter-century before the devastating quake, the Central Japan missionaries garnished the humdrum business sessions with a blend of fun, fellowship, and inspiration. Their feet nestled in soft slippers, they sang familiar hymns in their native tongue and joked without restraint. A visiting couple, former U.S. Congressman O. K. Armstrong and journalist Marjorie Moore Armstrong, brought greetings from the States, adding a pleasant whiff of home. But the high point of the meeting was a farewell address by the station's senior member, Elizabeth Watkins. Her address survives on audiotape.[1]

Chairman Dewey Mercer introduced the speaker. "Three or four years ago," he said, "Elizabeth paid me one of the nicest compliments I have ever received. She was talking to Ramona about me, and she referred to me as 'our husband.'" The audience laughed knowingly. For two decades the Mercers and Elizabeth had been the only Southern Baptist missionaries on Shikoku, the smallest of Japan's four main islands. The Mercers had seen her hair turn white, her shoulders stoop, her wrinkles deepen.

"On April 21, 1970," Dewey continued, "Elizabeth will be seventy years young. At that age she has no choice but to leave Japan and retire from the Foreign Mission Board. But knowing Elizabeth as I do, she will not retire from mission work. She never will."

Dewey knew her as well as the precious gems in his rock collection. True to her timeless calling, Elizabeth was to spend the rest of her life serving Orientals and international students in Utah and other western states. Dewey was less accurate, however, in saying she had no choice but to leave Japan at the age of seventy. Adept at circumventing rules and regulations, Elizabeth would stay an extra three months.

The veteran with a mind of her own first came to Japan in 1929 as a "tentmaker" and supported herself by teaching English. The Southern Baptist Foreign Mission Board (now International Mission Board) had turned her down repeatedly, citing a shortage of funds. In the prosperous era following World War II, when it was debt-free and hence less selective, the Board appointed Elizabeth on the field even though she was forty-eight, well past the formal age limit of thirty-five. Given to headstrongness and firmly set in her ways, the latecomer never made the transition from a freelance guided by instinct to a team member bound by common rules. When she put her mind to a task, she was unstoppable, like a runaway freight train going downhill.

Elizabeth was aware that her freewheeling ways annoyed and sometimes enraged her missionary and Japanese colleagues. One pastor, calling her a "senseless old woman," demanded her expulsion from Shikoku.[2] But like a cornered cat with her back arched, she managed to keep her attackers at bay. Besides her detractors, Elizabeth had a corps of loyal supporters. "I know a great many missionaries," wrote Katsuji Sugimoto, a sometime teaching colleague and governor of Fukuoka Prefecture, "but Miss Watkins is unique in the way she has renounced the comforts of life and identified with the lower classes, sharing her all with poor and needy Japanese. If anyone is truly charitable and worthy of praise, she is."[3]

Elizabeth was frugal by instinct, having drunk the tears of poverty in her teens. Her philosophy was the Congregationalist motto, "Make it do, use it up, do without."[4] She never owned or drove a car. During her furloughs in the States, her "white-glove cousins" sometimes waited awkwardly in bus stations for the quizzical old maid who thought air travel a waste of God's money.[5] Even so, the cousins admired her religious commitment and showed her more than a dollop of respect. One praised her as "an exceptionally hot-hearted Christian and tireless worker."[6]

Though average in grace and poise, Elizabeth clearly excelled as teacher, social worker, and church planter. She had little patience with mediocre efforts. Lois Carter, one of her students during her year as an instructor at Converse College, recalled having to learn the "I am" sayings of Jesus in the Gospel of John. On a test, Lois named all the sayings but one. Elizabeth shocked her with an F, explaining, "You didn't do your best. From now on, always do your best."[7]

"Elizabeth Watkins must have been born in high gear," a coworker said.[8] Her thin and delicate five-foot five-inch frame notwithstanding, she was hyperactive, ever pursuing a killer schedule, always caught up in a whirlwind of good works. There were temporary setbacks—times of illness or self-doubt or frustration—but she would rebound with a fresh burst of manic energy, with astonishing pluck and grit.

This tenacious woman was also intense. She could be so engrossed in a table conversation that she would bring her food-laden fork toward her mouth and miss the target. Whoever or whatever had her attention was all-important at the moment. Her capacity to focus on individuals was outstanding. And her curiosity was insatiable; she had to know everything about her friends and kinfolk, among them the thirty-five first cousins on her mother's side.

Although an extrovert—"I like people" was her explanation for years of service as a hospital volunteer[9]—Elizabeth was intuitive and spiritually focused. She was convinced that every true Christian has a direct pipeline to God. Hers she put to use without hesitation, and if God spoke first with timely advice or a premonition, it was no surprise. When a telegram reported the death of an aunt who had helped raise her, Elizabeth calmly said, "I already knew it."[10]

Missionary Helen Sherer recalls that Elizabeth "misplaced a treasured fountain pen, while we were crossing the ocean together from California to Japan. She went to her cabin to pray about it, then came out and went straight to the spot to reclaim her pen. As a harried young mother of four, I was very impressed."[11]

Elizabeth's faith was simple, her theology conservative, and her sense of mission as unshakable as her belief in heaven and hell. A Japanese pastor dubbed her a "fireball evangelist,"[12] and among her heroes were evangelists R. A. Torrey and Mordecai Ham. While she was a student at Columbia University, her pastor was I. M. Haldeman, archfoe of worldliness, modernism, and Harry Emerson Fosdick. Elizabeth adored Haldeman. Later she would have spent a year at Bob Jones University, only thirty miles from her home in South Carolina, had not friends warned her that if she attended this fundamentalist school, "our Southern Baptist churches would not accept me."[13]

Even so, Elizabeth never made orthodoxy a test of friendship. Though dogmatic, sometimes calling the less orthodox "unsaved," she was not as belligerent as, say, Bertha Smith, a long-lived China missionary who helped Elizabeth start one of the churches on Shikoku. Elizabeth "accepted advice even from young people," said Hiroko

Tsuda, a coworker. "She acknowledged her faults and apologized sincerely."[14]

Her chief failings were the temper tantrums that persisted from childhood, when her nickname was Spitfire. Elizabeth called herself, only half impishly, "a red-headed, hot-tempered woman." She was like live coals, warming everything around with her glow but sparking and sizzling when provoked. She could scorch the unwary who riled her.[15]

"Elizabeth is one of the most colorful persons ever to serve in foreign missions," summed up George H. Hays, the Foreign Mission Board's East Asia director.[16] She was never dull, but always distinctive and animated, a compelling presence. Her sense of humor, like that of many other eccentrics, was legendary. During stunt night at the annual meetings of the Japan Baptist Mission, her drollery would bring down the house.

Even her talks on serious occasions were usually folksy, a seamless blend of wit and wisdom that would bring gales of laughter interspersed with calms of tingling awe. So when she rose to give her valedictory to the Central Japan Station, a hush fell over the room. The members knew they were in for a treat.

Single Life in Japan

"The first thing I want to do," Elizabeth said, "is have Pete sing the chorus of the song 'He Will Keep His Promise to Me.'" The slur in her speech, a lifelong trait, merely invited rapt attention to her words.

"The reason she asked *me* to sing it," A. L. (Pete) Gillespie responded, "is that it is so old, none of the rest of you know it." At fifty-eight, Pete was the senior missionary after Elizabeth. The two had worked together in Kokura amidst the rubble of World War II, and he had later sung and preached in Elizabeth's church meetings on Shikoku. In his sonorous baritone voice, Pete belted out the chorus:

He will keep his promise to me,
All the way with me he will go.

He has never broken, any promise spoken,
He will keep his promise, I know.

"The reason I wanted this sung," Elizabeth explained, "is that I wanted to talk to you about how God has always kept his promises to me. But unfortunately, I was given the subject of 'Single Life in Japan.' I have to stick to this subject." Her horn-rims could not hide the impish look in her hazel-brown eyes, nor could her firmly set jaw avoid an ostensible shift from gravity to gaiety. Her words came fast:

The poet said, "It is better to have loved and lost than never to have loved at all." I don't believe it. I never have. You will understand when I tell you about my would-have-been husband. It's a long story that goes back about fifty years to my courting days. So put on your sleeping togs and get ready to sit up all night.

My courting days followed the First World War, which left many girls without husbands. Since I did not snare a man, it occurred to me that my would-have-been husband must have died in the war. So when people asked me about my husband, as they often did, especially after I came to Japan, I used that as my excuse. I would say, "Well, I reckon he was killed in the war." . . .

Being single in Japan has both advantages and disadvantages. It is sometimes good and sometimes bad. The worst time is at mission meeting. I see these fine-looking men all dolled up with their hair oil on. They have their wives by their sides, and they parade into the meeting, on Sundays especially, and each one sits by his wife. I look around and I say, "Where is mine?" I feel sort of embarrassed at first, and self-conscious, and jealous, and full of self-pity, because I don't see anybody I can sit with. And then I look around again and see somebody's funny-looking husband, and I say, "Huh! I'm glad he's not mine!" That comforts me. I'm not jealous anymore, and I'm willing to sit by myself or with some of the other pitiful-looking single women. So through the years I've learned to live with being single, even at mission meeting.

The next worst time for being single is when you have a dress with a zipper in the back. You just don't have anybody to zip you up. Then there are times when something mechanical goes wrong in the house—a leaky faucet, for instance. And there is income tax time, with those forms to fill out that I don't understand. I think, "Oh, it would be good to have a husband. These women who do have husbands, how fortunate they are."

There are people who ask about my husband, as I said, and there are also curiosity cats who ask me about my children. They ask, "Whose mother are you?" I say, "I'm not married yet." I've had people to say, "Please tell us at what age you expect to marry."

In the Confucian culture that pervaded Japan, marriage was the norm, childbearing a duty. It was customary to address any mature woman as *okusan* (housewife). Most people frowned on single women as odd if not freakish, and at best incomplete. Foreigners were only partially exempt from this reproach.

In prewar Japan, Elizabeth noted, she was sometimes mistaken for the mother of Maxfield Garrott, a single missionary ten years her junior. Both were teaching at Seinan Gakuin, the Baptist boys' school in Fukuoka. Even police officers, more intrusive than their postwar successors, would stop Elizabeth on the street and enquire whether she was Garrott's mother. "I must have looked motherly," she quipped.

Yet she was also mistaken for a man. "I taught only boys," Elizabeth continued, "and got to be very mannish in my dress. I wore blouses with collars and a kind of tie, and I wore a long overcoat. When I walked down the street, I would hear people discussing me. They would say, 'It's a man. No, it's a woman. I think it's a man. No, it's a woman.' They couldn't figure out which I was."

Several of those present had seen the musical spectaculars at the four-thousand-seat opera house in Takarazuka, some twelve miles away. The opera house featured lavish sets and moving stages, svelte dancers and gorgeous costumes, stirring songs and throbbing drama. Most appealing, perhaps, its four hundred performers were all women, in sharp contrast to Japan's all-male Noh and Kabuki theaters. Some were male impersonators widely acclaimed for their courtly skills.

Elizabeth could identify with these "beauties in men's clothing." She had taken male parts in student plays at Judson College in Alabama and the Woman's Missionary Union Training School in Kentucky. Her masculine jaw and flexible features had served her well in these roles. Then she had taken a puckish delight in befuddling her spectators on the streets of Fukuoka. Had circumstances dictated, Elizabeth would have disguised herself as a man in order to carry out a dangerous mission, as did Lottie Moon in China.[17]

But spunk had its limits in the chauvinistic culture of prewar Japan. As Elizabeth pointed out, there was no substitute for the identification that a husband provided for a woman. She further cited the danger of having male visitors in her home, even for Bible classes, and the demand for constant vigilance to forestall gossip. A churlish missionary once accused her, Elizabeth recalled, of "having men in my house all hours of the night."

But despite the proprieties imposed on single women, marriage might have been worse than spinsterhood. "If I had had a husband," she declared tongue in cheek, "he would have died of starvation or indigestion. If I had had children, I would have brought out the worst in them. Or they would have been like their father—no good." Yet she had often quoted from Genesis, "It is not good that the man should be alone," quickly adding, "nor the woman." By the age of thirteen she had planned her family and named the four or five children she expected to have. The Sherers recall that when asked why she was leaving Japan, Elizabeth would reply with a straight face, "Because I never found a Japanese man who would marry me."[18]

In her heart of hearts, Elizabeth was glad she had never vowed away her life to a male. When asked if she had ever been in love, she could say with Lottie Moon, "Yes, but God had first claim on my life."[19] She had settled the matter at the age of twenty-one, after breaking up with a blind seminary student, Sam Lawton. Elizabeth found fulfillment, she said, in the words of Isaiah 54:5: "For thy Maker is thine husband." She cherished the freedom to talk audibly to God in her home and "make love to him out loud." This intimate relationship, she believed, made her fruitful. Indeed, her spiritual offspring were numerous, and some called her Mama.

Promises That Were Kept

In the latter part of her speech to the Central Japan Station, Elizabeth turned to the theme she preferred: How God kept all his promises recorded in the Bible, especially the promise to supply her every need if she would do his bidding. But having used up her time already, she dealt with the theme only briefly. Shortly afterwards she provided a fuller account that was mimeographed and sent to all members of the Mission.[20] Then a decade later, when she wrote her autobiography, she titled it "How God Kept His Promises to a Teenager."[21]

God provided her with the means, Elizabeth testified repeatedly, to obtain the requisite education for a missionary career. God enabled her to gain valuable experience working for the Home Mission Board (now the North American Mission Board), the Woman's Missionary Union of Oklahoma, and the International Grenfell Mission in Newfoundland. He never failed to meet her needs while she was a freelance in Japan.

One of her favorite scriptures was Matthew 19:29: "And every one that hath forsaken houses, or brethren, or sisters, or father, or mother, or wife, or children, or lands, for my name's sake, shall receive an hundredfold, and shall inherit everlasting life." After one Christmas season she claimed to have received a hundred presents, a hundred cards, and two hundred dollars in Christmas money. "Everything worked out in hundreds," she said, "another experience of Christ keeping his promise."[22]

Besides praising a God who never breaks his Word, Elizabeth often paid tribute to the person most responsible for her sturdy faith. "My mother gave me to God for his service before I was born," she wrote. "Later, as the leader of my Sunbeam Band [for children under the age of nine], she gave me my first interest in foreign missions."[23]

Later still, the mother—Lizzie Watkins—lived and worked with her daughter in Fukuoka and in a wartime camp for Japanese-Americans forcibly removed from their homes on the West Coast. She practiced what she taught. During the years they were apart, these two "women on mission" exchanged letters frequently, usually every week. The salutation Elizabeth used most often was "Precious Mother."

Elizabeth thought of her faithful God and her precious mother when, four days before leaving Japan, she stood awkwardly in front of a battery of TV and flash cameras. She was being honored by the government for her forty-one years as a "maidservant" to the Japanese people. Through a proxy, Emperor Hirohito (posthumously known as Emperor Shōwa) conferred on Elizabeth Taylor Watkins the Fifth Class Order of the Precious Crown.[24]

It is unlikely that the slight American woman had anticipated that "dazing and dazzling occasion."[25] It is more doubtful that anyone who knew her as little Spitfire could have foreseen this imperial award. A mischievous child, rebellious at home and at church, she was fatherless at nine and filled with dread at eleven, when her mother suffered a temporary mental breakdown. Her psychic scars were deep. They could have been debilitating had not her religious faith been deeper still.

Like Amy Carmichael, Mother Teresa, and thousands of other single women missionaries who have left an indelible mark on peoples around the world, Elizabeth Taylor Watkins was committed to a role in life's drama that she accepted as from God. She was resolved to fulfill this role whatever the cost in sorrow and pain. So despite the many obstacles strewn on the course of her pilgrimage, Elizabeth persevered. She blazed a trail of adventure well worth pursuing from its "Precious Mother" origin to its "Precious Crown" climax and beyond.

1

Spitfire in Spartanburg

---

june 11 1908

GENERAL HEADQUARTERS
SPARTANBURG, S. C.,_____190___

My Dear Mother
   I thank you and thank you
and thank you for making
that pretty dress and take so
much trouble to make it.
                                   I wish
you all had more money so you
and father could do what you
wanted to do
        from your dear little 8 year
old girl Elizabeth

NO ONE INFLUENCED Elizabeth Watkins more than her mother Lizzie. Her father Eddie was a towering figure in her childhood, but even if he had not died when Elizabeth was nine, his imprint on her life would have paled beside Lizzie's. "Precious Mother" and her only daughter were knit together heart and soul.

Elizabeth Cleveland Bomar, called Lizzie, was born in Spartanburg, South Carolina, February 7, 1866. She was the fifth of ten children born to John Earle Bomar and Louisa N. Bomar. Lizzie's parents, like Franklin and Eleanor Roosevelt, were distant cousins with the same surname. Both their families were predominantly Baptist, a denomination so entrenched in the state that it was virtually the established church. At the turn of the century, in both Spartanburg County and South Carolina as a whole, Baptists outnumbered adherents of all other denominations combined.[1]

Lizzie's father was a Civil War veteran customarily addressed as Major Bomar. As versatile as he was prominent, John Earle served at various times as district judge, editor of the *Carolina Spartan*, member of the state legislature, and moderator of the local Baptist association. His wife Louisa, barely eighteen when they married at her father's plantation home three miles south of Spartanburg, devoted herself to the nurture and care of their brood. The tenth child died early, but the other nine grew up and married and produced thirty-eight offspring, greatly enlarging the clan and swelling its pride.[2]

John Earle and Louisa took their children to Spartanburg's First Baptist Church and gave them religious training at home as well. Their piety bore fruit. Three of five sons—Edward, Paul, and John—became doctors of divinity in charge of prestigious churches. Another son, Horace, walked in his father's footsteps as a public-spirited lawyer, lifetime deacon, and Baptist college trustee.[3]

Lizzie, baptized at thirteen years of age, was likewise devoted to her church. She was one of twenty-four charter members of the "Young Ladies' Missionary Union of the Baptist Congregation of Spartanburg, S.C.," organized in January 1884. As chairman of the committee on missionary intelligence, she read avidly in the field, giving priority to the monthly *Heathen Helper*.[4]

Lizzie attended two Baptists schools. The first was the Cooper-Limestone Institute for Young Ladies (later called Limestone College), which was owned by the Spartanburg Baptist Association. Lizzie's father was a trustee. The second school was the Richmond Female Institute, which under a different name later merged with Westhampton College of the University of Richmond. Lizzie graduated from the Virginia school in 1887 with diplomas in English, English literature, and philosophy. She held in high esteem the trustee chairman who signed the diplomas: H. A. Tupper. A South Carolinian from a well-to-do family, Tupper was widely known among Baptists as corresponding secretary of the Foreign Mission Board.[5]

Returning to Spartanburg, Lizzie taught school two years, then resigned because of recurring illnesses. This left her free to substitute for other teachers, help her mother with housekeeping chores and entertainment, visit scattered relatives, and devote long hours to her church. She took on a Sunday School class of "factory boys" and, in February 1891, organized a Sunbeam Band for teaching missions to children. Her stature in the church grew yet more in 1895 when, still single, she was elected president of the Woman's Missionary Society.

Over the years Lizzie earned an array of certificates for Sunday School teachers' courses and Woman's Missionary Union study courses. These certificates she cherished no less than her Richmond diplomas.[6] Religious education was her lifelong pursuit.

Though religion was her chief passion, it was not all-consuming. Lizzie was remarked for her dashing beauty and style. She frequented concerts and other cultural events, loved games and costume parties, and even danced and played cards, though with discretion to avoid censure. Liquor she abhorred. Lizzie wore the white ribbon badge of the Woman's Christian Temperance Union even on her nightgown.

Lizzie's Courtship and Marriage

In the fall of 1890, Lizzie paid a month-long visit to her brother Paul and his wife Nannie in Camden, where Paul was pastor of the First Baptist Church. One day she accompanied Nannie to see off a friend at the depot, which bustled with travelers headed for Gala Week in Charleston with excursion tickets that would admit them free to several dazzling events.[7] By happenstance, it seemed, Lizzie was introduced to Edward Fleming Watkins, a twenty-nine-year-old bachelor. Eddie, as he was called, was little more than another name and face to cross her mind's horizon and sink into a boundless sea of names and faces. She already had several ardent admirers, though none had captured her love. But Eddie knew only that his prominent eyes fastened instinctively on the twenty-four-year-old single who bore his mother's first name.

His mother, Elizabeth Calvert Taylor Watkins, was a daughter of William Taylor, the Richland district (Columbia) sheriff known as "Black-eyed Billy."[8] His father, Dr. Benjamin Fleming Watkins, had practiced medicine in Columbia until the city was occupied by General Sherman. The doctor's office and home had both been destroyed in the fire that ensued, along with the family possessions except for the silverware a slave had cleverly buried. Benjamin and Elizabeth, with their children Mary and Eddie, had taken refuge in Newberry, then had settled in Camden, where their roots lay. The doctor had died of kidney trouble when Mary and Eddie were in their teens.[9]

One day Lizzie found herself in the home of the widowed Mrs. Watkins, then sixty-seven. She was merely accompanying Nannie on her usual rounds of church visitation, but Eddie reciprocated by calling on Lizzie twice. After her return to Spartanburg he kept in touch through frequent letters. Her replies were polite but restrained. "I don't know how to treat him," she told her journal. "I like him well enough for a friend, but I fear he wants more."[10]

More indeed! Eddie pursued her like a hound after its prey, visiting her home whenever he could, always bearing gifts. His Christmas gift in 1891 was a gold pen that she accepted as the "handsomest present" of all. When she was thrown from a buggy and ruptured a blood vessel, he seemed to share her pain throughout the weeks of recovery. Still, Lizzie would not give in. "Poor fellow," she said after one visit. "I fear he was little paid for his trouble in getting to see me."[11]

Eddie was resolute. In June 1892 he proposed by mail, asking that they get married as soon as possible. Lizzie said no; they could only be friends. "My entire heart must go with my hand," she wrote. "Sometimes I wish I could love him. God help me and direct me in this important step!"[12]

In the face of Eddie's dogged persistence, Lizzie came to believe that God was leading them together after all. He was strikingly different from her other suitors, among them Messers Crout, Matthews, and McCravy. The matter settled in her mind, one hurdle remained: stiff opposition from her father, who earlier had forbidden her to marry J. D. McCravy. In John Earle Bomar's gentry eyes, Lizzie was too good for an unsettled, small-scale merchant like Eddie, who lived in four different Carolina cities during the five-year courtship.

Unlike his parents, Eddie was not even a Baptist. He had joined the Presbyterians, who in South Carolina were outnumbered by Baptists ten to one. Baptized in 1866 in Camden's Bethesda Presbyterian Church, in the landmark building where the congregation still worships today, Eddie faithfully transferred his church membership each time he moved to another city.[13] So stern and puritanical was his religious demeanor that he seemed a mismatch for the more worldly Lizzie. John Earle must have respected Eddie's piety, but he frowned on a comedown marriage that would erode the Baptist solidarity of the Bomar clan.

That mattered not to Lizzie, and she was no less strong-minded than her parents. Marry she would, no matter what. Gracefully bowing to the inevitable, John Earle and Louisa hosted the wedding at their home on November 12, 1895. Lizzie's brother Edward, then pastor of the First Baptist Church in Aiken, led the couple in repeating their vows.[14]

Five days after the wedding, Bethesda Presbyterian Church signalled its approval by electing Eddie an elder. Upon returning from his honeymoon, however, Eddie declined the office. Perhaps he felt disqualified by having taken as wife a Baptist no less committed to her denomination than he was to his. Predictably, Lizzie promptly joined the Baptist church in Camden, though Paul and Nannie were no longer there, having moved to a pastorate in Kentucky. Each Sunday, husband and wife went their separate ways.[15]

From the outset, Lizzie felt at home in Camden. As a student of history and active DAR member, she was fascinated by Camden's role as a major British garrison in the Revolutionary War. As a year-round resident, she was pleased that it was now a "gentle town of kindly people"[16]—3,533 by census count, and more when the Northerners came down for the mild winter season. Springtime was heavenly, so gorgeous were the pink and white dogwoods and fragrant magnolias.

Lizzie's blissful life was jarred in January 1898 when her mother Louisa died of gallstones. Then on the first anniversary of Louisa's death, John Earle lingered too long at her snow-covered grave and came down with the grippe. Six days later he was gone.[17] Eddie's mother also died in 1899, completing the loss of both sets of parents.

Benefitting from the settlement of two estates, Eddie and Lizzie invested in a new brick building for his Camden Grocery House. The handsome structure on Main Street included space for rental offices on the second floor and a restaurant on the first.[18] When the year ended and a new century dawned, Eddie and Lizzie were not only financially secure but happily expectant, eagerly awaiting their first child.

Elizabeth Takes the Stage

On April 21, 1900, Lizzie gave birth to a five-pound girl so fragile-looking that her parents carried her about on a pillow. They named her Elizabeth Taylor Watkins after Eddie's mother, who had died during the pregnancy. It was a pleasant coincidence that the child's mother also was an Elizabeth—a queenly name that harks back to the mother of John the Baptist.

Bethesda Presbyterian Church joined in the celebration by electing the new father a deacon. This office Eddie accepted. The deacons had two main functions: caring for the poor and assisting the elders with business matters not considered routine. Probably because of the close connection between these two offices, Elizabeth would mistakenly remember her father as a Presbyterian elder.[19]

Two more children were born into the Watkins home at Camden: John Earle, in 1901, and Edward Fleming, in 1903. Both boys were healthy, handsome, and bright, with prominent ears like their father. Elizabeth took immense pride in her brothers, but she also contrived to outshine them, like Venus when configured with Jupiter and Mars in the evening sky.

In 1904 the family moved to Spartanburg, where Eddie joined W. Beverly Montgomery in the wholesale grocery trade. Montgomery was the husband of Lizzie's sister Mamie. Business was good in Spartanburg, a city strategically located in a cotton-growing region. Since 1870 the population had soared from one thousand to more than twelve thousand. The cotton mills bustled with their clackety-clack and whir, among them the South's largest with thirty-five thousand spindles under one roof. So prosperous was the burgeoning city that by 1908 it would claim "the best paved streets in the South."[20]

The Watkins family lived in a spacious two-story house built to their specifications at what is now 481 Irwin Avenue, about two miles south of downtown. As can still be seen today, a covered porch, punctuated with four double columns, wrapped around the front of the wood-frame structure. In back was a screened-in porch that stood thirteen steps above the ground because of the slope of the land.[21] One of the dearest memories Elizabeth had of her childhood was sleeping on that lofty porch in the summertime. She savored the heavenly feeling of lying in the tops of the water oaks and poplars that swayed round about.

Eddie was a no-nonsense merchant who dressed conservatively, wore a mustache, and slicked down his thinning hair. Lavishly protective of women and girls, as was expected of gentlemen in the old South, he often walked Elizabeth to the school gate and carried her books. Eddie also doted on his sister, Mary, making her a full member of the family. A tubercular, Mary was so nervous and frail that she was confined to the house most of the time.

Eddie and Lizzie had knelt together on their wedding night to dedicate their lives anew to the Lord, and it was their practice to work out disagreements prayerfully without a fuss. Every morning, before going to work, Eddie read the Bible to his household. They sat in a semicircle while he read, then knelt by their chairs while he prayed.

Families who prayed together and stayed together were not uncommon in those less complicated times. In this case, the family altar helped to atone for the cleavage each Sunday when Eddie attended the First Presbyterian Church and Lizzie the First Baptist Church. The children went with their mother. All three were baptized by immersion before the age of twelve.

Sunday meant more than going to church, for Eddie and Lizzie kept the Sabbath as strictly as old-time Puritans. Yard work, housecleaning, laundering, sewing, baking, washing of hair—all were taboo. No one used the tennis court that lay invitingly on the south side of the house. The children did not play with toys, look at the funny papers, or study their lessons for school. Sunday afternoons they spent mostly in memorizing Bible verses and taking quiet walks with their father in the nearby woods.

Yet no amount of parental devoutness and discipline could prevent outcroppings of what theologians call original sin. Elizabeth was jealous of her parents' love for one another, and resentful of their being together when she could not be present. She quarreled with her brothers, especially when they teased her. According to her autobiography, she was "willful, selfish, and stubborn." As if that were not confession enough, she described herself as "dictatorial, dogmatic, high-strung, nervous, afraid, self-conscious, self-pitying, easy to cry, highly sensitive, and easily angered."[22]

Elizabeth's late-in-life portrait—or reconstruction—of her childhood temperament is overly negative and harsh. Following in the train of John Bunyan and like-minded evangelicals who stressed human depravity, she had a penchant for confessing her sins with almost pathological candor. Lizzie had made similar confessions to her journal, such as "I am so selfish and so often cross and ugly."[23] But surely there were redeeming qualities that Elizabeth—and Lizzie before her—failed to disclose. For instance, a letter she wrote to Lizzie at the age of eight expresses a normal concern for both parents. "I wish you all had more money," Elizabeth said, "so you and Father could do what you wanted to do."[24]

Still, the darker side to her nature was no less real than her nickname Spitfire. Almost any affront she suffered could spark a tantrum. "I did not like to be disagreed with or to be criticized," Elizabeth wrote, "even to the extent of being told that my slip was showing."[25] She took pleasure in pestering others, especially Aunt Mary. When Mary was nursing a headache, little Spitfire would stand on the rockers of her chair and jiggle her up and down.

It fell to her mother to discipline the little miscreant. Lizzie did so reluctantly, sadly. Following a set ritual, she would take Elizabeth into the parlor, explain why her action was wrong, kneel down and pray for her, and then spank her with her hand or switch her with a twig from a peach tree in the yard. But even this measured approach to discipline was no cure for Elizabeth's defiant mood. "I thought that my temper was hot because my hair was red," she recalled.[26]

Spitfire rebelled against going to church, partly because it was a two-mile walk each way even with shortcuts through woods and yards. She sometimes went into Sunday School assembly crying out loud in protest. She would leave her own class and sit in Lizzie's class sniffling while her mother struggled to teach the lesson with composure. Elizabeth also resisted efforts to make her a Christian. When the pastor called, she would hide in a closet.

Her attitude began to change in 1908, after a band of volunteers from the First Baptist Church organized Southside Baptist Church only a few blocks from the Watkins home. Lizzie became one of 114 charter members of the new church, as did her brother John, who was moderator at the organizational meeting and the church's first Sunday School superintendent.[27]

The meeting place on Church Street was first a tent and then a frame tabernacle with a sawdust floor. Both tent and tabernacle were a comedown for Lizzie, who admired the Romanesque Revival architecture of First Baptist Church. In the downtown church's four-year-old sanctuary, built at a cost of $65,000, there were art glass windows given in memory of Lizzie's parents and grandparents. Still, she calmly made the adjustment to the new situation. Southside Church built a respectable $30,000 auditorium in 1911, and its proximity to the Watkins home compensated for its plainer style of construction.[28]

At the new location Elizabeth found Sunday School and church far less irksome than before. There was an air of excitement and expectancy among the people. Besides, going to Southside Baptist Church was as easy as walking to her elementary school just across the street. For some time, in fact, Elizabeth's Sunday School class met on the inside steps of the school. There Elizabeth learned to sing "G-O-O-D good, / G-O-O-D good, / We will try to be like Jesus, / G-O-O-D good."[29] She passionately wanted to be good, yet thought herself hopelessly wicked.

A One-Parent Family

In the spring of 1909 Elizabeth and her brothers came down with whooping cough. From them Eddie caught a "nurse's cough" that hung on for weeks after the children were well. Now in real estate rather than the grocery business, he got caught in the rain one day and developed pneumonia. The infection was too much for his weakened constitution. Eddie died at home June 1, 1909, aged forty-seven. The next day his pastor, the Reverend J. S. Watkins (no kin), conducted the funeral at the deceased's home and the interment service at Oakwood Cemetery.[30]

Lizzie's stalwart faith sustained her in grief. She replaced her husband as the leader of family worship at the breakfast table. When the children wanted to rush off to school, Lizzie would say, "No, I'll not give you a bite of breakfast until we have read God's word and prayed." She prayed for each child by name. It was mainly due to Lizzie's prayers, Elizabeth believed, that all three children consistently made good grades.[31]

At Sunday School one week Elizabeth had a substitute teacher who said, "I want to ask you children to do something. Take your Bible to bed with you. Put it by your pillow. As soon as you wake up, before you hear anyone's voice, let God speak to you through his Word as you read a little of it. And before you talk to anybody, talk to Jesus in prayer."[32] Taking the words to heart, Elizabeth formed the habit of starting each day with private Bible reading and prayer.

She also became a lifelong tither, following her mother's example. She received no allowance, but Lizzie entrusted four or five hens to her care and taught her to tithe the eggs. In later years, however meager her income, Elizabeth always set apart the Lord's portion first. God honors his promise to tithers, she often testified, to "open you the windows of heaven, and pour you out a blessing" (Malachi 3:10).

While still not a baptized Christian, Elizabeth felt a growing sense of religious mission. This was natural, for she had as food and air the missions promotion of Southern Baptists and the evangelical spirit of the Bomars. Her uncle Edward had served as assistant corresponding secretary of the Foreign Mission Board from 1900 to 1906.[33] Her mother had taken the three children to study missions from an early age and had taught them to sing "Be a little Sunbeam everywhere you go; / Help to drive the darkness from this world below." Endued with this missionary impulse, Elizabeth saved all her Sunday School papers for the time when she would teach the less privileged children of the world.

In time, her resistance to baptism wore thin. On Sunday morning, October 16, 1910, while Southside's pastor R. E. Neighbour was preaching in the tabernacle, Elizabeth felt a tingling within. "With the eyes of my heart," she later testified, "I saw Jesus hanging on the cross, and knew He died for me."[34] During the singing of the invitational hymn "Just As I Am," she walked down the sawdust aisle to the front. The pastor greeted her warmly. After the hymn, when Neighbour presented her to the congregation as a candidate for baptism, he spoke prophetic words that Elizabeth came to cherish as though an heirloom necklace: "Who knows but that this little girl will be a missionary."[35]

The pastor's sermon and invitation provided the occasion for Lizzie's own efforts to come to fruition. "It was you who talked to me about being a Christian," Elizabeth once wrote her, "and begged me to accept."[36] To commemorate the sacred event, Lizzie gave her daughter a Bible in which she wrote Proverbs 3:5, 6: "Trust in the Lord with all thine heart; and lean not unto thine own understanding. In all thy ways acknowledge him, and he shall direct thy paths." These verses became Elizabeth's guiding motto, and a beacon pointing her to Japan.

Elizabeth was baptized one week after her public profession of faith. Since Southside had no baptistry, Pastor Neighbour administered the ordinance at the mother church downtown. Little Spitfire was hardly dry before she learned an important lesson: even the rite of baptism is no sure cure for a volatile nature. When her brother Edward aggravated her in some way, she threw a rock at him. It missed, but the next minute the "babe in Christ" was crying her heart out, ashamed of her impetuous act and frightened at the harm she might have done.

This was the first of recurring lapses that caused Elizabeth much anguish. Fond of sweets, she would pass up the pie or cake or candy whenever her conscience hurt. At times like Christmas, New Year's, or Lizzie's birthday, she would write her mother a note saying that she was giving up this or that bad habit. But neither ascetic acts of penance nor well-meant resolutions did any good: "Every night I repented of the same sins, and without fail committed them all over again the next day."[37]

Elizabeth also suffered nagging fears. Sometimes when she was sleeping on the high back porch she would be jolted awake by the crash of thunder. Terrified, she would run to her mother's room and jump into bed with her. Lizzie never scolded the trembling child. She would embrace her and quote softly, "Thou wilt keep him in perfect peace, whose mind is stayed on thee: because he trusteth in thee" (Isaiah 26:3).[38]

Lizzie's soothing assurances were undercut by Mary's excessive fears. During electrical storms Aunt Mary made everyone huddle together in the central hall, away from all windows or anything that might "attract the lightning," as she would say. She warned the children not to hold even a needle, and forbade them to sing or talk above a whisper. They would wait in silence till the storm had abated.[39]

As if to vindicate Mary's obsession, lightning once struck the telephone, launching a ball of fire that danced on the carpet at the family's feet. A thunderbolt also struck the next-door neighbor's house, knocking down the chimney. Later, Elizabeth had a college roommate whose mother had been struck and killed by lightning before her very eyes. The cumulative effect of these experiences was manifest in the nervous tension that Elizabeth would never overcome.

The Most Haunting Fear of All

Elizabeth entered public school at the third-grade level, after two years of home schooling under Lizzie. She was eight years old. In the new environment Spitfire was more subdued than at home. Her deportment grade was 95 the first month, and afterwards, except for two 99s, it remained at the 100 mark through high school. Her academic grades were similarly high, always averaging above ninety.

Many of her cousins and friends received money for making the honor roll, some as much as a dollar. Elizabeth and her brothers asked their mother for like treatment. "The idea of being paid to do your duty!" Elizabeth recalled Lizzie replying. "I would be ashamed of you if you did not do well in school. It is your duty to work hard and make good grades. Certainly I am not going to pay you to do that."[40]

In the sixth grade, Elizabeth made the honor roll by only a hair. Her report card shows a grade average of ninety-one, the lowest yet, and fourteen absences, a new high. For the first time she was not exempt from final exams. It is apparent that something was amiss. Indeed, Aunt Mary, not Lizzie, signed the report card every month that term.

This deviation from the norm reflected a crisis in the home. Earle came down with typhoid fever, a life-threatening disease, and fire gutted the store building in Camden, the rental income from which was crucial to Lizzie's budget.[41] This double whammy floored the single parent, then going through the menopause. She suffered a complete breakdown. Her siblings placed her in Broadoaks Sanitorium, a private mental institution in Morganton, North Carolina, noted for its advanced therapy.[42]

Elizabeth dreaded coming home from school lest she hear the news that her mother had died. Losing one's father is traumatic enough, and Elizabeth was now more perceptive. The threat of being placed in an orphanage hung over her like a pall. Her interior pain was severe.

Lizzie's brothers and sisters gathered in her home, knelt in the parlor, and pleaded with God to spare her life and restore her health. Considering the store of piety in the Bomar family, few people could have had stronger prayer support. By Easter of 1912 Lizzie had shown marked improvement. "How I wish I could gather all three of my treasures in my arms tonight," she wrote to eight-year-old Edward. "I am so lonely for you darlings. . . . Be thoughtful of your Auntie, save her all the steps you can. . . . I must say good night and go to rest so I can gain strength and soon be able to come home."[43]

Lizzie was back home that summer, having recovered within a year. Elizabeth was jubilant, but her mother's ordeal had left its mark on her impressionable mind. "For the next twenty years," she later recalled, "I was haunted by the fear that when I reached my forties, I, too, would go insane."[44]

Elizabeth also recalled the sting of poverty. "I was never given five cents to go to a movie, or to buy an ice cream cone or a stick of candy."[45] Only at Christmas was there fruit in the house. After the fire in Camden and the financial drain of a long, disabling illness, Lizzie had no choice but to husband the money with rigor. She bought the daily necessities and no more. The family members read or studied by lamplight and bathed in a little tin tub placed in front of the fireplace. In 1920, toward the end of her college days, Elizabeth reminded her mother in a letter that the family had endured "eleven years of constant anxiety."[46]

While a student at Converse Street High School, Elizabeth often wore secondhand clothes. Most were castoffs of an aristocratic schoolmate whose mother was a friend of Lizzie's. Since the girl was an attention getter, even riding to school in a buggy drawn by a handsome pony, Elizabeth felt uneasy wearing her clothes. She worried that other students would recognize the once-spiffy garments and treat her with disdain.

After school, when young people skated, rode bicycles, went to the movies, or danced, Elizabeth sat at home doing her lessons. The parlor where her aunts and uncles had prayed for Lizzie's recovery served as a study hall, a place where Lizzie enforced quiet as though someone were dying in the next room. Under this discipline, Elizabeth continued to make grades in the mid-nineties. An added incentive was seeing her name published in the honor roll each month, an answer to her inner need for social recognition.

Elizabeth looked back on her social development in those years as "abnormal." But the relationships and activities she recalled from her early years seem to contradict that perception. Many of the relatives on her mother's side—aunts, uncles, and cousins—lived in Spartanburg or visited there often. Elizabeth joined them for family gatherings, picnics, and Christmas trees. The cousins played dolls, Elizabeth remembered, until "we became ashamed for people to see such big girls carrying dolls through the streets."[47]

Elizabeth also played tennis on the family court with her brothers and their friends. She romped with them in the backyard and raced with them over the wooded hills. Together they acted out her history lessons, pretending to be early American settlers and Indians. They played in tree houses and made tents out of corn stalks. This idyllic side to Elizabeth's childhood and youth should not be obscured.

True, she had no boy friends, no beaus. If Elizabeth went to a school function where girls had escorts, she would be squired by her brother Earle, nineteen months her junior. But in retrospect, that was not the calamity it seemed at the time. Converse Street High School, like many others at the time, offered only grades eight through ten. Elizabeth was barely sixteen when she graduated, and awaiting her at college were pleasant dates with young men who had never heard her called Spitfire.

2

Coming Out at Judson

Judson College
Marion, Ala,
Nov. 17, 1919.

Precious Mudder,
In the book room
here, I want to tell you I love
you. You already know I do,
but you said one day you
want me to tell you so. I

LIZZIE WATKINS ADVISED HER DAUGHTER to choose between
Converse College in Spartanburg and Judson College in Marion,
Alabama. These small, private schools for women were both so
attractive to Elizabeth that it was like choosing between chocolate cake
and apple pie.

Converse College was fully accredited and less than three miles
from home. Though not a church-related school, it was influenced
strongly by Presbyterians and to a lesser extent by Baptists. John Earle
Bomar, Elizabeth's grandfather, was an early trustee, and several of
her relatives had studied or taught at the school. Its appeal was well
nigh irresistible.[1]

Judson College, an older institution founded in 1838, stood in a small but historic Baptist enclave. The town of Marion was the site of Howard College (now Samford University) and the Southern Baptist Home Mission Board until these institutions moved to Birmingham and Atlanta respectively in the 1880s. Judson College stayed put, clinging like a vine to its twenty-acre campus near the Perry County courthouse, where it represents the Baptist heritage to this day.[2]

To Elizabeth, Judson had two drawbacks. Marion was nearly four hundred miles away, and the college, although academically challenging, was unaccredited at the time. Nevertheless, she chose Judson over Converse. Her uncle Paul Bomar was Judson's president, and her cousin Virginia Bomar, a sophomore majoring in French, offered to be her travel companion during the long train rides from Spartanburg and back. Moreover, Elizabeth felt a spiritual kinship with Ann Hasseltine Judson, the missionary heroine whose name graced the Alabama school and undergirded its virtues and ideals.

Fortunately for Elizabeth, Judson's lack of accreditation would prove no barrier to graduate study, and separation from home for months at a time speeded her transition to adulthood without ill effects. The separation was not without pain, however. During Elizabeth's freshman year, her aunt Mary, who had always been like a second mother in the home, died of the tuberculosis which had sapped her strength for a dozen years or more.[3] Yet all Elizabeth could do during the final, wretched weeks of Mary's life was to write comforting letters and pray for "dearest darling Auntie." Two years later, her brother Edward lay flat on his back for six weeks, recovering from severe hip and leg wounds sustained in a car mishap. Again Elizabeth could only pray and write, this time using humorous prose and jokes to amuse her battered sibling.[4]

It took far less than a family tragedy to make Elizabeth homesick. During her freshman year, her brother Earle wore long pants for the first time, and the next year Edward had his turn. These were pivotal rites of passage, unrepeatable, and Elizabeth yearned to celebrate them in style. Christmas too was a trying time in her junior and senior years, when she forewent the train trip home to save the forty-dollar fare.

The geographical separation from a family she adored spurred Elizabeth's development as a writer. Only by letter could she share her novel experiences at Judson with her mother and brothers—and with Mary while she lived. Only by letter could she express her innermost thoughts and tell her loved ones how much she longed to throw her arms around them and kiss them. Often this meant writing by candle or bathroom light after room lights were out, for her weekly missiles were seldom short.

Elizabeth not only wrote home often; she expected her letters to be answered without delay. She felt let down when the mail bell rang and her name was not called. Earle and Edward wrote occasionally—more often when nagged—and Lizzie usually sent a weekly narrative of the goings-on at home and church. But Elizabeth begged for more and longer letters, more gossip on relatives and friends, more words of affection and concern.

First-class postage went up from two cents to three cents, but Elizabeth still insisted on more letters. And when Lizzie apologized for using cheap stationery, she wrote back, "I'd love to get your letters written on shavings or tree leaves or toilet paper."[5] In her senior year she pressed Lizzie to do more than report the news. "What do you think of as you wash the dishes all by your lonesome? What do you dream of, what do you long for? Do you know we have been just acquaintances these 19 years and don't after all know each other?"[6]

Adjusting to College Life

Soon after entering Judson, Elizabeth had her first date, a buggy ride with Willie Hare, whom she met through an Alabama cousin, Harriet Bomar Ellis. Willie aroused her suspicion by slyly encouraging the horse to walk as slowly as possible, and in conversation she found him "mentally slow."[7] Afterwards he made a futile effort to sustain a courtship by mail. "I wish you would tell me if you love me or not," Willie wrote as if a dolt. "If you do not say yes, you make me think that I have been spending money for candy and never get any good out of it."[8]

Elizabeth lived in the dormitory but often visited her uncle Paul and aunt Nannie at the president's mansion, a colonial-style home fronted with four tall columns nestling upper and lower porches. Having Paul and Nannie close by was pleasant, but being the president's niece had its awkward side. One day when Elizabeth was in the college office her uncle walked in with the Bible teacher, Richard Hall.

"Dr. Bomar," Hall said, "that niece of yours is one of our shining lights."

"Oh yes," the president replied, "she gets that from me."[9]

Determined not to embarrass her uncle or the family back home, Elizabeth not only studied diligently but strove to overcome her social ineptness and spruce up her looks. At New Year's, for example, she resolved not to lose her temper, use bad words, bite her fingernails, put her fingers in her mouth, or scratch her head. On the positive side, she promised to join the "Morning Watch," a society whose members covenanted together to begin each day with Bible study and prayer.[10]

Another motivation for being a model student was Elizabeth's awareness of the financial burden she was placing on the family. Lizzie's income was small and unsteady, dependent on transient boarders and property lessees who were often careless with their payments. The money she sent Elizabeth was never enough, even though it was supplemented with gifts from aunts and uncles. For her part, Elizabeth worked part time in the school bookstore, made some of her clothes, bought second-hand books (a used English text was $1.75), kept expenses at a minimum, and—to ensure God's unswerving support—tithed every cent of her income.

Elizabeth was under financial strain all four years. In March 1918, eager to see the silent movie "Joan of Arc" but worried that her mother might not consider it a wise use of twenty-five cents, she explained that the picture show was half-price for students and that "Joan of Arc" was both educational and patriotic. America being at war added to the force of her argument. On another occasion, after Lizzie authorized her to buy a spring hat in Marion, she selected a pokelike feathered one at a modest six dollars (most were "beyond the church steeple in price"), then had it laid away until her mother could approve so large an expenditure and send a check.[11]

Judson College discouraged parents from giving their daughters excessive spending money or expensive items of any kind. It sought "to inculcate simplicity of taste and to discourage the love of display." Even so, Elizabeth's letters reveal, some students regularly received generous checks known as "butterflies" and lived a cut above the others. And in spite of the rule that "borrowing text-books, clothing, jewelry, and other articles is positively forbidden," there was a lively traffic in articles as well as cash. On a few occasions when she was desperate, Elizabeth borrowed money from an affluent student, reported the transaction to her mother, and repaid the loan as soon as Lizzie's check arrived.[12]

Elizabeth Begins to Blossom

During summer vacation at home, Elizabeth worked off the stress of her freshman year. She played tennis with Earle and Edward on the family court and went with them to hike, hunt, or pick blackberries. Her garden and chickens enjoyed extra care. She was active in her beloved church, teaching a girls' Sunday School class. When she returned to Judson in the fall, her eyes sparkled like diamonds.

"The girls say I look different from last year, that I always look happy," Elizabeth wrote. "I have such cute, funny, congenial roomies though, and am crazy about such a lot of others that I cannot help it."[13] She shared Room 60 with three girls and came to know nearly all the 240 girls who made up the student body, three-fourths of them Alabamians. They were all sisters and, as the college catalogue put it, "members of the President's family." Elizabeth was breaking out of her cocoon of introversion, though still committed to hard study and good grades,

Life was more joyful than ever. There was a fresh magnificence about the well-kept hedges on the campus, the stately magnolias, the large rose garden surrounding a bed of pansies. There was soul-lifting music in the sound of the triangle rung by Abe McCliney, the former slave who awakened the students from their slumber and called them to their meals. "Uncle Abe" was chief and chaplain among the blacks who served the lily-white school as gardeners, janitors, maids, and cooks. One of his prayers in behalf of Judson girls is a classic: "O Lord, give us pure hearts, clean hearts, and sweethearts."[14]

Sports were more pleasurable than before. Elizabeth was mediocre in anything physical, no match for her brothers on the tennis court at home and no candidate for any varsity team at school. Yet she would jump up and down and cheer loudly when Judson played basketball against Woman's College or Alabama University. At the intramural level, she played basketball as a Tiger, on an outdoor clay court that was oozy and gooey when wet. Archery became her favorite sport, and swimming, traditionally a male activity, ran a close second. Responding to the times, Judson had added an indoor pool lined with gleaming white tile.

Elizabeth was caught up in the swirl of social and cultural events that enrich college life: lyceums, plays, pageants, operas, and concerts—even a performance by the Russian Symphony Orchestra. She was elected to the student council and joined the Pierians, one of two sections of the literary society called Conversational Club. Especially enjoyable were the social contacts with the boys from Marion Institute, the "Army and Navy College" in the town.

Marion Institute (now Marion Military Institute) was successor to Howard College, whose president and certain faculty members had chosen to remain at the old campus when the college moved to Birmingham in 1887. M.I., as it was called, offered courses at the high school and junior college levels, preparing its better students for senior colleges and universities as well as the service academies at Annapolis and West Point. It was more cosmopolitan than Judson, the three hundred cadets hailing from thirty-nine states.[15]

The cadet who made Elizabeth's heart flutter was John Burks, an Irish redhead self-described as "a lonesome Kentuckian" and "hopeful."[16] They had their first date at a reception Judson threw for the boys. After the stiff formality of a long receiving line, Elizabeth and John strolled about the campus in the moonlight, listened to music in the students' parlor, and drank punch in the YWCA hall. She felt warm and squishy inside. When the bell rang for bedtime, her heart turned sad as she watched John and his fellow cadets "melt away in the darkness."[17]

When M.I. in turn held a reception for the Judson students, the boys formed a half-moon on a field lit with fires laid at intervals. The girls went through the line, each introducing the one behind her and repeating the names of the boys. Then the line broke up, and couples arm-in-arm wandered off to chat and stroll. Some of the pairing was steady, but it was casual for most, Elizabeth included. Her relationship with John cooled quickly, like an autumn day at sundown.

Though dating the boys ranked high in popularity, the Judson girls were adept at entertaining themselves. Most hilarious were the faculty take-offs at Saturday night club, when students with the gift of mimicry would dress in the teachers' everyday clothes and ape them to the delight of all. There were other parties at which everyone dressed in a peculiar manner, such as with clothes and hair backwards. At a George and Martha Washington masquerade, Elizabeth's costume was a funny black basque with huge puff sleeves and a long, full black skirt. With her hair all powdered, she felt in the style of the period.

These "dress-up" affairs helped relieve the monotony of school uniforms, which Judson required until 1921. The fall and winter uniform, purchased from the school for thirty dollars, was a dark-green woolen suit with a green Oxford cap balanced on the head like a plank. One outfit did for the season. The warm-weather uniform was a plain white middie suit made of washable goods. Colored one-piece dresses were also permitted at times, as when the girls had to walk the long mile to M.I. for a reception.[18]

One's personal appearance was especially important on Sunday mornings, when Lady Principal Margaret Brown inspected the students before marching them off to church. If a girl's uniform was rumpled, Elizabeth said, she was punished with a week in study hall. If a girl had excessive makeup, Miss Brown would snatch her out of line and rub her face with a washrag. Elizabeth was never at risk, for she had been taught from childhood that "nice girls don't use rouge and lipstick like circus women."[19]

The students marched to the church of their parents' choice. For most, this meant the historic Siloam Baptist Church, an antebellum brick structure enhanced with stained glass windows befitting a gothic cathedral. Paul Bomar had been pastor there in earlier years and, to Elizabeth's delight, still supplied the pulpit from time to time. She called him "one of the best preachers I ever heard."[20]

Upon arriving at Siloam Baptist Church, the girls were seated as a group on one side of the sanctuary. A student usher—visibly nervous, as Elizabeth was when her time came—would work the pews from front to back, standing at the end of each pew until a set number of girls had entered to fill it. When the student body was in place, the usher would walk back down to the front and call out "Seats," the signal for all to sit down together. The girls had been forewarned to sit up straight, not "on their backbones."[21]

Arrayed on the opposite side of the church were the khaki-clad boys from M.I. During worship, the cadets and the Judson girls would smile at one another across the townspeople, who occupied the middle section. After church the girls were allowed to have the cadets as their personal guests for Sunday dinner at the college.

There were "churchless Sundays" also, such as when the weather was nasty or the town had a hundred cases of flu. But there were no Sundays without religious instruction, for the college conducted a Sunday School on campus that was no less compulsory than weekday chapel. Sunday evenings, students were free to attend YWCA meetings and church services or to ignore them.

For all its variety, college life for Elizabeth was primarily academic, a succession of courses that opened up new and fascinating worlds. For the first time she viewed the moon through a telescope, exclaiming over the "big holes." In chemistry lab she produced "beautiful crystals and delightful vapors." In geology class she was introduced to the theory of evolution, which she called "the most interesting thing I ever studied." Evolution raised haunting questions about Adam and Eve and where Cain got his wife.[22]

Elizabeth took three foreign languages—Latin, German, and French—and did well in all three except for misspellings. This "besetting sin," as she called it, afflicted her English writing as well. Good grades did not come easy. Elizabeth would get up as early as 3:30 to cram for final exams. Writing home after one exam, she said, "I felt like our cat looked after we tried to wash it."[23]

Elizabeth studied English under Anne Kertley, later described as "one of the most respected, admired, loved, avoided, and feared teachers in all of Judson's history."[24] Kertley was the recipient of the first honorary degree awarded by the college, a doctor of laws. Some of her considerable energy, however, she devoted to palmistry, and some of her students seem to have taken her readings seriously. "I will have a love affair," Elizabeth reported after a session with Kertley, "a slight one and a serious one, the latter resulting in marriage. . . . I have great faith in what she says."[25]

Elizabeth called her teachers "sweet" and told funny stories about them with respect and admiration. Mattie L. Jones, the math teacher, "looked like a chicken" and had a way of saying, "Girls, you better mind out; a teacher may see you!" When one student slipped out the window during a math lesson, Miss Jones looked up in time to see a foot disappear. "Well, never mind," she said. "I guess rest will do Miss Sadie Lee more good than staying in here."[26]

But Elizabeth complained about the strict supervision of young maids by old maids, branding it "oppressive." Miss Brown, whose duty was to maintain "a motherly oversight" of the students' interests, was more like a "big policeman watching over criminals" when she sat by Elizabeth in the dining hall and regaled her with jokes to keep her from stuffing herself. The 115-pound "criminal" saw nothing wrong with trying to put some fat on her bones.[27]

Elizabeth welcomed the less rigid controls in her third year. Juniors could sleep through breakfast on Mondays, go to town once a week without a chaperon, take walks any afternoon, and keep their lights on until 10:30 instead of 10:00.[28]

Even laxer was the fourth year, when Elizabeth lived in Senior Hall, Room 140. Seniors could keep lights on until eleven, be late to seven meals a week, cut chapel once a week, and skip Sunday School and church once a month. They could also go to the picture show any night except Saturday, provided they went in groups of no less than four and had no school duties to perform. Previous engagements with men in town were still forbidden, but seniors could speak with men on the street if they should meet by chance.[29]

Judson had little attraction for the flappers of that era, the young women who rolled down their stockings below their knees or otherwise defied convention. Only a handful of students dared to flout the rules, but they could be the envy of their peers. One of Elizabeth's classmates, Lydia Fuller, won acclaim by finessing Miss Brown and eloping with her boy friend. After a quick marriage in the next county, the couple passed through Marion on their honeymoon. The entire senior class, waiting at the depot, sang to the newly-weds, snapped their pictures, and showered them with rice.[30]

A New Missions Commitment

Each time Elizabeth went home for a summer or Christmas vacation, she was astounded at the changes in Spartanburg, mainly due to World War I. After America's entry into the war in 1917, thousands of Army engineers and civilian construction workers converged on the city to set up a camp for training soldiers. Within weeks they created Camp Wadsworth, a thousand-building complex about three miles west of downtown, a site now occupied by Westgate Mall. Some thirty thousand men were stationed there, most of them members of the New York National Guard, and their relatives followed in droves, grabbing all available housing in the area. Soldiers swarmed into town for entertainment, taxing facilities to the limit. Block-long lines formed at theaters and soda fountains. Prices soared. Spartanburg was transformed into a little New York.[31]

In the summer of 1918 the camp's population was hovering around forty thousand, nearly twice the population of the city. Draftees had come from every part of the United States, among them Slavics, blacks, and full-blooded Cherokee Indians. The camp also had British and French trainers, distinguished by their colorful uniforms, and a bevy of Germans under guard.[32]

Elizabeth helped to entertain the troops, as this was deemed a patriotic duty of young women. She was icy towards soldiers who wanted to pet, but others seemed to enjoy her company. One evening her date suggested that they go to a dance. Elizabeth said no. During the "protracted meeting" in her first year at Judson, she had pledged never to dance. Surprisingly, though, her mother encouraged her to go with her date. "You don't have to dance," Lizzie said. "Just go and talk with the boys."

The evening was a disaster. Since the men greatly outnumbered the women, they urged Elizabeth to dance, and some of the mothers present added their pleas. After some hesitation, the wallflower "broke over and had a jolly time out on the floor." Between dances, however, a soldier to whom she had attempted a Christian witness walked up to her and said, "I thought you were a Sunday School teacher."

"I am," she replied.

"Then, what are you doing here!" he exclaimed, quickly walking away.[33]

Stunned, Elizabeth promptly went home and told Lizzie, who cried and said that she should never go again. Elizabeth would continue the once-a-week folk dancing in Judson's gym, but dancing with the opposite sex was ever after taboo.

That autumn, the terrifying flu epidemic that swept most of the nation's eastern metropolitan areas stretched its tentacles into the isolated town of Marion. Scores of people fell ill and sought treatment in the hospital or, in the case of Judson girls, a quarantined section of a dormitory. As a precaution, teachers sprayed the students' noses and throats twice daily. Classes were suspended each morning from 10:30 to 11:30, and all who were able went outside to breathe fresh air. Every afternoon the students were required to walk in line through the woods, avoiding contact with others. They kept up one another's spirits with corny jokes such as "I opened my window this morning, and in flew Enza."[34]

By some fluke, Elizabeth escaped the flu but succumbed to German measles. At breakfast one morning another student gasped, "Look at her face!" It looked like a "flower garden." Elizabeth was consigned to the infirmary—or "prison"—where she pined away in a dark corner, forbidden to look out the window lest she damage her eyes.[35]

Whether because of the dance-floor incident or the measles attack or something else, Elizabeth's spiritual interests took on a fresh life. She was more appreciative of, and cooperative with, Eula Dawson, the Latin teacher who directed the school's religious activities. Dawson encouraged Elizabeth to attend church-related conferences and sometimes paid the travel expenses out of her own pocket. Her teachings on prayer and personal witnessing began to sink in, helping prepare Elizabeth for a life in missions.

With respect to foreign missions, Judson College had strong and tangible links to Japan in particular. The school's dean of women, Drucilla Collins McCollum, and her late husband J. W., had established Southern Baptist work in Japan in 1889. Dru was a Judson alumna; J. W. had graduated from Howard College before its removal from Marion, and he had attended seminary with Paul Bomar. One of Judson's former lady principals, Daisy Pettus Ray, had been appointed a missionary to Japan with a glowing recommendation from Bomar.[36]

In November 1916, while on furlough, Daisy Ray visited the campus with daughters Emma and Elizabeth. Inadvertently, she became a stumbling block to Elizabeth Watkins. Her speech to the students was emotional, and her clothes were dowdy. "If that is a foreign missionary," the freshman thought, "excuse me. I'll never be one! I'll work for God here in America, but I'll not be any foreign missionary!"[37]

Offsetting the negative impact of "the tacky and tearful" Daisy Ray were the admirable qualities of several members of the Student Volunteer Band. Elizabeth named two members in particular who served her as role models and later lived up to her expectations by going to China. They were Mabel Williams (Mrs. Frank T. Woodward) and Marguerite Pierce (Mrs. John Thomas Littlejohn).[38]

Elizabeth was no less committed to missions than Mabel, Marguerite, or the Rays. But she interpreted her call as to home missions rather than foreign, and she planned to do Christian social work in the slums of an American city. Still, it came as a jolt that she was elected YWCA president for her senior year. This meant "having the religious part of the whole school and the Christian activities of three hundred girls on your hands." Dru McCollum told her she was "the one and only one for the place."[39]

In the summer of 1919, between her junior and senior years, Elizabeth obtained work in the dining room at Blue Ridge, a YMCA-owned interdenominational retreat near Black Mountain, North Carolina. Like the other collegiate staffers, she earned fifteen dollars a month plus board. Girls had to be willing to work up to six hours a day and boys up to eight, but often the work load was lighter, allowing them time to attend some of the conferences and other events.[40]

During her two-month stint at Blue Ridge, Elizabeth gained work experience, made lasting friends, and acquired a taste for bacon. She cut her name and address in the tower atop Mount Mitchell, the highest peak east of the Rockies. Visiting Asheville with her mother, she explored the grandeur of Grove Park Inn and toured George Vanderbilt's 250-room French chateau at the Biltmore Estate. By summer's end, she had gained a treasure chest of memories and a spiritual commitment that would shape the remaining course of her life.

The Blue Ridge season opened with the Southern Student Conference sponsored by the YWCA (not YMCA). Elizabeth heard inspiring messages from the Reverend Henry Sloane Coffin, the eloquent Presbyterian from New York, and outstanding missionaries to many nations.[41] The messages convinced her that she had not given the challenge of foreign missions a fair hearing. Spiritually discontent, she asked to talk with J. Lovell Murray, educational secretary of the Student Volunteer Movement and a former missionary to India.

As they sat on the broad plaza overlooking an expanse of green grass, Elizabeth asked, "Why should I be a foreign missionary? Isn't settlement work in America important? Wouldn't this ministry be pleasing to God?"

"Suppose the man in charge of the Conference Center told us all to go and cut grass," Murray replied. "Suppose many people began cutting near the steps where the grass was just about an inch high. But way over there the grass was almost as high as your head, and there were only two or three people cutting it. You see, Christian work is the same all over the world. It is cutting the same grass. But in some places the grass is very high and there are few people to do the job. That's the only difference."[42]

Elizabeth hurried to her room and fell on her knees. "I can't be a foreign missionary," she told the Lord. "I have no money. I have just one more year in college. Were I to become a foreign missionary, I'd have to have much more education. But there is no more money." The Lord's answer, she said, was clear: "My child, don't worry about the money. Leave that to me. You put yourself in my hands and be willing to do what I ask you to, and I will supply your needs."[43]

Elizabeth recalled Pastor Neighbour's remark at the time of her conversion: "Who knows but that this little girl will be a missionary." She remembered a similar remark from her uncle Horace, the one who walked in his father's steps as a lawyer and deacon. Fresh in her mind was a Blue Ridge lecture on the widespread squalor and misery found in India. "My eyes were opened," Elizabeth wrote to her mother. "I found that we really have no slums. The real ones are in India, China, and Africa. There are hundreds of workers entering our fields here and over there they are few."[44]

On June 9, 1919, halfway through the first conference of the season at Blue Ridge, Elizabeth signed the Student Volunteer pledge: "It is my purpose if God permit, to become a foreign missionary." Lizzie shed tears of joy at the news, the answer to her prayer of nineteen years. Ever the realist, however, when she heard Elizabeth say that maybe God wanted her to go to Africa, Lizzie retorted, "No, the Lord has certainly not called you to Africa. You're no good to me in the kitchen in the summer. You wilt with the heat like a leaf. No, you are not called there. God has too much common sense."[45]

The Crowded Fourth Year

Her senior year was the most hectic. Elizabeth was not only YWCA president but a member of the Student Government Council, then in its first, formative year. She was active in the Volunteer Band, which now had ten aspirants for foreign missions and twenty-seven for home missions. There were socials to attend, such as the senior-sophomore party at which the seniors dressed as boys and the sophomores as little girls. And there were time-consuming special events, notably the school's fund-raising drive in connection with the Seventy-Five Million Campaign of Southern Baptists.

At President Bomar's request, Elizabeth enlisted and trained students as "four-minute speakers" to visit country churches and ask for campaign pledges. The churches where she herself spoke turned out to be shockingly different from the ones she had attended in Spartanburg and Marion. One she described as a "typical church where the men all sat on one side and the women on the other, where the women got up all during church and prayer to take their whole families out to the toilet . . . where babies were given huge biscuits to eat to keep them from crying, where hats were in the form of sun bonnets . . . where women's mouths were stained with tobacco juice, and where the music was led by the drawling voice of an old man who acted instead of any piano."[46]

The most exciting event of her senior year was the eighth international convention of the Student Volunteer Movement, held in Des

Moines, Iowa, from December 31, 1919, to January 4, 1920. Elizabeth was one of three elected representatives from Judson. Most of her travel expenses were paid from funds raised at a freshman stunt program and at a gift-shop tea, but she still had to rely on the generosity of her uncle Horace. To be properly attired, she borrowed a warm dress and a dark-plum coat from two schoolmates. A special train carried the Alabama delegation from Birmingham to Des Moines at a reduced rate.

The SVM convention brought together 6,890 delegates from 949 institutions of higher learning in the United States and Canada. Among these delegates were four hundred foreign students from thirty-nine countries.[47] Never had Elizabeth been in so cosmopolitan a gathering. Nor had she experienced such cold weather. She slept between wooly blankets on a huge "sinky" featherbed, walked on blocks of ice, and saw icicles hang from her nose and form on her coat collar where her breath struck it. "If only my mother could have been there!" Elizabeth exclaimed.[48]

Inside the heated coliseum the delegates listened to gifted speakers—among them missionary statesmen Robert E. Speer, Sherwood Eddy, and John R. Mott—while facing visual reminders of the challenge before them. Displayed above the platform was the famous watchword: "The Evangelization of the World in This Generation." Behind the platform hung a sprawling world map with markers where more than eight thousand student volunteers had served. On the platform sat hundreds of missionaries returned from their fields.

The impact on students was immense. Donald A. McGavran, later a missionary to India and now renowned as the "father of the church growth movement," was one of many who heard and answered a call to carry out the Great Commission.[49] Elizabeth too had her spiritual horizons broadened, her heart set ablaze. She returned to Judson College with her missions commitment firmed up for life.

As YWCA president, Elizabeth hosted the second annual conference of the Student Volunteer Union of Alabama, which brought seventy delegates to the campus in March. Most came from the women's colleges in the state, but sixteen were male students from Howard, Auburn, and Birmingham-Southern. Among the conference speakers were Lovell Murray, who had counseled Elizabeth at Blue Ridge, and missionaries from India, China, and Korea.[50]

Local merchants and others who had cars at their disposal met delegates at the train and chauffeured them about the town. Elizabeth herself rushed to the station several times to greet delegates and see to their needs. She presided at some of the sessions, and at a Blue Ridge dinner skillfully carved the roast.

Being in the spotlight hardly fazed her. The president's niece had come a long way in the four years since she arrived on campus bringing her big rag doll. She had made many "good friends," and the school's yearbook called her the "biggest gossiper" in her class. Her only disappointment was that she seemed to be "man-proof." She wrote: "I am one of three seniors out of a class of 30 who are not engaged—or just the same as. Woe is me!"[51]

Elizabeth completed her three-thousand-word graduation essay and was ready for commencement Tuesday morning, May 25. Clad in cap and gown, and wearing her class ring on the little finger of her right hand, she received her B.A. degree and a diploma in home economics. Elizabeth graduated as an "honor student" and won "final honors" in education and English. Even with rigorous elective courses—geology, bacteriology, advanced analytic geometry—her transcript shows a total of 48 A's and 8 B's.

A beaming Lizzie was present at the commencement exercises, proud of her daughter's exemplary record at Judson, pleased that Elizabeth would continue her education in preparation for overseas work, thankful that the sacrifices of four long years had not been in vain.

3

Life at House Beautiful

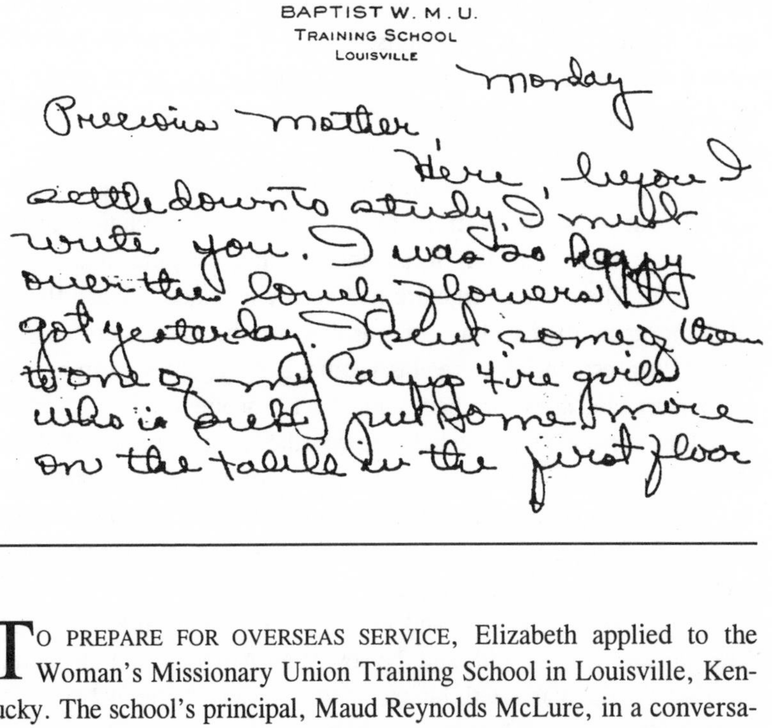
BAPTIST W. M. U.
TRAINING SCHOOL
LOUISVILLE

Monday

Precious Mother,

Here, before I settle down to study, I must write you. I was so happy over the lovely flowers I got yesterday. I put some of them on one of my Camp Fire girls who is sick, put some more on the table in the first floor

TO PREPARE FOR OVERSEAS SERVICE, Elizabeth applied to the Woman's Missionary Union Training School in Louisville, Kentucky. The school's principal, Maud Reynolds McLure, in a conversation with Elizabeth at the student convention in Des Moines, had assured her of a welcome. All the applicant needed was the means to pay for the two-year course of study. Tuition was free, but room, board, laundry, and books ran about two hundred dollars a year. Since Lizzie could no longer help, Elizabeth thought she might have to delay her enrollment and teach school a while.

Before graduating from Judson, however, she received a letter from her uncle Horace. "If you want to go to the Missionary Training School," he wrote, "I'll pay your expenses."[1] It was a magnanimous offer. Though a successful attorney with a butler in his employ and extensive property holdings in Spartanburg, Horace Bomar had six children of his own to educate. But he had a soft spot in his heart for his widowed sister and her children, and his belief in Christian missions made Elizabeth a special case.

During the summer in Spartanburg, as was her custom when at home, Elizabeth taught a Sunday School class at Southside Church. The Sunday School expressed its gratitude with the gift of a Bible that would serve her throughout life and be returned to the church after her death. Invited to speak at a Baptist assembly in Greenville, Elizabeth related her call to foreign missions and won the friendship of Mrs. J. D. Chapman and other WMU leaders who would be her faithful supporters in the years ahead.

In mid-September, after an emotional farewell service at Southside, Elizabeth went by train to Louisville. The Training School occupied a three-year-old, three-story Gothic building at 334 East Broadway. The elegant structure had been christened "House Beautiful," the name of the house of learning for the "daughters" in *Pilgrim's Progress*. Inside were classrooms, library, chapel, dining hall, sun parlors, and sixty-two bedrooms for 125 women.[2]

More attractive than the building was the school's principal, Maud McLure, a former voice teacher who exuded beauty and charm. She had been brought up in a fourteen-room colonial mansion—"Mount Ida" in Talladega County, Alabama—and taught by private tutors before attending Judson College. The regal lady had also been tempered by sorrow. Her husband had died of a dental infection when their son was one year old, and the son as an Army captain had barely survived World War I with his face and right leg shattered.[3]

"Mother McLure," as she was called, strove to make her charges the finest and best prepared Christian workers possible. She taught them Personal Evangelism, a one-semester-hour course, and she prayed with them daily, giving House Beautiful its reputation as "The Power House of Prayer." Elizabeth revered McLure and frequently sang her praises in letters to Lizzie. Oddly, though, Elizabeth's grade in Personal Evangelism was a mere 83, her next to lowest grade at the school.[4]

The Training School students took many of their courses at the Southern Baptist Theological Seminary, a male bastion six blocks down Broadway. Lest they be distracted by the seminary's four hundred men, the women were required to "sit together in both class room and chapel, and not linger in the halls. . . ." Nor were they to go out on the street with any of the "brethren"—a term the women mockingly pronounced "brethern."[5]

To Elizabeth, it was an awesome privilege to sit under the intellectual giants who taught the seminary classes. She had seminary president E. Y. Mullins for theology, the tall and dignified John R. Sampey for Old Testament, the quippish A. T. Robertson for New Testament, the well-traveled H. C. Wayman for Biblical Introduction, and the inspiring W. O. Carver for missions. All were eminent scholars who delivered breathtaking lectures and enjoyed high respect.

In Professor Wayman's class, Elizabeth sat on the front seat "under the drippings of the sanctuary," she reported, quoting Dr. Robertson. Wayman was "perfectly wonderful & interesting."[6] Yet Dr. Carver charmed the women students even more. "Often it seems when he speaks," Elizabeth wrote adoringly, "as if Christ himself stood before you."[7] She helped the Training School raise $625 toward the expense of Carver's 1923 tour of the Orient, and she was delighted when, thirty years later, the school was renamed Carver School of Missions and Social Work.

Elizabeth's first exam was in Sampey's Old Testament. The seniors at the Training School prayed that she and the other juniors would all pass. When the grades were posted, House Beautiful resounded with laughter, especially in the sun parlors where the women gathered to celebrate the answer to their prayers. In contrast, the seminary dormitory, five-storied New York Hall, echoed with cries of anguish, for some of the men had failed. Elizabeth not only passed this first test in Old Testament but went on to earn a course grade of 98.

This pitting of the sexes against one another came in the wake of the August 1920 ratification of the women's suffrage amendment to the U.S. Constitution. The Training School women celebrated their new voting rights with a surge of confidence in their ability to compete with the seminary men.

Even so, some of the women complained that the seminary courses were too demanding. The "chief bugbear," Elizabeth reported, was Josephus, the Jewish historian whose ponderous works were read as preparation for comprehending the New Testament. One dazed student had been studying so hard that when she stopped to write a letter home, she began it with "Dear Josephus." Another student, after reading about the gruesome Maccabean wars, dreamed that she was being killed. Her roommates were awakened by her shrieks.[8]

Before graduating from Judson, Elizabeth had noticed in the Training School catalogue that the core curriculum included music and sight singing. It was a time when the ability to play and sing hymns was considered standard equipment for female missionaries at home and abroad. Elizabeth's friends had kidded her about the requirement, knowing how slight was her aptitude for music, and the satirical writer of her "Class Prophecy" had even cast her as concert leader and soloist in a circus. Elizabeth acknowledged the deficiency, blaming it on her early instruction at home. When she entered public school at the third grade level, she explained, the other children had already learned the scales, and the latecomer never caught up.

Elizabeth could have opted out of private piano lessons but took them anyway. She had as little time for practice as she had a feel for rhythm, so that when she turned twenty-one in April, her repertoire consisted of but one hymn: "Love Divine." Even so, the passage to adulthood was so special an occasion that Elizabeth gave a private one-piece recital for her closest friends. During her second year the plodder mastered one more hymn, "I Gave My Life for Thee."

The Training School day began with the rising bell at six o'clock. Elizabeth and her roommates would take turns reading the day's selection from *Daily Strength for Daily Need*, after which they would kneel and pray. Then they would go to a student-led chapel in Heck Memorial Chapel, the worship center with stained glass windows across each side and a portrait of Fannie Exile Scudder Heck at the front. Heck was the longtime WMU president who had led in the founding of the Training School. The student body gathered in this chapel for services at 6:45 each morning and 6:30 each evening.[9]

After morning chapel came breakfast in the many-windowed dining room, where graceful tables were arranged among upright pillars and set with crocheted place mats. Meals were served by students in crisp white aprons, who also scraped and washed the dishes, scrubbed and reset the tables, and swept the floors. All students were required to do one hour of domestic labor daily. In addition, they had to keep their own rooms reasonably free of the grimy soot deposited by Louisville's ever-belching smoke stacks.

Classes and related activities consumed the daylight hours. Evening study time began at 7:30. A five-minute recess bell rang at 8:30 and the retiring bell sounded at 10:00, followed by lights out at 10:30. So regimented a life of study, work, and religious devotion was the Baptist version of a nunnery—a cloister of vestal virgins without the black and white habits.

The *Students' Hand-Book* of the time consistently refers to the students as "girls," which is what the students chummily called themselves. Yet some of the women were gray-headed and many had taught school for years. Twenty-year-old Elizabeth may have been the youngest among them, for the catalogue specified that no one under twenty-one would be "admitted in training" for home or foreign mission service.[10] Her first roommate, Nonie Stephen Gravett, a senior, was so mature that Elizabeth called her "Grandma." When a third student, Birdie Lou Clark, was assigned to their room, Elizabeth gave her a nickname based not on age but on pecking order. Birdie became "Thirdy."[11]

Though chummier with the women in their lower twenties, Elizabeth liked her schoolmates of all ages. Never, not even at Judson College, had she seen women so congenial and lovable. Elizabeth thought them "the jolliest, happiest, healthiest, heartiest bunch of girls to be found in the world."[12]

Parties Galore

Elizabeth adored the school's social chairman, Juliette Mather, calling her "the joy of the house."[13] Juliette had an irrepressible enthusiasm for life and a genuine interest in others. Alma Hunt well described her as "original and clever, vivacious and warmly winsome."[14] Upon her graduation in 1921, this gifted woman became the first national secretary of the WMU's Young Woman's Auxiliary.

Juliette returned to Louisville the next March to lead the annual YWA rally and WMU conference, a weekend event that opened on St. Patrick's Day. At a boisterous party that evening, the students staged a pig race with three pigs—actually three students—named after the conference leaders. The racers, among them "Juliette Mather Airedale," were down on all fours, cleverly dressed in blankets, long white snouts, little curly wire tails, and little green caps. Three other students, dressed as Irish washer women, had the racers in tow. Each washer woman announced the pedigree of her pig, throwing in some Irish jokes. The race was so hilarious, Elizabeth said, that not even real pigs were equal to the "grunting and squealing" that resounded through the hall.[15]

The lively parties and rollicking good times in that Baptist convent would have shocked its primmer supporters had they but known. One memorable skit was based on Sir Walter Scott's *Lochinvar*, a poem about knighthood. Elizabeth, playing the frustrated bridegroom, galloped in on a feather-duster horse fully looking the part. Her costume consisted of blue velvet jacket, pink satin sash, red stockings, pink garters, high-heeled slippers adorned with big gold buckles, and tricornered hat with a big plume. Her hair was powdered and tied in a queue at the neck with a black bow. "As I slipped the ring on the bride's finger," Elizabeth wrote, "[I] was interrupted by the bold knight Lochinvar who soon took her off and left me brideless." All the other knights then galloped off in pursuit.[16]

Throughout the performance, entertainers and spectators alike often glanced at two VIPs in the audience to catch their reactions. Maud McLure and her younger cousin, Kathleen Mallory, corresponding secretary of Woman's Missionary Union, were a sideshow of sorts. Though models of decorum, they munched on peanuts while sitting in soap boxes ("box seats") and wearing ear puffs.[17]

Even the Training School's daily meals were fun times. The students sat at the same place in the dining room for two weeks, then were assigned a new set of table companions. The members of each new group would give themselves silly names and weird identities. After one of the two-week shuffles, those at Elizabeth's table became the Amy family: Mama and Papa and three sets of boy-girl twins. The youngest twins were three-year-old Jack and Jill Amy. Next were Bill and Frill Amy, age six. The oldest were Pill-Jerk-Peter-Pope-Pius-II Amy and his twin Peggy. Elizabeth played the role of three-year-old Jack.

At one evening meal, Elizabeth unwittingly served up an extra helping of merriment. Some necessary work after gym class had forced her to take a hurried bath, scramble into her clothes, and rush to supper, arriving just in time to preside over her table. Unknown to Elizabeth, her dress was on "hind side before." The other women broke into uncontrollable laughter. Her face flushed, Elizabeth had a bodyguard escort her to a nearby room where she could "get turned around."[18]

To keep dining room conversations pleasant during exams, anyone who mentioned lessons at the table had to pay a small fine. Still, the forbidden subject popped up so often that the fines collected during Elizabeth's first year paid for a special party in the basement, at which the women chattered over hot chocolate, marshmallow cream sandwiches, and pickles for spice.

As at Judson, Elizabeth enjoyed sports and recreation. She cheered the Training School High Heels in their traditional baseball game with the Seminary Low Heels. She was one of forty-nine women to take a cruise down the Ohio River on the steamboat *Nashville*. More interesting than the scenery along the river, Elizabeth reported after the cruise, were "the real grisly seamen with wooly white hair, wrinkled faces, and pipes in one side of their mouths and a wad of tobacco in the other."[19]

During the brisk winters in Louisville, Elizabeth sometimes had to trudge through deep snow. The flakes came down thicker and faster and more steadily than she had ever seen before—perfect for snow cream. She was surprised to see horses used to remove snow from the street car tracks. If the weather got her down, and she felt as if she might be getting a cold, Elizabeth would take a bottle of Wampole's (a tonic) and feel renewed.

The Training School often received gift packages from WMU organizations, especially at Thanksgiving and Christmas. The packages could be designated for all the students, for those of a particular state, or for an individual. Everyone welcomed goodies to eat and yet blamed them for unwanted pounds. "I smiled my face out of shape,"

Elizabeth said upon receiving a large Christmas box from her mother. Inside were cake, candy, fruit, and nuts to nibble on. There was even a fur to wear. For days Elizabeth went around "as proud as a peacock and feeling like a Croesus." Her thank-you note to Lizzie still shows chocolate smears.[20]

Out Beyond the Campus

As Elizabeth soon discovered, Louisville was a world apart from tiny Marion. Its population of 234,891 (1920 census) was more than ten times that of even Spartanburg (22,638). This metropolis on the Mason-Dixon line had attracted immigrants—many of them poor—from various parts of the world. A vital part of Training School life was ministering to the city's needy, whether immigrants or not. Every student did practical work under the direction of Emma Leachman, a faculty member and "city missionary," whose "criticism could be as biting as her praise was genuine."[21]

Elizabeth was one of seventeen women assigned to the Good Will Center at 524 East Madison Street, which was said to have the only bathtub in the neighborhood. The facility offered a supervised playground, a small library, and a wide range of social and religious activities, including Penny Banks to encourage thrift. This assignment was Elizabeth's initiation into teaching immigrant boys and girls with "funny names." She had her first run-in with Catholic nuns who warned children away from the Baptist Center, but she also experienced the thrill of little Italians greeting her with the cry, "Be my teacher!"[22]

On Wednesday afternoons Elizabeth taught a sewing class of twelve-year-old girls, and on Thursday afternoons she and her partner, Jessie Dye, would visit the girls' homes to learn about their families. Elizabeth had heard and read of people living in crumbling tenements, in tiny attics and on back alleys. Yet she was poorly prepared for the squalor she found. "The way some of those people live!" she exclaimed. "It is worse than animals."[23]

One day Elizabeth and Jessie spoke to some children playing in the street and told them about the Sunday School classes and the various clubs in the Good Will Center. They touted the Blossom Shop (ages seven to nine), Blue Bird Club (nine to eleven), and Camp Fire Girls (eleven to fourteen, with a separate unit for working girls). When they inquired about a pupil named Lena, the children replied that they did not associate with her because "she goes riding with strange men whom she doesn't even know."[24] But they gave directions to Lena's home.

Elizabeth and Jessie climbed a little stairway squeezed between two stores. They approached a door but withdrew when they realized it was the front door. Miss Leachman had told them that "the people of the slums use their front doors only in case of funerals."[25] Elizabeth and Jessie then made their way to a dirty alley, climbed a rickety stairway, fumbled along a dark hall, then halted at the odor of onions and cabbage floating in a wave of intense heat. Seated in a grungy room, sewing, was Lena's mother. She did not invite them to sit down, and they soon left to visit other shabby places.

One afternoon Elizabeth and Jessie Dye took twenty-seven Camp Fire girls on a hike to Cave Hill Cemetery. The girls wore club uniforms that they rented from the center. The younger ones still attended school, but others worked in dingy factories or shops. All seemed to enjoy running down the green slopes, rustling in the leaves, sitting under trees, and watching snow-white ducks swim on the lake. At handicraft time, they made owls out of peanuts, paper, and glue. Then before returning home, they reviewed the law of the Camp Fire Girls: "Seek beauty; give service; pursue knowledge; be trustworthy; hold on to health; glorify work; be happy."[26]

In their meetings at the Good Will Center, the girls learned sewing and cooking. Some with working mothers had to prepare the meals when they came home from school, and nearly all were undernourished. Since they knew little about cereals, the girls were shown how to cook oatmeal and cream of wheat. One day they made custard bread pudding; another day they cooked potatoes with white sauce. The girls also learned table settings, how to eat with knife and fork, and other practical knowledge not taught them at home. Elizabeth happily reported that three of the girls and one of the mothers were baptized.

One Sunday morning Elizabeth went with Phebe Lawton to her field work in the King's Daughters Home for Incurables. On the second floor of the spacious building the two students found some thirty women gathered for Sunday School, eagerly awaiting the songs, prayers, and Bible study. Each woman was in a wheelchair. One was blind and deaf. One had palsy, another cancer, another rheumatism, her hands in knots. After the fifteen-minute service Elizabeth and Phebe spoke to the patients individually and tried to "cheer up the cheerless souls." They in turn were gladdened by some who seemed happy and bright even with deformities and pains.[27]

Big-name revivals that came to Louisville offered further opportunities for service. One featured Rodney ("Gipsy") Smith, the English evangelist born in a gypsy tent and knighted by King George V for his YMCA work during World War I. Elizabeth worked each night in the tabernacle's inquiry room as a counselor. She also helped in a protracted meeting led by George W. Truett, the eloquent pastor from First Baptist Church in Dallas. These revivals were a buttress to Elizabeth's spiritual life even if a detriment to her studies.[28]

The off-campus activity also helped to keep her physically strong. Elizabeth once calculated that she was walking about twenty miles each week doing her field work, and eleven miles a week going back and forth to classes at the seminary. And all that exercise did not excuse her from gym classes.[29]

In her senior year, when enrollment peaked at 142 boarding students and 44 day students,[30] Elizabeth succeeded Juliette Mather as Chairman of Social Life. One of her duties was to visit all the new students and help them get adjusted to Training School life. Also responsible for keeping the domestic work records, every other Saturday night she read out the new list of table assignments in the dining room.

As social chairman Elizabeth further had to oversee state parties, BYPU parties, seasonal parties, and other social events such as the annual "open house" for the seminary men. For open house the women decorated their building with hearts, hatchets, cupids, and arrows. When the guests had arrived, the men and women played different games simultaneously, the groups progressing from room to room.

One evening the seniors were invited to a reception given by Isla May Mullins, the seminary's First Lady. Elizabeth donned her canton crepe, long gloves, and fur, then joined the others for the half-hour streetcar ride to the Mullins home. The evening turned out to be

Elizabeth's, for she and the hostess were the only Judson alumnae present, and Mrs. Mullins wanted to chat about their alma mater. When Elizabeth was free to wander about the house, she playfully sat in the chair that supported Dr. Mullins's six-foot, two-inch frame when he was studying or writing at home. She gleefully threw her head back in imitation of the brilliant theologian—he was out of town—and rocked a "wee bit."[31]

One Friday evening the school's dietician and house director, Mary Louise Warren, invited Elizabeth and two other seniors to go out with her to supper at a luxury hotel and then to a style show. The four slipped out quietly so others would not envy them and want to go also. When the beautiful, elegantly dressed dietician told a hired man she was going to the style show, he replied, "Miss Warren, you sure will get the prize!" The show featured children and dogs and grown-ups, not to mention the beautiful costumes, and it gave Elizabeth much to talk about for days.[32]

Choosing a Man and a Mission

Training School students were allowed to go out with an escort only three times a year. Elizabeth, no wallflower, used up her three privileges before Christmas. Fortunately, this restriction did not apply to church activities, such as Baptist Young People's Union socials. Third and St. Catherine's Baptist Church, which was within walking distance, had a BYPU exclusively for seminary and Training School students, making it a popular place for dates. Elizabeth would doll up in her red trimmed dress with long gloves and feel like she was walking in the clouds. One escort she described as "smart, intelligent, interesting, traveled, experienced." Another one was "such a nut."[33]

One escort became a steady boy friend. Sam Lawton was a first cousin of Phebe Lawton, from a clan well known among South Carolina Baptists. Like the Bomars, the Lawtons produced ministers and missionaries of distinction. Sam was distinctive in another sense: he was blind from birth with retinitis pigmentosa. That did not hinder him from walking Elizabeth to church each Sunday night, one pocket filled with peppermint candy for them to enjoy while walking home. The two often talked in the Blue Room, House Beautiful's courting parlor graced with elegant rosewood furniture, and they went out to dinner with other couples. Sam gave her a triple-layer box of Liggetts chocolates for Christmas and sent corsages on other occasions. He visited her home in Spartanburg and had her to visit his family at their summer cottage in the mountains. Marriage seemed to be their aim.

Months before Elizabeth and Sam graduated in 1922, however, the sparkle in their courtship began to fade. One day Elizabeth told Sam he could come for a visit at eight o'clock that evening. He arrived on time, but her mind was on other matters, and she forgot about the date until Sam had been waiting in the parlor for an hour. He sweetly agreed to come another time, but she knew he felt offended.

When the two were together, Elizabeth sometimes yawned and seemed bored. Like her mother, who was known to sleep in church Sunday nights while the preacher droned on, she was "plagued with a makeup that insisted that she get sleepy when the chickens went to roost."[34] Sam could not see her drowsiness, but he could sense from the tone of her voice that her attention had drained away. "What's the matter?" he would ask.

The courtship fizzled and died when a schoolmate told Sam that Elizabeth was neglecting him and paying a great deal of attention to other men. Elizabeth called it "a misconception and misunderstanding on some one's part."[35] If Sam could have seen for himself, she felt, he would have known the charge was untrue. It was her duty as social chairman of the school to greet the dates, notify the women, and make herself generally pleasant in the parlors. Still, Elizabeth seems to have fallen short of Sam's expectations. Though she reveled in the courtship, she knew down deep that it was on a collision course with her commitment to foreign missions, since Sam would never be able to meet the physical requirements of the Foreign Mission Board. Her heart was never fully his.

Their courtship on the rocks, Elizabeth nudged Sam into the arms of Alice Stockton, a schoolmate at Judson as well as the Training School. Sam married Alice in 1924, after touring Bible lands with a group led by Professor A. C. Wayman, and the couple taught at Mars Hill College in the mountains of North Carolina. Sam went on to earn a Ph.D. from George Peabody College for Teachers and to carve out a stellar career as minister, educator, and humanitarian. A daughter,

Mary Elizabeth (Mrs. Karl J. Myers), served in Nigeria as a missionary physician, opening the way for Sam himself to do a stint there as a foreign missions volunteer.[36]

Elizabeth gave priority to mission over a man. In the summer of 1921, at the end of her first year in Louisville, she wrote to the Foreign Mission Board and offered herself as a missionary candidate without specifying the field. Afterwards, the Board's T. Bronson Ray visited Louisville and interviewed Elizabeth along with other candidates. He informed her that appointees were expected to be twenty-six years of age, though exceptions were made for some at twenty-four or twenty-five. "You are handicapped somewhat with youth. . . ," said Ray in a follow-up letter, "but this is an impediment which can be overcome with patience."[37] Elizabeth thought his words patronizing and insensitive, but she had no choice but to grit her teeth and wait.

Even though her appointment was to be shelved for a time, Elizabeth reached the conclusion that God wanted her to serve in Japan, where several of her favorite schoolmates were headed. Among them was Phebe Lawton, the winsome "chairman of general culture" at the school. At Phebe's invitation, Elizabeth joined the Japan study group, where she learned much about that country from the discussions and stereopticon slides. Phebe's roommate, Florence Walne, had grown up in Japan and had been an appointed missionary since 1919. At one of the group meetings, blue-eyed Florence, dolled up in a bright kimono and clutching a huge Japanese umbrella, told marvelous stories about her native land.

Florence's parents, Ernest and Claudia Walne, also in Louisville on furlough, were themselves a showpiece of missions in Japan. Appointed in 1892, they towered above their colleagues in achievement as well as years. Dr. Walne contributed to Elizabeth's orientation by showing a movie about his missionary life titled "From New York Hall to Japan."

The Walne family coveted Elizabeth for Japan. "She is a glorious girl," Florence wrote to T. B. Ray, "with a radiant Christian personality and great charm of manner. She is quite young, but very able mentally and thoroughly consecrated."[38] But Ray kept the candidate on hold.

The graduation ritual for the Training School seniors began with the baccalaureate service at Walnut Street Baptist Church Sunday evening, April 30, 1922, with preaching by Louisiana pastor M. E. Dodd. At ten o'clock the same evening, the seniors attended the traditional "Vigil Service" at the school, a time of solemn consecration led by Maud McLure. Before retiring for the night, Elizabeth wrote in her Bible these words: "Have I a message to give? Am I willing to deliver it at any cost? Is it my purpose to deliver it at all times? I have——I am——it is——with God's strength."[39]

At the commencement Monday evening, May 1, Elizabeth and her fellow seniors marched single file into Heck Memorial Chapel, each wearing a simple white dress and carrying a palm branch symbolizing victory. The juniors followed double file. The assembled body sang "How Beautiful upon the Mountains," Maud McLure handed out diplomas, and the seniors passed their garlands to their kneeling junior sisters. Now holding the Bachelor of Missionary Training degree, Elizabeth was well equipped for her first assignment in full-time Christian work.

4

Among All Nations at Norfolk

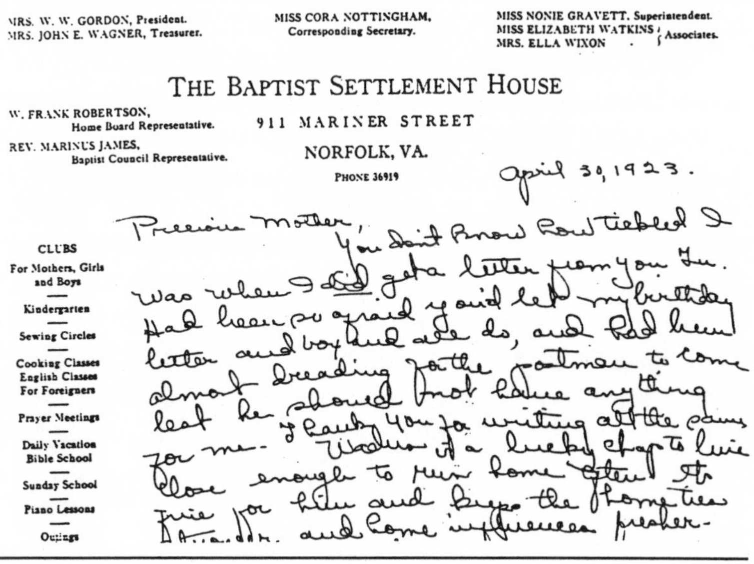

[handwritten letter, largely illegible]

Precious Mother,
You don't know how tickled I
was when I did get a letter from you. I
had been so afraid you'd let my birthday
letter and boy and all do, and had been
almost dreading for the postman to come
lest he should not have anything
for me. I thank you for writing...

DURING HER FIRST YEAR at the Training School, Elizabeth came to know and esteem Nonie Gravett—the one she called Grandma—as roommate, prayer mate, and soul mate. When Nonie graduated in 1921, the Home Mission Board appointed her superintendent of the Baptist Settlement House in Norfolk, Virginia. The next year Nonie invited Elizabeth to be her associate.

"I feel I can never be supremely happy," Elizabeth wrote, "until I begin my real work 'over there.'"[1] But since the Foreign Mission Board would not send her to Japan at age twenty-two, she welcomed Nonie's invitation as a call from God and signed on with the Home Mission Board. While waiting to go abroad, there was no better place to work than a port city teeming with immigrants. Norfolk was a microcosm of the world, a mission field where Elizabeth could serve "in his name among all nations" (Luke 2:24-27).

After graduating from the Training School, Elizabeth returned to Spartanburg and took a crash course in typing, gaining a skill that would serve her well the rest of her life. In early June she rode the rails to Portsmouth, boarded the ferry at Pinner's Point, crossed the Elizabeth River to Norfolk, and took a taxi to 911 Mariner Street. The driver let her off in front of a two-story dwelling with "Baptist Settlement House" displayed above the front door. This was the right house, obviously, but the neighborhood seemed wrong. The street was broad and clean, and the houses on either side, though tightly packed, had a respectable look about them. Neat, pretty children were playing on the sidewalks. Elizabeth had envisioned a slum with dirty people and crummy shops.

The Woman's Missionary Union of the Norfolk-Portsmouth area had initiated a social and religious ministry to immigrants in 1910—the "first Good Will Center in Virginia"—and had purchased the Mariner Street house in 1913. Besides raising five hundred dollars for this purpose, the women had arranged for the WMU of Virginia to supply maintenance funds and for the Home Mission Board to appoint workers and advise the local committee in the direction of the work.[2]

The settlement house was as modest inside as it appeared from without. Upstairs were a bedroom, a kitchen-dining room, a bath, and a cutely appointed kindergarten room with little white chairs. The first floor had club rooms and a large assembly room. In the basement were workshops used exclusively by boys. A backyard served as overflow space.

Elizabeth moved in with Nonie and their "chaperon," Mrs. Ella Wixon. Mrs. Wixon's daughter, also named Ella, was the previous superintendent, having resigned to become Mrs. James Merritt. The senior Ella, "a lovely, cultured, gentle, lovable lady," was variously called "Mother Wixon," "Pretty Lady" and "Grandmother."[3] Under the spell of her venerable presence, Elizabeth quit calling Nonie Grandma.

The three women shared the one bedroom on the second floor, stowing their personal belongings in suitcases and boxes under their individual beds. Despite the cramped quarters, the threesome lived in harmony, as though they had a natural affinity for one another. Elizabeth complained of loneliness the few nights the other two were away.

The situation might have been deplorably different. When Florence Allshorn arrived at her mission station in Uganda, she found that the only sitting room was divided into two halves. One half was filled with the senior missionary's furniture; the other half was bare. "That's your half," Allshorn was told. Shocked at the loveless reception, she read the same passage of scripture every day for a year—First Corinthians 13, Paul's enchanting "Hymn of Love."[4]

The settlement house property was adjoined by the yards of people from a dozen foreign countries. There were days when Elizabeth and her "congenial roomies" heard no English spoken except as they used it themselves. From their windows each evening they could see the neighbors sitting out on porches, steps, and curbs, and hear them speaking in unknown tongues. The women would be knitting or tending babies while babbling and enjoying the out-of-doors.

It was Elizabeth's habit to rise an hour before her roommates. She took "gymnastic exercises," had her devotional, and practiced on the piano (Nonie sometimes gave her lessons later in the day). How the other two slept through that hour Elizabeth did not say, but doubtless they had acclimated themselves to noisiness as native to their environment. The loud and incessant Greek music from a graphophone nearby competed with "the howling baby, the barking dog, and the shouting boys" in an upstairs apartment next door. "Wish I could stick their mouths together with adhesive tape!" Elizabeth grumbled.[5]

The three women shared in the daily housekeeping chores, making beds, washing and drying dishes, dusting and mopping. The only laborious part was having to pull everything out from under the beds when they mopped the bedroom floor. More extensive cleaning they left to a hired woman who came each Saturday. None of the housework, Elizabeth claimed, was as hard as the mental work required to run the place.

Elizabeth did most of her own washing and ironing. In Louisville she had grown accustomed to the sight of people's laundry hung out from upstairs windows. "I little dreamed," she wrote, "I'd be hanging mine on a clothesline stretched between our window and the one of our next-door neighbor!"[6]

The women took turns shopping and fixing meals. Shopping was convenient, for the city market, with its vast offerings, lay only a few blocks away. They bought most of their groceries from Quakers in picturesque dress. Potatoes were a penny a pound, and other prices were comparably low. After a new market building was completed in 1923, one of Elizabeth's prize purchases was a tender rabbit.[7]

Each woman had a distinctive skill to offer in food preparation. Elizabeth was keen at dressing a hen, since her mother raised chickens at home. Occasionally the women had to adjust their menus and appetites to make use of unexpected gifts, such as a beef roast some friends brought when they had just cooked a veal loaf. "We had cow for so long," Elizabeth joked, "that I thought certainly I would begin to moo."[8]

The most welcome gifts were a long-awaited three-hundred-dollar piano from the Home Mission Board and three new beds from some WMU societies. The beds had thick, three-quarter size mattresses in three different colors: pink, blue, and gray. Ella took the pink one and Nonie the blue. Elizabeth, now in the position of her former roommate "Thirdy," had last pick but found the gray one no less comfortable than the others. "I'm in danger of getting the big head!" she chuckled, lounging on her pristine bed.[9]

Since one new thing calls for another, Elizabeth spent most of her month's salary on bed linens and on a $37.50 trunk—a sale item—to replace the battered one she had borrowed from Lizzie. The old trunk she moved to the kitchen and filled with canned goods received in a shower.

Elizabeth was always on the lookout for bargains. She snapped up a pair of black patent-leather slippers for $1.98 and a twenty-five-cent brassiere for eleven cents. At a bankruptcy sale on Main Street she bought a nice-looking woolen dress for $2.98. Another fall dress came "from our dear Church St. where Negroes, foreigners, and we poor folks trade and save much money thereby. The same dress on stylish Granby St. would have doubtless been beyond my pocketbook."[10] Church Street was the heart of the black business district, although Jews, Italians, Greeks, and Asians also ran shops there.[11]

Elizabeth had to be frugal. Out of her meager salary came not only living expenses but a tithe for the Lord's work and a portion for her future needs. The tithe went to her home church, usually designated for foreign missions, and the savings were stashed in Spartanburg's First National Bank, where her brother Earle was employed. Elizabeth needed to guard her money carefully, Mother Wixon advised, because "the Yankees might get it."[12]

Classes for Young and Old

Soon after Elizabeth arrived in Norfolk, the settlement house conducted its annual Vacation Bible School. More than a hundred children crowded in daily. Scores of Jews and Catholics attended along with Protestant children, attracted by classes in clay work, mat weaving, hammock making, rag rug manufacture, knitting, crocheting, and basket making. Also appealing were the lively stories and songs and games.

One day when Elizabeth was telling the life of Jesus to all the children in assembly, some were starry-eyed, hanging on to every word. When the session was over, a Jewish girl named Ida stepped up to the teacher, her face aglow. "Please tell me the rest of the Bible story," she begged. "Don't make me wait until tomorrow. I want to know what comes next."[13]

All the Jewish children seemed bright and eager to learn. They liked to repeat the stories about Jesus and sing songs about him such as "Sweet By and By" and "The Touch of His Hand on Mine." They saluted the Christian flag with no less vigor than the Gentiles.[14]

Discipline was never a major problem, though a few boys tended to grow restless and turn mischievous. Elizabeth devised a way to use up their energy and also procure some needed seats. Asking the ring leader to come help her, she explained how she wanted a nice bench to place under the tree in the backyard for her basket class. Half a dozen boys went into action. Wielding saws, hammers, and brushes, they turned lumber, nails, and paint into a useable bench, and a few days later they made six more benches for other groups.

At the close of the Vacation Bible School the children gave a demonstration at the new Baptist encampment in Virginia Beach.[15] Among the performers a Jewish boy named David recited Romans 10, and a Jewish girl named Esther told the story of the widow's mite and of Jesus' triumphal entry into Jerusalem. All the participants together quoted eighteen Bible passages on the theme of salvation, Elizabeth beaming as though she had won a Tony award.

The settlement house experienced little opposition from the surrounding churches and synagogues with the exception of St. Mary's Catholic Church. This church almost adjoined its backyard, and St. Mary's school and orphanage stood only a few doors away. The fine Catholic buildings overshadowed the modest, ill-equipped settlement house that encroached on their turf, and the priests and sisters disdained it as a sore and a menace. They were said to gather up the Bibles that the Baptists distributed and to keep the children after school lest they attend the beguiling clubs.

Despite the warnings and the risk of punishment, some of the children would run to the settlement house the minute they were released from school, even if it meant skipping a meal. A sixteen-year-old named Katherine persisted in coming even though her Italian parents beat her for the offense. To guard against recriminations, Elizabeth and her associates never published the names of their pupils. Nor did they put up any posters or notices around town, since advertising would only fuel the resentment against their work.

The settlement house sponsored group activities for all ages throughout most of the year. Among these activities Elizabeth was proudest of the "Jesus kindergarten." Children from many nations sat in the little white chairs for Bible stories and songs, or played with blocks and spools and dolls. Onea, Itamocea, and Sive were Greek; Nicolas was Polish; Gloria, Rose, and George were Syrian; Miriam and Helen were Chinese; Billy and Ruth were German; Walter was Swedish; Violet was French; Virginia was Canadian; Ethel was English; Peter and Maria were Spanish; Nisi was Russian; Jack and Bud were Irish; Martha, Mac, Mildred, Hazel, and Charles were American. One of the children's favorite songs was "Everybody Ought to Love Jesus."[16]

Cooking classes were much in demand. Under Elizabeth's direction, Blossom Shop girls baked apples and other dishes. The Camp Fire girls made Valentine cookies in the shape of hearts with red icing and their own initials. In other classes the girls sewed gingham dresses, dainty underskirts, and doll aprons. The Royal Ambassador boys, who called themselves "The Starvation Gang," produced a large variety of woodwork.[17]

An evening English class that Elizabeth taught for adults attracted a Russian mother from just across the street. During class everyone would hear her baby crying, but the mother of eight would stick to the lesson and show no signs of distraction. Obviously her motivation to learn was strong. One night Elizabeth asked, "Why do you take the trouble to come to study English when it is hard for you to get away from your big family?"

"Oh Teacher," the mother exclaimed, "if only I can read the funny paper!"[18]

Black Coffee and Warm Milk

Elizabeth and Nonie often visited the sick and needy, taking medicine, clothing, and the flowers that Lizzie would send as "a whiff of home." They tried to cheer the many doleful and despondent folk, such as lonely "Miss May," who at forty-five so yearned for the children she never had that she spent a great deal of time dressing and playing with a big doll. Visitation was also a means of winning the support of families and finding new pupils for the kindergarten and clubs.

In one Greek home, the mother served cakes and black coffee, which posed a dilemma for Elizabeth. She had never tasted coffee, always spurning it as "black pison." But the mother had so thoughtfully prepared the beverage, Elizabeth realized, that to turn it down might hurt her feelings irreparably. "So I made as if I dearly loved it," she said, "and sipped and sipped. All the same I don't want any more."[19]

Elizabeth was willing to compromise on black coffee more than on unseen germs. At times she seemed fastidious, as when she and Nonie visited an Italian home and the family sent out for ice cream. The visitors liked the cream and thought it safe, but they worried about the cleanliness of the spoon and saucer. As a precaution, they left the part of the cream that was touching the saucer and avoided licking the spoon.

Elizabeth and Nonie often took club members on outings. One cold day—Washington's birthday—they took sixteen of their Blossom Shop and Camp Fire girls on a hike to a dairy more than four miles out in the country. A wooded area they passed appeared to be an animal cemetery. Scattered about were the bleached, snow-white bones of cows and calves, including some perfect skeletons that showed "the wonderful construction of the body."[20]

After taking in the vivid anatomy lesson, the group went to the dairy and watched half a dozen men milk 170 cows by hand, strain the milk, then bottle and stopper it. Each visitor was given a bottle of warm milk to drink and another bottle to take home. Topping off that holiday's entertainment, a calf was born before their eyes!

One day Elizabeth and her colleagues took the kindergarten children across Chesapeake Bay by ferry. When the water grew rough, one little Greek boy apparently recalled the Bible story about Jesus and his disciples being caught in a storm. Without saying a word to anyone, he walked out on the heaving prow, stretched out his arms, and said, "Peace, be still." To Elizabeth's astonishment, the sea grew as calm as the child's beatific smile.[21]

Another time Elizabeth took the kindergartners to see a circus parade. Since Nonie was tied up with guests, Elizabeth had exclusive charge of the wriggling, restless tots. She worried that the elephants would trample them or some other catastrophe would befall them. One spectator saw Elizabeth's plight and offered his empty truck to hold her charges. No sooner had she piled them in than two of the children cried to go home. Elizabeth entrusted the others with two mothers while she rushed the fussy ones to their homes. When she returned, breathless from running, the parade was over except for the fading strains of the steam piano. Although thankful to find her kiddies safe, Elizabeth was downcast at missing most of the show.

Sunday was the most welcome day of the week, for there were no services at the settlement house. Elizabeth attended Freemason Street Baptist Church—now a Virginia historical landmark—and taught a class of Intermediate girls, usually with twenty to thirty present. Some of the men of the church regularly provided transportation for her and the settlement children. "You should have seen us piled up in Mr. Rhode's little five passenger Ford coupe—fifteen of us—some three deep," Elizabeth wrote. "Mr. Petty's was the only other one of our cars 'runable' today."[22]

Fun and Tacky Times

Though her work schedule was heavy, Elizabeth found time for recreation alone or with Nonie. There were street cars bustling to and from the beaches, and Elizabeth went as often as she could, taking her skirted, one-piece wool bathing suit. Never before had she lived near the ocean. She loved to frolic in the surf, to sniff the salty air, to watch and hear the waves come crashing in.

On a Tuesday night, their only free night in the week, Elizabeth and Nonie were invited to a church tacky party. Tuesday being a hectic day with three club meetings, they had no time to think of costumes until after supper. Then, with several of the neighbors watching in amusement, they rummaged in their trunks and began combining and fixing assorted pieces of clothing.

Nonie dressed as an old crippled granny, a backwoods creature hopping on a stick. Elizabeth was her daughter, Andy, in quest of some "eddication." She wore black slippers, white hose, long narrow blue skirt sagging off her hips, brown ribbon sash, white waist with high collar and variegated tie, a handkerchief pinned near the belt, and brown Bib gloves. Her hair was screwed in a knot, and a white georgette hat with a pink ribbon trailing around it hung off the back of her head. To complete the effect, she had gold front teeth and carried a huge bouquet of mixed paper flowers.

The two women walked to the church furtively, using the darkest streets. For her part in the "tacky" program, Elizabeth recited "Father Francis, Sister Sue." The climax came when all the revelers joined in a grand march around the room so that the judges might choose the most outrageous costumes. Elizabeth was declared the tackiest woman. She and the winning male were coaxed to the platform to receive their prizes. His was a mouth organ, and hers was a huge box wrapped with an excess of tissue paper, which she had to unwrap on the spot. Inside was a yellow pumpkin.[23]

There were times when Elizabeth looked tacky without meaning to. "Nonie and Pretty Lady have gotten after me repeatedly lately to get a slip," she told Lizzie, "saying that my clinging dresses call for one."[24] Lizzie sent her a princess slip, silk and shadow-proof, and Elizabeth put it to use. But she resisted, at least for the present, the hair style that was the rage: "All the mothers and grandmothers around here—white and colored—have theirs bobbed. I've about gotten disgusted with it."[25] The only concession she made on hair was to allow John LaBrie, her cousin Catherine's husband, to remove her "mustache." "He burned it off with acid," she told Earle, "and now I'll have no more funny place on my face. So you can't tease me any more about it, goodie."[26]

Elizabeth sallied forth to Portsmouth one evening to visit her aunt Jennie and uncle John Bomar (he was the new pastor of Westhaven Baptist Church). While walking to the ferry, she felt something wrapping about her ankles. A ragged fringe was protruding from beneath her new frock and hanging about two inches below it. Inside the lighted waiting room, Elizabeth saw clearly that the hem had come out of her slip, not the one Lizzie had sent but a blue one she had bought to go with the frock. Fortunately, she had grabbed up a handful of hairpins and put them in her pocket before leaving home. So when Elizabeth boarded the street car on the Portsmouth side of the river, she found a quiet private nook and pinned up the stringy raw edge while passing through the town.

Another day, seeing some children in uptown Norfolk with advertisement balloons, she asked a little boy where he got his and was told that a ten-cent store was giving them away. Having a sweet tooth for toy balloons, Elizabeth walked several blocks to the store. "I prissed up and got in line to get a balloon," she told Lizzie. But the clerk asked, "Where is your child?" Elizabeth went away red-faced and empty-handed.[27]

At a deeper level, she could not help but be sensitive to questions about the children she did not have, and as a defense mechanism she would joke about wanting at least twenty-three of her own. Some of Elizabeth's and Nonie's friends openly expressed pity for these "unclaimed blessings," urging the women not to throw away their lives as old maids. For her part, Elizabeth secretly derided these unwanted advisors as "field hands." But even Lizzie, who had remained single until the age of twenty-eight, expressed concern about her daughter's chances. "Please cheer up," Elizabeth retorted, "and get happy again about my old-maidenly state of mind."[28]

The widowed Lizzie was herself a prospect for marriage. "So you enjoyed your dear friend, Dr. V— this morning!" Elizabeth teased her. "I'm curious to know if his eyes were still closed and if your jim-jams returned."[29] The banter persisted, but Lizzie never wed a second time.

Elizabeth attended two lectures given at her church by a Mr. Jenkins. The lectures were titled "Making Love in Automobiles" and "Would You Marry Your Companion Again?" "Especially did I enjoy the first one," Elizabeth reported, without giving details. "He certainly believes in girls getting married."[30]

Her former boy friends Willie Hare and Sam Lawton still hovered about in her memory. When Sam wrote her of his upcoming trip to the Holy Land—this was twelve months before his marriage to Alice Stockton—Elizabeth excitedly sent a reply to his ship.[31] After hearing from Sam again, she wrote to her brother Earle: "I have one more chance to live a life different from an old maid's. Heard from my old beau! What do you think of that? If Sam would just start off again, I'd be all fixed, for poor Sam can't see, and poor Willie can't walk without limping. 'My beaus and I' would be a good subject for a column of funnies."[32] "There's hope for me yet," she wrote to Lizzie. "How would I look as 'Mrs. Willie Hare'?"[33]

Thoughts of Japan

Elizabeth had been in Norfolk less than six months when she again queried the Foreign Mission Board about an appointment to Japan. This time the Board sent her application forms, requested a medical examination, and began its routine background check.

Accompanied by Nonie, Elizabeth went to a physician for the exam. "I dreaded it," she wrote, "but Dr. Smith was lovely and did not make me take my shoes off even." The doctor found that her heart, lungs, and kidneys were all in good condition, and assured her there was no medical reason why she could not be appointed for overseas work.

"Why am I so thin?" Elizabeth asked.

"Probably because of undernourishment, not enough rest, and using up all your nervous energy," the doctor replied.[34]

Elizabeth felt she was eating enough. As insurance, she drank a half-pint bottle of cream every day—though not all at once. She mixed the cream with Horlick's malted milk and enjoyed it three or four times a day. As for rest, she was getting at least seven hours sleep. Though concerned about her weight, she was reassured by the doctor's report and eagerly awaited good news from Richmond.

The neighborhood had mail delivery twice a day. The letter carrier, a friendly black man, would whistle when he had anything for the settlement house. Though the house had a mailbox, Elizabeth or one of her colleagues would run out to take the letters from his hand. Until the all-important letter arrived from the Foreign Mission Board, Elizabeth monopolized the run.

"You are still being afflicted by that complaint we have discussed before," Secretary Ray's letter said. Elizabeth was not yet twenty-three, and she needed to be a full twenty-four or twenty-five. True, that same year the Board appointed twenty-three-year-old Helen Bagby to Brazil and twenty-two-year-old Frances King to China. But these women were MKs (missionary kids), already at home in the language and culture and eagerly awaited by their biological and spiritual families on the field. The other appointees were up to ten years older than Elizabeth.

"A number of people in writing about you," Ray continued, "speak of your tendency to nervousness and of your tendency to overwork yourself. All recommend you in the highest terms, mentally, spiritually and socially. More than one of them says, 'If she is strong enough physically, she ought to be appointed.'" To Ray, this "if" was a flashing caution light. He urged Elizabeth to work with more deliberation, do fewer things, and conserve her strength. "I want you, when you are appointed, to be in the pink of condition," he explained.[35]

The next year Lizzie urged her daughter to come home and fatten up by "doing nothing." Elizabeth declined. "When I lived in Spartanburg," she reminded Lizzie, "I was always pitifully thin. Am no thinner here than I was there. Maybe some place will turn up that's 'guaranteed to fatten' and then all the family will be happy and I'll be off for Japan."[36]

Elizabeth had her thoughts turned to Japan afresh when she and Nonie were invited to Norfolk's First Baptist Church to meet Lucile Clarke. Lucile was a gifted vocalist who had entertained wounded soldiers during the Russo-Japanese War, a service recognized by Emperor Meiji with the gift of a silver cup bearing the imperial crest. The veteran missionary was dressed in an elegant Japanese costume, and the eight members of the Lucile Clarke Circle who served the tea, cakes, and peanuts were similarly arrayed in kimonos and chrysanthemums. After the meeting in that "upper-crust church," Elizabeth and Nonie were "brought home in a handsome limousine with our heads high in the air."[37]

The next afternoon the pair attended a reception in Lucile's honor at a private home. "There, mingling with the elite, polished women," Elizabeth wrote, "Nonie and I rose on wings to the ranks of the privileged."[38] The reception was also a surprise shower for the charming guest. After refreshments and a program of readings, two little children dressed as Japanese entered the room. They were drawing a wagon that was covered with crepe paper of the WMU colors—purple, white, green, gold, and blue—and piled with white gifts. Several women brought in more gifts by the armful. When the procession of packages stopped before Lucile, she gasped in disbelief, then opened each gift and read out the name of the giver. Elizabeth's offering was a rose rubber apron that her aunt Louise Montgomery had given her for Christmas. Everyone exclaimed over the apron, but Elizabeth discreetly chose not to tell Louise what a hit her gift had made.

During Elizabeth's second year at the Baptist settlement house, the European and Asian immigrants began moving out of the neighborhood, and Afro-Americans began moving in. "A good size Negro boy," Elizabeth reported, "was actually found in our yard this past week playing with the white children!"[39] Apparently there was insufficient interest in refocusing the ministry on the new residents. In the spring of 1924, when the piano with black and white keys and the beds of three different colors were less than one year old, the Home Mission Board, on recommendation of the local board, voted to close the work and sell the property. The neighborhood has since become a complex of two-story brick apartments, but it is still overshadowed by towering St. Mary's Catholic Church.

5

Mountain Schoolma'am

WHEN THE HOME MISSION BOARD decided to close the settlement house in Norfolk, B. C. Hening, Superintendent for Work among Foreigners and Negroes, offered to reassign Elizabeth Watkins and Nonie Gravett to a place of their choice. Positions were open, he said, "with the Mexicans in Texas, with the Italians in Oklahoma, and with Indians in Oklahoma."[1] The two women asked instead to teach at one of the thirty mountain schools connected with the Home Mission Board. They were delighted when a telegram from Hening informed them of two openings at Lee Baptist Institute in Pennington Gap, Virginia. Nonie signed on at once. Elizabeth wavered.

A week after her twenty-fourth birthday, the Foreign Mission Board's T. B. Ray had authorized Elizabeth to have another physical examination. "You are still young," he reminded her, "and we may ask you to tarry yet a while. . . . Our real rule is to require young women to be 26 years of age before they are sent out. We have strained a point and allowed some to go at 24 and some at 25." In earlier correspondence, Ray had stated the age requirement as "a full 24 or 25" and "at least 25."[2] He seemed to regard this ambiguity as flexibility.

Elizabeth passed the physical, and a follow-up letter from Secretary J. Franklin Love asked that she "be available for foreign mission service."[3] Her fate hinged on the June meeting of the Foreign Mission Board, which was faced with a serious shortfall from the Seventy-five Million Campaign. Elizabeth and the other candidates were asked not to make other plans until after that meeting, in case they could be invited to Richmond for appointment within the next several months. "I'm at last accepted full-fledged," Elizabeth told Lizzie, "and he's saying he wants me to go if the money comes in."[4]

The June decision was a disappointment. No new missionaries would be sent out unless funding was available apart from the Board's own budget. Elizabeth was further disappointed to learn that the position with Nonie at Lee Institute had been filled. But the Home Mission Board found her a similar teaching post at Watauga Academy in Butler, Tennessee, which was just as well since Nonie did not go to Lee Institute but rather to Tampa for work among Cubans.[5]

After a summer vacation in Spartanburg, Elizabeth rode a "dirty, waterless train" to Johnson City in the mountains of East Tennessee. There she changed trains, walking with other passengers to a different station. After an hour's wait, she went on to Bristol, where she put up at the Hotel Virginian. After breakfast the next morning Elizabeth walked to State Street, so named because the Tennessee-Virginia state line runs down its center. An old photograph of a State Street parade shows the governors of Tennessee and Virginia riding in the back seat of an open car, each remaining in his own state as the car straddles the center line.[6]

Elizabeth found pleasure in going down the street in Tennessee and, after crossing to the opposite side, coming back in Virginia. She entered five-and-ten-cent stores in both states. After killing time in that novel manner, Elizabeth ate lunch and then boarded the Southern

Railway train that ran the half-loop to Mountain City by way of Elizabethton and Butler. The "funny little train" clattered across terrain deeply scarred by the devastating flood of June 1924. A twelve-inch downpour had sent the Watauga River on a rampage, causing twelve deaths and washing out fourteen miles of track between Hampton and Butler. Great chasms and piles of debris still lay along the tracks.[7]

When Elizabeth got off at Butler, a festive crowd awaited, for meeting the train each afternoon was a major diversion in this isolated town. It was a community of five hundred souls, three churches (Baptist, Methodist, Christian), and two industries (lumber and furniture). There were two schools: a public grade school and Baptist-owned Watauga Academy. The latter was a middle and high school with an enrollment of sixty-four.

Elizabeth's first impression of the campus, located a quarter-mile southwest of the depot, was anything but good. The approach was marred by a worm-eaten board fence and a creaky gate. The two dormitories were old and nondescript. Heating was poor and crude, and plumbing but a future dream. Water and coal had to be carried up the stairs, "slops" and ashes down the stairs. In Farthing Hall, the dormitory for girls, some of the rough wooden boards in the floors upstairs were so far apart that when they were swept, dirt fell on the girls in the rooms below.

The school's centerpiece, the administration building with a four-column porch, was more imposing and better equipped than the dorms. On the first floor was a library with five hundred books, not a haphazard collection as was often the case in mountain schools, but each volume carefully chosen. There were twenty periodicals, all kept in attractive, homemade covers. On the second floor was a chapel with shiny seats free of scratches, mute testimony that the students showed respect for the furnishings. Indeed, they spoke proudly of *our* school.[8]

The four-acre campus had such a homey atmosphere that it was more like a cozy yard. And what a lovely setting! Roan Creek flowed audibly at the back of the school, making its way to the Watauga River at the other end of town. A rustic bridge spanned the meandering creek. Round about were picturesque mountains and boundless forests of hardwood trees.

These redeeming features notwithstanding, Watauga Academy and its environment severely tested Elizabeth's capacity to adjust. "I might as well be in Kalamazoo as here, as far as civilization goes," she wrote. ". . . It is disgusting to find people so backward." When she went shopping for gloves and wool stockings in Elizabethton, the closest town to Butler, she complained: "Everything is both tacky and high or 'they don't have it.' You pay about twice the amount for a purchase in these small mountain towns that you do in a city. . . . I just don't see how people stand living in desolation." Elizabeth had been spoiled by living in downtown Norfolk "where in fifteen minutes after you decided you wanted something you could have it."[9]

Some of the people, Elizabeth charged, were "as dinky as the stores." Even professionals could arouse her ire. Dr. U. G. Jones, an eye, ear, nose, and throat specialist she consulted in Johnson City for her sinus trouble, was "too brusque, unsympathetic, and rough."[10] The doctor said she had a bad catarrhal condition of the nose that would take a long time to get rid of. Elizabeth was skeptical of his diagnosis and was of a mind to ignore his prescription. Back at Watauga Academy, however, the other teachers persuaded her to give the doctor's orders a try.

Elizabeth sprayed her throat three times a day with "some vile stuff after dropping some black or brown viler stuff in each side of my nose. . . . This medicine in my nose and throat makes my handkerchiefs all brown and terrible looking in one using." The convenience of paper tissues still in her future, Elizabeth wished for "a room full of old rags."[11]

Sponge Baths and Raw Milk

Elizabeth occupied an upstairs room in Farthing Hall, where she endured the same rigorous life as the other occupants. Bathing was crude. She would heat a small kettle of water on the little coal stove in her room, pour it into a wash basin, and sponge her shivering body. "I've not had a bath now for three months!" she wrote Lizzie in November. "Such is life."[12]

Elizabeth had her brother Earle to send her a flashlight. The electricity was cut off at 10:15 each night, and she usually had to take her sponge bath after that time. She also used the flashlight to go down into the milk cellar to get her daily quart that Rheta Williams, a senior, brought as she came to school. Elizabeth drank the milk religiously, hoping to put some fat on her bones.

Later she was able to get fresh milk from the school matron's cow, after its calf had been weaned. With Lizzie's encouragement, she began drinking an extra quart a day, taking some at meals as well as between meals. But she cut back on consumption after her face got bumpy and she thought the milk was to blame.

Elizabeth paid ten dollars for board out of her monthly salary of eighty-five-dollars. The food was always clean, appetizing, and well cooked, with an abundance of delicious meat, vegetables, corn bread, pie, and cake. What a treasure the school had in Ida Dugger, the matron-cook! Mrs. Dugger would call Elizabeth back to the kitchen for some milk or a piece of chocolate pie, and would bring flowers for her room.

Elizabeth was the academy's assistant principal and one of five teachers, all unmarried. The only male, the Reverend C. C. Perry, also served as principal. A graduate of Wake Forest College, Perry was said to be "a rather small, compact man of about thirty, with ruddy complexion and thinning sandy hair. He was polite and congenial, but more or less reticent."[13] Elizabeth thought he needed a wife. "He is a lonesome kind of a creature," she wrote, "who's hankering for someone to talk to."[14]

Elizabeth helped meet the principal's social needs by playing tennis with him on the school's court, a rough surface dotted with growing grass and marked off with sharp sticks instead of lime. But romantic interest between the two was nil. At year's end Perry resigned to pursue a seminary degree.

Among the other faculty members, Loretta Stout was Lady Principal and teacher of history and Latin. Anna J. Merryman taught Bible and home economics. Like Elizabeth, Merryman was a graduate of the WMU Training School in Louisville and had done other mission work before coming to Butler. She was to write the school song and earn high respect in the community during the coming years.[15]

The music teacher, Bettie Thornton, befriended Elizabeth from the outset and gave her piano lessons. Trained at the Cincinnati Conservatory of Music, Thornton was "funny and old-maidish, wearing gloves to work in . . . and walking gingerly along for fear she get a speck of dust on her shoes."[16] Elizabeth loved her more than any of the other teachers and, when the two were alone, called her "Simpie," meaning Sympathizer. Simpie had a big heart combined with common sense and a deep spiritual life as well as a refreshing sense of humor.

From Mountain and Hollow

Most of Watauga's boarding students came to school Monday mornings from the surrounding mountains and hollows and returned home Friday afternoons. Many walked; others rode on an animal or in a jolting homemade wagon. One of Elizabeth's duties as assistant principal was to look after their dormitory expenses. The room charge was $2.50 per term, plus the actual cost of electric lights and coal for heating. Electricity was $1.50 per month for each pupil if a sixty-watt bulb was used, and $1.75 if a seventy-five-watt bulb was used. Board, furnished at cost, averaged $7.50 per month for those who went home on weekends and $10.50 for those who remained on campus.[17]

Figuring individual expenses was complicated because one student would come to school on Monday with a pig, the price of which had to be deducted from his or her bill, and another would bring so many pats of butter, a peck of apples, or some potatoes. Elizabeth's arithmetic nearly broke down under the strain. Tuition, ranging from $3.00 to $4.00 per month, was also subject to adjustments. Jake Miller, she reported, "rides in to the school on a mule daily and makes fire in the schoolhouse to help pay for his tuition."[18]

Elizabeth taught English, French, algebra, and geometry in the tenth, eleventh, and twelfth grades.[19] She was impressed by how clever her English pupils were. Several knew the textbooks so well that they consistently made grades in the upper nineties. But come Friday afternoon, they shed their "larnin" like a garment and put back on their mountain dialect—"Appalonics"?—which they continued to use as they returned to school on Monday morning. Then when the nine o'clock bell rang, they switched back to good English as if by magic and used it until Friday again.

THE
SCHOOL
TEACHER

Just think of what it means, alas!
To be a pupil in your class;
The only joy that's to be found.
Is when dismissal time comes round.

Geometry Class
'25

Teaching French was more stressful, since Elizabeth had no ear for foreign languages. Fortunately, her French teacher at Judson College had been a competent instructor. Watauga offered only first-year French, encouraging juniors to take it as an elective. The college preparatory course required two years of Latin.

Algebra and geometry were also required of college-bound students. "I enjoy my math so much more than English," Elizabeth wrote. But she had never been a whiz at it, as her mother had. When stumped by a geometry problem, as sometimes happened, she prayed to God for the solution.[20]

One day a student named Sally came in "a bit late, pale and shaken." She had been walking the railroad track to school, Sally explained, when an approaching train caught her by surprise in the middle of a trestle that spanned a ravine. There was no time to run to the end of the trestle. Clutching her school books in one arm, she swung down between the crossties with the other arm just before the train thundered by overhead. Remarkably, Sally was able to pull herself up without dropping a book.[21]

The boys at the school, some of them older than Elizabeth, knew "all the secrets of paper wads, mirrors, and the other foolishness."[22] They also had a great sense of humor. Some of the boys took a naive new student to Bristol. "Now, in the city," they told him, "a gentleman takes off his hat to ladies." They left him on a busy corner and then ran away to hide and see what he would do. There he stood, conscientiously jerking off his cap to every woman who passed him. Then, catching sight of the manikins in a store window and thinking them real women, he took off his cap to them also, while the scamps around the corner snorted with glee.[23]

The mountain people were generally retarded in formal education because of poor schools, a shorter school year, and their isolation from and neglect by the outside world. Watauga was ranked in the C class of Tennessee high schools.[24] But the mountain people were hardy and resourceful, making many of their tools and utensils by hand. They were marked by strong individualism and personal faith, as Elizabeth realized increasingly from visiting in her students' homes. She also learned of "several bastards in the school. That sin is so terribly prevalent in this section."[25]

One Thursday afternoon classes were cancelled so that the teachers and students could go as a group chinquapin hunting. After a long and pleasant tramp over the ever-changing and scenic mountain road, they reached an area of chinquapin trees, where they played "Jack in the Bushes" to see how many nuts they could win from each other, and "Pretty in Her Hand." Elizabeth had never heard of these games before and was amused to watch the couples as the gallant and attentive boys helped the girls find the nuts. On the way back to the school the boys played tricks on each other, and all had a merry time.[26]

Indoor socials were rarer than outdoor treks, and few students seemed to know or care about them. The trustees, whom Elizabeth called "poor blind moles," frowned on social activities and seemed to think that studying was the only thing school was for. Some of them had no patience with even the BYPU (Baptist Young People's Union), saying "it is only a courting machine."[27]

Not until January did the school have its first social of the school year. The girls' literary society (Calliopeans) entertained the boys' literary society (Philomatheans) at a Friday night party. As Elizabeth happened to be society critic, it fell her lot to oversee the party. She listed the obstacles she perceived and found the task daunting. Many students would be gone for the weekend, more of them boys than girls; the social committee seemed helpless and short on ideas; and there was little time for preparation. Elizabeth dreaded the whole affair.

It happened, though, that the students carried out their assignments splendidly. The decoration committee made the room attractive with fluted red paper festooned from the light fixture to the corners of the room. The refreshment committee got their own mothers to make and donate some delicious cakes—devil's food with marshmallow icing and caramel. The girl responsible for the games planned and took charge so well that everything went along without a hitch. Everyone laughed uncontrollably.

The most fun occurred when they were drawing partners for refreshments. Helen Goodwin, a ninth grader, was coupled with Mr. Perry. She looked stricken, he seemed bewildered, and the others howled, but all enjoyed eating the ice cream and cake. Some of the students had such a good time, they said, that they "forgot there was such a thing as a lesson."[28]

Kneeling at the Mourners' Bench

Watauga Academy was strict, and the teacher's word was law. "It was almost like being in the army," said one alumna.[29] Religious activities were a part of the regimentation. Not only were Bible courses required of all students, but each morning at ten they were marched to chapel for a solemn worship service.

The religious program of the school was closely linked with that of Butler Baptist Church. Active in the church as always, Elizabeth started a Young Woman's Auxiliary and introduced the six-point record system to the Sunday School. She also ordered *Girls' Weekly* for her own class. "Sunday School is so backward, stupid, and uninteresting here," she explained, "I feel you have to do something to attract them."[30] The girls were enthusiastic about reading the material and doing the written exercises. One of them, nestling close to Elizabeth, looked up with loving eyes and said, "You are the first teacher we ever had to get us papers and nice books."[31]

One church duty piqued her. "It's a joke, but true," she wrote Lizzie, "that your melodious daughter *must* grace the choir. There is no way out. I've tried in all ways to keep from disturbing the already varied strains issuing forth from that important nook—but to no avail. The superintendent will walk right back to me before the whole Sunday School and argue that I go 'to fill up the chairs if I can't sing' so that I'm thoroughly embarrassed and wish I'd gone before." Sometimes she would open her mouth, singing in her heart but making no noise to disturb others. No one knew but what she was singing, Elizabeth thought, and she was "doing her duty."[32]

The charade was suspended when Elizabeth's mother visited her at Thanksgiving and the two went to church together. "As long as I am here," Lizzie said, "I am not going to see any such joke. Get out of the choir and sit by me." The cowed daughter obeyed.[33]

The teachers were also required to help at the mourner's bench. Anyone who wanted to be saved had to go to the front of the church auditorium and kneel at the designated place. A teacher knelt with the penitent and "prayed him through." For timid and self-conscious

Elizabeth, this chore was unpleasant, but she endured it as another facet of teaching in the mountain mission school.

Elizabeth admired the pastor, R. M. DeVault, as a faithful, consecrated man of God. She was amused at how his status and schedule differed from that of a pastor in the city. Although DeVault lived in Butler, he preached at the Butler church only on the second and fourth Sundays of the month. The other Sundays he ministered at two other churches of which he was pastor. His annual salary at the Butler church was $660, and at the other two churches combined, $322.[34] His salary seems to have averaged about $82 per month, less than Elizabeth's $85, and he had a large family to support. Fortunately, he was able to do part-time farming, and church members gave him potatoes or other produce and fed him Sunday dinner. This pattern of support was typical of country churches.

But life in the region was far from idyllic. Elizabeth sat bug-eyed one Sunday morning when a bevy of Ku Klux Klansmen marched into the church at the close of the offertory. Representing a movement that boasted four million members, the white supremacists in ghostly robes presented the pastor with a check for thirty-five dollars to help pay for new pews then being installed. Elizabeth had never seen money contributed to a church with such drama and flair.

Less friendly to the church were the region's moonshiners and bootleggers, another flourishing breed in that prohibition era. Despite an occasional bust by the "feds," rural stills operated at full capacity, producing booze of uneven and often dreadful quality. The citizens of Butler, led by the Baptists, strongly opposed the "whiskey crowd," as Elizabeth called them, despite the threat of retaliation. One morning it was discovered that generous amounts of kerosene had been poured over most of the town's stores. Why they had not been set afire, no one knew. A store burned down a few miles away, but the Butler stores survived.

In late January, Juliette Mather wrote to Elizabeth telling of two job openings and offering to recommend her for either of the two. One position was "student worker" at Florida State College for Women in Tallahassee, promoting YWA and other activities among the Baptists. The other, which Juliette recommended, was young people's leader of the Oklahoma WMU.

Elizabeth hesitated to leave Watauga after only one year but felt she had no choice. Her debut as a schoolteacher had not come off well. "The work has grown more distasteful and irksome daily, " she told Lizzie, "causing me to feel I am such a failure and a misfit. Such a large percent of the students failed completely in my classes this month that I am concerned I can't teach."[35] She discussed the matter with Perry, who said it would be perfectly honorable for her to resign, since he could get a replacement. She then wrote to the Foreign Mission Board and learned that its financial difficulties would almost certainly rule out her being appointed soon. That door closed, Elizabeth told Juliette she would accept the Oklahoma position if it were offered her.

Toward the end of the school year the church experienced a stirring, fruitful revival. There were thirty-five additions, almost all by baptism. At revival's end, all but one of Elizabeth's twenty-two Sunday School girls were believers and all but eight were members of the church or candidates for baptism. The revival provided a needed boost to Elizabeth's spirit as she prepared to leave for a greener pasture.

Long-needed improvements came to Butler and Watauga Academy the following year. A water system was installed in the town and plumbing in the school. The dormitories were painted, and the living rooms and society halls were equipped with elegant new chairs.[36]

But years of struggle lay ahead. The Home Mission Board began to disassociate itself from mountain schools because of a burdensome debt and the progressive spread of public schools. In 1931 the local trustees of Watauga Academy entered into contract with the Johnson County Board of Education to operate the school under a "dual-control system." In 1940 the Baptist association sold the school to the county, which closed it in 1948 when the Tennessee Valley Authority completed construction of Watauga Dam and moved the entire town of Butler to higher ground two miles away. The site where Elizabeth taught—and wished for running water—has since lain 160 feet beneath the surface of Watauga Lake.[37]

6

Wandering the Sooner State

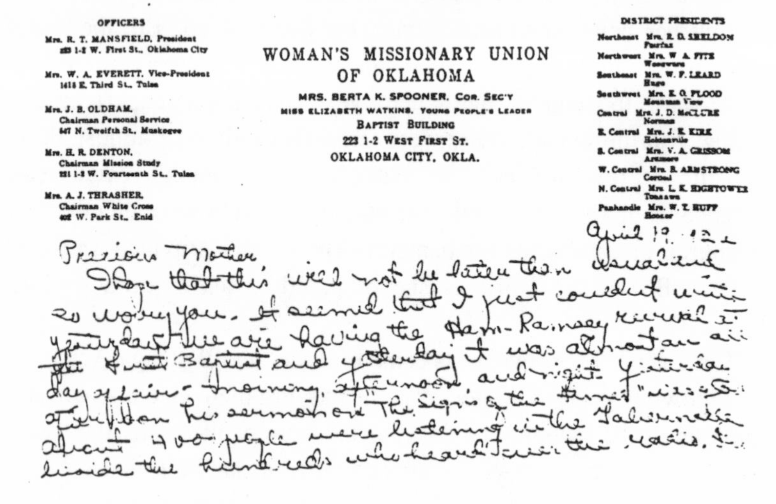

[Handwritten letter:]

Precious Mother,
I hope that this will not be later than usual and so worry you. It seemed that I just couldn't write yesterday. We are having the Ham-Ramsey revival at the First Baptist and yesterday it was almost an all day affair — morning, afternoon, and night. I listened to [Mordecai] F. Ham's sermon on "The Sign of the Times" over the radio about 400 people were listening in the Tabernacle beside the hundreds who heard him on the radio. I...

JULIETTE MATHER INSTRUCTED ELIZABETH to be in Memphis the second week of May for the tandem sessions of the Woman's Missionary Union and the Southern Baptist Convention. There Elizabeth would meet with the delegates from the Oklahoma WMU and be interviewed for the position of young people's leader. Having never attended a Southwide Baptist event, the candidate was doubly excited over the trip.

Elizabeth made a hurried visit to Spartanburg, then joined her uncle Edward Bomar for the train ride to Memphis, where she stayed in Hotel Chisca. Southside Baptist Church had elected her a "messenger" (delegate) to both the "women's meeting" and the "men's meeting." Women had been seated as messengers to the male-dominated

SBC sessions since 1918, but they were still a tiny, voiceless minority. The Memphis convention's 5,600 messengers heard even the WMU report from the mouth of a man.[1]

Besides the mass gatherings in Municipal Auditorium and First Baptist Church, Elizabeth attended group meetings such as the WMU Training School banquet at the Chamber of Commerce, which brought together alumnae from around the world. She talked and laughed with scores of relatives and friends, among them Jessie Dye, her social-work partner at the Training School and now director of the Good Will Center in Memphis. Less happily, she found herself an object of curiosity to the hundred or so women from Oklahoma. The word had spread that she would likely be their new young people's leader.

Elizabeth was interviewed and scrutinized so often that she "felt like a little boxed mouse being passed from hand to hand for inspection."[2] The chief inspector was Berta Keys Spooner, the state WMU's corresponding secretary, a position later called executive secretary-treasurer and more recently, director. The fifty-year-old widow had proven her business acumen by successfully running her late husband's hardware business for six years before training for religious work at Southwestern Baptist Seminary in Ft. Worth. A native of Decatur, Alabama, Mrs. Spooner was remarked for her clear, commanding voice with a "beautiful Southern accent." She stood tall and erect, "with shoulders squared like a military leader."[3] Her calculating mind, common sense, and gentle wit made her an ideal supervisor for Elizabeth, who, when formally offered the young people's post on Saturday afternoon, promptly accepted.

Elizabeth's collapsing hope of being appointed to Japan had been further battered Friday night when J. Franklin Love announced that the Foreign Mission Board was $1.2 million in debt and might have to "call home some of our workers."[4] That discouraging word was a convincing sign to Elizabeth that the Oklahoma post was God's will for the present. As Secretary Love had tried to explain, when Southern Baptists launched the Seventy-five Million Campaign in 1919, the response was overwhelming. Pledges totaled more than $92 million, to be paid over the next five years. With $20 million of this amount earmarked for foreign missions, the Board set out to double its overseas force—a move premature if not reckless. When the campaign came to a close at the end of 1924, less than $59 million had been collected, and foreign missions had reaped only $10.5 million. The shortfall left the overextended Board near collapse.[5]

To WMU administrators like Berta Spooner, this was no way to run a business—certainly not the Lord's business. Fannie E. W. Heck scorned debt as "extravagance," "disgraceful," and "unnecessary," even suggesting that using mission funds to make interest payments was robbing God. "Like all other women," said another leader, "I hate the three D's—Debt, Dirt, and the Devil."[6] Yet WMU societies in Oklahoma and throughout the South continued to stand by the debt-laden mission boards, both home and foreign, with their generous financial support.

On Saturday night, "foreign missions night" at the "men's meeting," Elizabeth felt an uneasy peace within as she gazed with envy and admiration at the nineteen missionaries on stage. Three were furloughees from Japan: Frances Fulghum, who sang a Japanese song on the program, and Norman and Fannie Williamson. Elizabeth could not know how these three would impact her life in the next decade. Throughout the evening she struggled to keep her confused thoughts focused on her commitment to Oklahoma.

On Sunday morning Elizabeth went to the First Presbyterian Church to hear the noted evangelist and prolific writer R. A. Torrey ("perhaps the greatest sermon I ever heard"). In the afternoon, at Municipal Auditorium, she heard the preaching of Dallas pastor George W. Truett and the singing of a hundred-voice Negro choir that made her tingle all over. After a final conference that evening, Elizabeth boarded the 11:40 train for Oklahoma. She shared a Pullman berth with Mrs. Spooner, who, acting more like a mother than a boss, gently kissed her ward good night.[7]

To the Work in the West

Juliette Mather had advised Elizabeth to be prepared to go directly to the work in Oklahoma, but no one had warned that she would begin by speaking at ten district meetings of two days each. First came the East Central District meeting in Wilberton on Monday and Tuesday, followed by the others in rapid succession. Accompanying Elizabeth and Mrs. Spooner was Mabel Swartz Withoft of Georgia, the author of *Oak and Laurel*, an eyewitness account of Southern Baptists' mountain schools. Several years had passed since Withoft's visit to Butler, Tennessee, so Elizabeth briefed her on recent happenings there.

The three women buzzed around the Sooner State by train and bus, staying in hotels and in homes. They spoke in "beautiful city churches facing a great crowd of beautifully dressed women" and in "plain country churches" filled with "plain country folk." The lavish church dinners and tasty home meals, Elizabeth said, were "enough to make us all as fat as hogs."[8]

Near Muskogee they observed the three hundred students at the Northern Baptist-directed school for Native Americans. "One girl with her long black hair, fair complexion, and delicately chiseled features was beautiful," Elizabeth noted. "Such must have been Pocahontas and Minnehaha." Elsewhere she was fascinated by the "blanket Indians," some with platted hair under a straw hat with a red feather stuck in the band.[9]

The traveling trio were entertained by "the most gracious folks anywhere," but one hostess, Mrs. Pennington, was unique. Not only was she Mrs. Spooner's sister, but among her eight children were ten-year-old quadruplets. "Three have dark hair and eyes while the fourth has light hair and blue eyes," Elizabeth observed. "Altogether they weighed something over 16 lbs. when born."[10]

During their travels Elizabeth had no money and needed none. Businesswoman Spooner made all arrangements, bought the tickets, paid the bills. One day a train conductor asked Elizabeth, "Lady, where are you going?"

"I don't know," she replied.

"Well, lady," he said, "what are you doing on this train if you don't know where you're going?"

Before Elizabeth could explain, another passenger spoke up: "This lady has a perfectly good chaperon close by."[11]

On the day she arrived in Oklahoma City, Elizabeth learned with embarrassment that the capital was different from the smaller towns which had served as her orientation to the state. A police officer "arrested" her for jaywalking. There were pleasant encounters too. Elsie (Mrs. R. T.) Mansfield, the state WMU president whom she had met in Memphis, extended her a gracious welcome as "our much-needed, long-looked-for Young People's Leader." And Lucy Smith, a YWA president and future missionary to China and Japan, became her friend.[12]

Elizabeth lodged for a season at the Baptist orphanage, where the Mansfields were employed. She was impressed that each child was "adopted" by a WMU society, which provided personalized clothing and gifts as well as linens, blankets, and food. Some children, moreover, were "borrowed" by their society during the summer vacation and lavished with affection.[13]

Then she moved up town, closer to her office in the three-story Baptist building on First Street. She slept at Mrs. Harper's rooming house and ate at Mrs. Mayer's boarding house. Mrs. Harper, a divorcée with two children and two or more "beaus," struck Elizabeth as "pitiful," "dressing with clothes to knees, no undershirt sometimes and a thin dress, paint thick on cheeks and lips, hair dyed and curled, and eyes blacked."[14]

If Mrs. Harper was brazen in appearance, Elizabeth was drab and out of style. Berta Spooner, who sported bright red hats, advised her subordinate that a permanent would improve her looks. Beauty parlors and permanents had recently come into vogue, but Elizabeth spurned the advice at first, thinking it extravagant to pay $12.50 for curls she could well do without. She hated "artificial looking things." Then she began to worry that if others saw her as tacky or unkempt, they might think Christian workers regarded themselves as different from everyone else, and this wrong impression might deter them from a Christian vocation. Elizabeth remembered her own experience at Judson College, where Daisy Ray's dowdy dress provoked the reaction, "If that is a foreign missionary, I'll never be one!" She recalled Maud McLure's prayers that the Training School students might be "winsome for Jesus' sake."[15]

Her mind now changed, Elizabeth made a date with the Permanent Wave Shop. The three-hour treatment with the fat hair-curling irons left her ecstatic. "Do you remember how you used to roll up my hair on rags to try to make your only daughter have curls?" she wrote Lizzie. "Well, you did your best to have a beautiful, curly-haired daughter, but the ugly duckling wouldn't be transformed. Now at last, after years of rolling it up, breaking it off, tangling it—I have . . . a permanent wave." And what was Mrs. Harper's reaction when she saw it? "Oh, what beautiful hair, naturally curly, too, isn't it?"[16]

Soon Elizabeth was striking out on her own by bus and train, and all the more thankful that her hair was always "ready to fix." She was "on the trot" so much that by July she felt like "an old dog in the field work." She led YWA house parties, taught mission study courses, organized new groups. The Radium Springs Assembly at Salina, featuring radium baths known for their medicinal powers, kept her busy for nine days. So did the Falls Creek Assembly in the Arbuckle Mountains—Arbuckle "hills" to Elizabeth after a year in Butler, Tennessee—where more than seven hundred were present. The Falls Creek faculty included Juliette Mather, who despite a painful crick in her neck, went home with Elizabeth for a weekend tête-à-tête.[17]

One Saturday night in July, Elizabeth arrived in Carmen by train, then hired a cab that rattled along to Fairview, where she was deposited at the hotel. "I was so sleepy," Elizabeth reported, "that I deferred even the bowl and pitcher bath and tumbled into bed about the time goblins walk."[18] The next day she taught a Sunday School class, preached at the eleven o'clock hour, talked to Sunbeams in the afternoon, and preached in the evening service. On Monday she had lunch with the pastor, then talked to GAs at three, RAs at four, YWAs at seven, and WMU members at eight. Elizabeth kept at it like a politician on the campaign trail.

In McAlester, where she stayed in Mrs. Allen's regal home, Elizabeth enjoyed a private sleeping porch facing the misty hills, with an adjoining sitting room and private bath. "I feel like the Queen of Sheba," she wrote. But in Custer City "I was entertained by dear people as poor as Mrs. Allen is rich. Only one bedroom for father, mother, two boys, one daughter, and three guests. They slept in the yard and all over the house. A tin wash pan of cold water for all bathing. Red-brown rain water from the roof the only drinking water." In other towns also she stayed in humble abodes where she sat on "boxes and cracked chairs" and slept out of doors on hay.[19]

Elizabeth loved the variety in her work and reveled in the uncertainty of what would happen next. "I feel that I have been let out of a cage or freed from behind iron bars now that I am away from Watauga and the schoolma'am life."[20] The adventurous life in the West con-trasted sharply with the monotony back at Butler, where the binding, repetitive schedule had frayed her nerves. Her only repetitive work in Oklahoma was preparing a weekly column ("Auxiliary Achieve-ments") for the statewide paper, *Baptist Messenger*.

By summer's end Elizabeth was convinced that Oklahoma was "a state where every young man has an equal chance and where you are accepted on your face value without reference to who your kin people are or where you came from. The man in the patched overalls is just as welcomed and important as the finely dressed dude."[21] The women in Oklahoma had to work harder, she noted, but they enjoyed consider-able freedom from convention, even going to church without hats. Most impressive to Elizabeth, at a large luncheon where each person had to give her native state, not one was an Oklahoman by birth. Because of Oklahoma's unique history as Indian Territory, home-steading came late and the state was still young.

Elizabeth was learning to swing along with the Sooners and the Boomers, and she was pleased that they seemed to accept her as one of their own. "I'm getting as brown as a young Indian . . . ," she wrote. "My white arms I brought out here are all gone. . . . I'm getting so brown that when I bathe, my arms don't look as if they are kin to my legs." A friend called her "a sure nuff black full-blood Oklahoma girl now," which was no surprise to Elizabeth "after the glorious swim-ming, hiking, and love-making with the sun and wind."[22]

At the state WMU convention in November, where she shared the platform with Kathleen Mallory, J. B. Lawrence, E. Y. Mullins, and other dignitaries, Elizabeth presented a lengthy report around the theme of diamonds. "Just as there are black, white, pink, blue, brown, yellow, and green diamonds," she said, "so the color of our Oklahoma jewel is not always white."[23] At this point in her report she paid tribute to R. E. Young, a black RA leader who had organized new chapters with great skill and enthusiasm. The tribute reflected the WMU's pioneer role in bettering race relations in Oklahoma and across the South.

A Wanderer on the Earth

During the fall Elizabeth spoke at seventeen of the forty-eight Baptist associational meetings held throughout the state. "I'm still a wanderer on the earth," she wrote. Her November report states that since coming to Oklahoma she had spent 101 days on the field as against 53 in the office, and she had stayed in 66 different homes.[24]

Elizabeth had to catch trains and buses all hours. She would be met at a station and driven fifty or a hundred miles in an open car across "treeless plains where the sun beat down on the sagebrush," over prairies "between fields of waving golden wheat that stretch as far as eye can see," past forests of oil derricks (Oklahoma had fifty thousand wells), through clusters of storage tanks that reminded Elizabeth of tombstones in a cemetery, by zinc and lead mines where people lived wretched lives in dog-kennel houses or big boxes. She would speak at a church with its own cyclone cellar out back, then be driven back to the station to catch another bus or train.[25]

Elizabeth had been miserably trainsick during her college days when she was going back and forth between South Carolina and Alabama, but that weakness she overcame in Oklahoma. Like the much-traveled Annie Armstrong, first corresponding secretary of the national WMU, she learned to relax and sleep on trains as though at home. Elizabeth would be seasick many times in the future, but never trainsick again.

Whether she ate biscuits and fried chicken three times a day or enjoyed more variety, the food was so sumptuous that she felt "like a toad fed with shot." In her chasing around, however, often she had to skip meals or skimp on them, so that actually she got thinner, not fatter. This added to the discomfort of sitting on a hard church bench all day and into the night. "I just wish I had a little thicker pads on me where I sit down," she groaned, "so my bones wouldn't rub the seat. . . . I'm trying to get up courage to begin wearing a corset but have so far treated this spell of self-respect as per usual." Her words might have interested Sears, Roebuck and Company, whose 1925 catalogue promoted corsets only as a way to "remove your excess fat."[26]

While teaching "Stewardship and Missions" one week at Oklahoma Agricultural and Mechanical College in Stillwater, Elizabeth attended her first rodeo, saw an exhibition of aesthetic dancing, and experienced dormitory life afresh. "I was in the room with a lively freshman," she wrote, "and in the heart of college pranks. The boys serenaded the girls one night. Another night while the rest of us were asleep, my peppy roommate got a number of girls lined up down the hall and at a given signal all slammed the doors. How the house mother and frightened girls from first floor rushed up! They could never discover what the crash was or who were the culprits, and I did not know until later."[27]

There were frustrating moments also. Once when Elizabeth was returning to Oklahoma City on a Pullman car, the conductor asked what time she wished to be called in the morning. Since the train was due to arrive at 6:15, she asked for 5:45, and the conductor wrote it down. The next morning she was "punched in the ribs" at 6:10. In pajamas, she hastily jerked on her clothes, then rang and rang for the porter to let her down from her upper berth. He did not come until the train had stopped. The other passengers were getting off, but he told her not to worry, that the train would wait there a while. No sooner had Elizabeth gone to the dressing room and started taking the curlers out of her hair—her permanent had worn off—than the train began to move, getting faster and faster. Elizabeth was angry and scared. She could find no one to stop the train, and she did not know where it was going. All she could see outside was the darkness. Finally she found the porter, who asked, "Did you want to get off at Oklahoma City?"

Elizabeth ran back to the dressing room, grabbed on her hat after stuffing her hair in, jerked the rest of her things into her pocketbook and coat pockets and dashed out to the end of the car again, where she told the porter she *had* to get off. He said to wait a minute. Finally the train stopped. "Where am I?" she asked. "In Oklahoma City," he said. "We just switched to these tracks."[28]

Elation and Depression

In May 1926 Elizabeth heard what William Martin called "the vivid, fire-breathing preaching of a colorful old war-horse named

Mordecai Ham."[29] Ham was the Kentucky-born evangelist and radio preacher who later claimed one million converts, including Billy Graham. On Memorial Day, the close of his seven-week campaign in Oklahoma City, the war-horse preached more than one hour on "The Battle of Armageddon." The effect was electrifying. "When he talked of Christ's return," Elizabeth reported, "people became so happy and excited that some Baptist women shouted in ecstasy, trembling, jumping up and down, and clapping their hands—in First Church! Dr. [Lincoln] McConnell was laughing and crying all at the same time. Mr. Ham was so happy his face shone radiantly. Old people tottered down the aisle to take his hand and rejoice that Jesus is coming."[30]

No less exhilarating than the Mordecai Ham campaign was a gathering of Native American Baptists. Many small tents were pitched around one large tent. The large tent sheltered a choir of young people and a pulpit from which a preacher poured out his heart. When his passionate sermon ended, nine other men stood up, representing nine tribes and languages. They spoke simultaneously, interpreting the sermon to nine groups of people seated before them. One elderly man who was converted in the meeting asked to be baptized that night, so that he could leave immediately and take the gospel to his own people. "Now I am the only Christian in my tribe," he said.[31]

Despite these and other spiritual highs, by September 1926, after fifteen months in Oklahoma, Elizabeth was feeling "bilious," "draggy," and "queer." She decided "to march myself down to the doctor to let him see if I have a tapeworm, malaria, laziness, or what." The doctor said she was merely suffering from nervous fatigue, that she needed no medicine except perhaps some iron tablets. "You should go out to the country, a camping park, or somewhere," he said, "and play and forget all your work. You need at least a month or two of rest."[32]

When Elizabeth objected, the doctor grew stern. "You are doing yourself an injustice by working too hard and not playing any," he chided. "If you keep on, you will get yourself in an awful mess." But what could Elizabeth do? Not only did she love her work, but she was allowed vacation time of only two weeks. And why should she be "in the pink of condition," as T. B. Ray desired, if she could not be appointed to Japan?

That frustration underlay her fatigue. There was a part of her work she did not like: making missionary talks. It tore her up emotionally to speak on "Go Ye," presenting the needs and calling for volunteers. She would go home and cry herself to sleep, so badly did she want to go herself. Attending the 1926 WMU convention in Houston (she roomed with Lizzie in the Rice Hotel) and hearing foreign missionaries speak added to her distress. Her home missions star was on the service flag that hung before the audience, but until she had a foreign missions star, there could be no peace in her heart.

Less than a month after the 1925 Memphis convention and J. F. Love's doomful report, the Foreign Mission Board had appointed Lolita Hannah to Japan. Just graduated from Carson-Newman College, Lolita was only twenty-two and not an MK. But she was thought qualified—indeed she was—to fill the "desperate need" for a music teacher at the girls' school in Kokura, and, more important, she had a guarantor for her support. "I was a complete freebee," Lolita said later, "or I'd never been sent."[33]

Elizabeth, by contrast, had been turned down at twenty-two although she had graduated from both Judson College and the Training School and the Foreign Mission Board was appointing missionaries in large numbers at the time. Moreover, she had been turned down at twenty-three as still too young. Since then she had been shunted aside for lack of funds rather than age, but she could not help but see an inconsistency in the way the age requirement was enforced. The process seemed erratic, and Elizabeth felt dumped.

A bit of hope had been kindled by an article written by George W. Bouldin, a professor at Seinan Gakuin, the Baptist boys' school in Fukuoka. "We need several new missionary teachers," Bouldin announced.[34] After reading the article, Elizabeth had written him for more information, explaining that she had been called to Japan but had been unable to go as a missionary. Bouldin had suggested that she might come as a self-supporting English teacher. "If you have work in our city," Bouldin had said, "my wife and I will be glad for you to live with us."[35]

The offer was genuine. The Bouldins, whose only child had long since died, boarded single missionaries in their home routinely. They were acquainted with Elizabeth through her Training School friends in

Japan—Phebe Lawton, Naomi Schell, Mary Walters, and Florence Walne. These women kept in touch with their stranded sister and tried to keep her spirits up.

On September 14, three days after Elizabeth had seen the doctor, Cecile Lancaster, a Texan on furlough from Japan, came to Oklahoma City for a speaking engagement. Cecile taught English and physical education at Seinan Jo Gakuin, the Baptist school for girls. "I asked her," Elizabeth told Lizzie, "if there is not some way I can work and support myself over there. She says I can get a position in a government school, get much more salary than a missionary, have a good deal of free time, and do all the missionary work I want to. All I'd teach would be English."[36] Cecile stressed the importance of an M.A. in English, which she herself would earn at Baylor University during her year in the States.

This contact was the tonic Elizabeth needed. "I'm happy," she wrote her mother, "happier than I've been for a long, long time." She was coming home immediately to enroll in Converse College. She would accompany Cecile to Japan the next September, when she would be "strong, fat, and capable of teaching English."[37]

Elizabeth had her fall college visitation and other engagements planned in detail. To bolt from her job at this point would inconvenience many and burden Mrs. Spooner in particular. Nevertheless, the decision made, Elizabeth resigned her post that very night and boarded a train for home the next day. Like an original Sooner, she could brook no delay in staking out her claim. She had to make a quick run for the M.A. that would open up the land of her dreams.

Berta Spooner was magnanimous, calling the decision "sensible" in view of God's call and praising the "wonderful work" Elizabeth had done. "The young people are splendidly organized," she reported. Elizabeth had accomplished in fifteen months what might have taken years.[38]

7

Manhattan Mission

Columbia University
New York City
Feb. 7, 1927

Precious mother-mine,
I waked this morning thinking of you on this your Birthday, hoping that you will have a happy one indeed. Then from the bottom of my heart I thanked God for such a mother as you. I believe it would have been an utter tragedy for me to have had any other mother — in fact I could not have had because you gave your life for me and I am part of you. That is a wonderful thought. I wish I were like

N OT UNTIL SHE ARRIVED IN SPARTANBURG did Elizabeth learn the shocking news. Converse College had discontinued its M.A. program. Forced to change her plans quickly, the headstrong daughter fell back on her mother's long-standing advice.

"While you are aiming," Lizzie had told her, "aim high. Go to Columbia University in New York. That is considered the best university in America, isn't it?"[1] Columbia was a prestigious temple of learning, with thirty-five thousand students drawn from around the world. It was also expensive. Tuition at its Teachers College was ten dollars per "point" (semester hour), or more than three hundred dollars for an academic year. At Converse, tuition and fees were only two hundred dollars. Living expenses also were higher in New York than in Spartanburg. Fortunately, Elizabeth's younger brother Edward had recently come of legal age for the three children to claim a delayed inheritance from their father. Her share of this money sufficed to meet her needs.[2]

Elizabeth withdrew one thousand dollars from the First National Bank, threw her things together in haste, and headed for New York. Upon arriving at majestic Pennsylvania Station in the throbbing heart of the world's greatest city, the would-be Ivy Leaguer broke into a cold sweat. For the past four years she had worked, not studied, and the academia that beckoned would be more rigorous than anything in the past. Was she lunging for a prize beyond her grasp? Would she fall flat on her face, her inheritance gone and nothing to show for it? If she failed to graduate, how could she face her mother? How could she teach in Japan?

Her anxiety was soon dispelled by kind and helpful personnel at Teachers College on Morningside Heights. The advisor of women graduate students arranged her appointment with a professor, who recommended that she major in English and helped her make a schedule. The advisor found Elizabeth an inexpensive room in an apartment building on the nearby Hudson River. The cozy, steam-heated room—317 Tompkins Hall—was an affordable $4.89 per week.

Elizabeth was delighted to find cafeterias in the two buildings where her classes met. "On rainy days you can study, rest, eat and all in practically the same place," she wrote. "There is a nearby rest room with cots where you can go and sleep all you will between classes."[3] The cafeteria meals were satisfying, though not aimed at Southern palates. The chicken was never fried, and the string beans never had grease added when they were boiled. Still, Elizabeth was pleased to have nutritious meals for a dollar a day.

"I was so anxious to gain weight," she said, "that I wished I could eat two dollars' worth of food in one meal!"[4] As an alternative, she kept a five-pound jar of Horlick's malted milk in her room and drank a glassful every night. This commitment to calories would boost her weight to 106 pounds by spring. She stimulated her appetite with a great deal of walking on Columbia's thirty-two-acre campus and twice-weekly swimming in the splendid indoor pool at Teachers College.

Her weekly missiles to Lizzie were generally positive and upbeat, though not free of gripes. "These Northerners don't believe in giving away a thing," she fumed. "You pay five cents for a piece of wrapping paper, ten cents for string, five cents to use a telephone." A month later she complained, "The men here at the university don't strike my fancy, somehow. So many seem so conceited—especially the lawyers."[5]

Columbia's office of admissions initially denied Elizabeth graduate status because Judson College lacked accreditation. After examining her school records from high school up, however, the office admitted Elizabeth on probation, her standing to be determined after satisfactorily completing sixteen hours of courses. Elizabeth enrolled for eighteen hours in the fall semester, paying tuition of $180 plus a university fee of six dollars.[6]

Her courses were Educational Psychology, "mainly how to teach"; Educational Sociology, which "really made me think"; English Literature, 1832-1880; Teaching of Composition; and Teaching of Literature. In lieu of writing a thesis, she signed up for Teaching English in Foreign Countries. The instructor for this course was a German, and the students, some of them "queer looking," were a cross section of the world.[7] Elizabeth had taught foreigners in Louisville and Norfolk. Now she sat where they sat.

She was unprepared for the heavy library work and report-writing her courses required. Everyone in Teachers College seemed to study from morning till night with a sense of desperation, for the failure rate was high and the rivalry intense. The 5,333 students all had teaching experience and were committed to the field of education.[8] Some were brainy products of Harvard or Yale; some were school principals. Such competition was daunting to Elizabeth. Had she set the bar too high?

At times Elizabeth had to read a novel a day to keep up with her assignments. There were many nineteenth-century works she had not read before, such as Emily Brontë's *Wuthering Heights*. Weaker still in twentieth-century literature, she raced through *The New Machiavelli* by H. G. Wells—480 pages long—and other recent novels. This frenetic pace worried her mother, who warned against eyestrain. "I am wearing my glasses," Elizabeth assured her, "so that my eyes, though constantly in use, are stronger and my frown is fading."[9]

Roaming Beyond the Campus

Elizabeth stuck to her books on weekdays and Saturday mornings, but Saturday afternoons and Sundays she devoted to other pursuits. On the first Saturday, she and three other residents of Tompkins Hall snatched some lunch and sallied forth, bound for Battery Park at the lower end of Manhattan. The quartet went by subway—Elizabeth's first time to thunder along below ground—and returned on the elevated train. "We didn't jump fast enough thru the subway door as we started," she told Earle, "and we were separated, part being shut up and whisked away while the rest were left standing and staring after the rushing car."[10]

Reunited at Battery Park, the foursome boarded a rolling, heaving boat and chugged past Ellis Island to the Statue of Liberty. The majestic lady's stone base rose the equivalent of twelve stories, and the greenish copper statue rose ten more. The students panted up the tiny, winding steps to the crown, from which they looked at the water and boats some 250 feet below. Elizabeth was reminded of the time she and Lizzie had labored to the top of the Washington Monument. That memory was still with her the next morning, when her muscles were sore and stiff.

Slightly limping, Elizabeth gamely accompanied some new friends to Broadway Presbyterian Church, where her spirit was nourished and her heart was warmed. That afternoon the women visited the Metropolitan Museum of Art and marveled at its rich fare. At day's end Elizabeth wrote her brother Earle: "My neck fairly aches from looking at so many pictures, my muscles are sore to touch from climbing, and my feet are growing corn patches, but I'm having the time of my young life seeing New York."[11]

Other weekends Elizabeth and her friends visited the Navy Yard, Coney Island, Bronx Zoo, Greenwich Village, Wall Street, the Museum of Natural History, and the Cathedral of St. John the Divine. They walked through the downtown canyons, past acres of plate-glass windows, on sidewalks so congested that police signs warned, "Keep moving!" They stared up in awe at the lacily ornamented Woolworth Building, a Gothic "cathedral of commerce" and the city's tallest structure at the time. "Our necks are two inches longer," Elizabeth joked, "from trying to see the top."[12]

They rode the rails through all five boroughs of the urban colossus, their train often packed. "People swarmed like flies around molasses or cabbage," Elizabeth said of one busy station. "I guess there were four or five hundred people who tried to get on our one car. For once I knew how the inside of a sandwich feels."[13]

Dynamic New York was pulsating twenty-four hours a day, giving succor to human life of every kind. It was a collection of foreign colonies as separate and distinct as carrots and cabbage, a Babel of sixty-six different languages and dialects.[14] "There are now more Russians in New York than in Moscow," observed the Brooklyn *Eagle*, "and more Italians by a hundred thousand than in Naples."[15]

Indeed, the number of foreign-born residents—over two million—exceeded the total population of Oklahoma. Elizabeth had contact with exotic peoples and languages off campus and on, far more than at Norfolk. She sometimes ate at Columbia's International House with students from thirty nations. The greater the variety, the more she loved it.

One Saturday Elizabeth joined two or three hundred others for an all-day trip up the Hudson River under blue skies. The brilliant autumn colors along the Palisades threw her heart into rapture. "Each moment the scene was lovelier than the second before, yet every one was too gorgeous to be improved and certainly to be described."[16] At the U.S. Military Academy in West Point she watched the cadets drill in their dress uniforms and saw Army defeat Syracuse in a football thriller. She returned home about ten that night, gloating over the perfect day.

The brother of one of her schoolmates sometimes took Elizabeth and her friends out into the country in his Pierce Arrow. "The leaves seem mad with flashing shades of all the hues of the rainbow," she wrote after a November outing. "The country around N. Y. City is glorious in gold, red, and green."[17]

Some of Elizabeth's sightseeing was an extension of the classroom. One school trip took her to Sleepy Hollow and Washington Irving's grave. She and her fellow students sat in the old Dutch church where

Ichabod Crane was said to have directed the choir, and they walked the path where the headless horseman allegedly galloped near the little stream. They also stopped by Edgar Allan Poe's tiny white cottage in the Bronx, finding it hemmed in by rows of identical apartment houses. The cottage had been restored to its condition when the genius poet lived there "trembling on the verge of starvation."[18]

Elizabeth went with the Sociology Club to the children's court and then to the model Children's Village, where problem boys and girls lived in groups in cottages and received individualized attention. The heartbreaking evidence of domestic failures made Elizabeth more grateful for her devout parents. Repeatedly in her letters she thanked Lizzie for being a good mother, in contrast to so many other mothers she had observed. "There certainly are a million ways," she noted, "in which women can turn fools."[19]

One Saturday Elizabeth visited in the immigrant slums with a Salvation Army lassie. They stumbled up the dark steps of crumbling brick tenements, using a flashlight even by day. They found people who were dirty, hungry, sick, and cold, people who lived in squalor and slept four or five to a room. It was painful even to catch a glimpse of the destitute in their wretched abodes.

To meet congenial people in better circumstances and enjoy a social life, Elizabeth joined the Graduate Club and the Southern Club. Every week there were teas, parties, and special programs to vie for her time. She heard lectures by the famous, including the American essayist and critic Brander Matthews and the British classical scholar Gilbert Murray. But whatever the occasion, Elizabeth kept her eyes open for other Southern Baptist women to befriend.

Religious Life to the Fore

At the beginning of school, as noted above, Elizabeth attended Broadway Presbyterian Church with a group of new friends. "It seemed real fitting," she noted, "that using Father's money here, I should first worship in a Presbyterian church."[20] On special occasions she visited other non-Baptist churches also. In December, for instance, she marched in an Episcopal "Feast of Lights" procession that took her to the grave of Clement Moore, author of "The Night Before Christmas."

But joining a church was a Baptist affair. After sampling Calvary and Judson Memorial, she settled on First Baptist Church. Its building at Broadway and Seventy-ninth Street was huge and elegant, and the people were so friendly, Elizabeth said, they "nearly ate us up." Later she commented that this church "doesn't seem like Yankees—more like angels."[21]

I. M. Haldeman, pastor of First Baptist Church for the past forty-two years, had just returned to the pulpit after several months' absence because of illness. So esteemed was the eighty-two-year-old cleric that parishioners overflowed the church Sunday morning and Sunday evening, and about five hundred attended the Friday night prayer meetings. While Haldeman preached, the congregation seemed to "hold its collective breath." "Words cannot describe him," Elizabeth wrote glowingly. "You feel that an angel or one from the gates of heaven is bringing a message straight from God."[22]

One of Haldeman's sermons was titled, "Is Mussolini the Antichrist?" "He surely is," Elizabeth agreed. The Napoleon-like fascist dictator was a prime candidate because of his identification with the Roman papacy, itself the Antichrist in the view of Martin Luther and others. Whether or not this sermon was "straight from God," it made Elizabeth "feel the close approach of Jesus coming for the redeemed so that we could almost feel his touch."[23]

A fundamentalist author and orator of world renown, Haldeman had written such books as *The Signs of the Times*, *The Second Coming of Christ*, *Why I Preach the Second Coming*, *Ten Sermons on the Second Coming*. He was radically anti-worldly and otherworldly, truly convinced that the end was near. "The outlook of the church . . . is not on this age but on one to come," Haldeman proclaimed. Reform movements, he believed, were of the devil, no more useful than "cleaning and decorating the staterooms of a sinking ship."[24] Haldeman's cultural pessimism clashed with the social work philosophy taught at the WMU Training School, but Elizabeth tried to accommodate both views. She focused her social work on individuals and used it as an evangelistic means of "pulling them out of the fire" (Jude 23).

Not everything at Haldeman's flourishing church pleased Elizabeth. The pews were rented, which meant she had to stand in the rear, as many did, or be seated as someone's guest, as was usually the case. The Sunday School seemed old-fashioned and inefficient, its attendance less than two hundred. There were no missionary organizations for the young people, no YWAs, GAs, or RAs.

The BYPU (Baptist Young People's Union), to Elizabeth's amazement, met on Monday night and used no "quarterlies." Each person on the program would give a Bible talk impromptu, after being handed a card that listed only a topic and some relevant scriptures. Only the leader of the meeting would prepare a speech in advance. The program participants were all men, since women were expected to keep silent in BYPU as in the other church meetings. This was most queer to Elizabeth, who muttered that the women "just go and sit or sing."[25]

True to her inner drive, Elizabeth organized a YWA (Young Woman's Auxiliary) for Southern Baptist women at Columbia. Teachers College alone had about one hundred Baptist women enrolled, half of them from the South. In search of prospects, Elizabeth called on many of the ninety-six residents of her own apartment. Even so, attendance at YWA meetings remained in the single digits.[26]

One member was Marjorie Terry from Oklahoma, a steady companion who accompanied Elizabeth to Sunday School, church, and BYPU, often dazzling her with the lovely clothes she wore. Ethel Gregg, a teacher at Mars Hill College in North Carolina, was an active member until January, when she quit Teachers College and returned to the classroom.[27]

The YWA met regularly for mission study and projects. Occasionally there were guest speakers, such as Doris Knight, Southern Baptist missionary to China who was doing furlough study at New York's Biblical Seminary. The meetings drew attention from afar. Ethel Winfield, secretary of the literature department at the WMU in Birmingham, wrote to say she never expected to see the day when there would be a YWA at Columbia. The Foreign Mission Board's J. F. Love also expressed interest, saying he expected to visit New York shortly and hoped "to see your group of Southern girls while there."[28]

As much as Elizabeth savored YWA work, it alone could not fulfill her ever-burning sense of mission. Each week she taught a children's group and a men's English class at the Chinese Baptist church near Park Place. Her work was supervised by Mabel Lee, a wealthy and cultured Chinese with a Ph.D. from Columbia. Lee lived with her mother, a petite figure who hobbled about on tiny bound feet, and they often had Elizabeth in their home. Everything about Mabel Lee showed signs of refinement and good taste. Thanks to her exacting standards, the black-headed children Elizabeth taught were little gentlemen and ladies, perfectly behaved.

Owing to her involvement in the Chinese community, Elizabeth learned to read a few Chinese characters that would later prove useful in Japan. At a stunt party, she and some classmates did charades of several ideographs and pictographs. The character for "wife," for example, pictures a woman with a broom; the one for "peace" shows a woman under a roof, implying that her proper place is in the home. Elizabeth and her colleagues displayed the Chinese characters one at a time and acted out their meanings.

She cultivated a taste for Chinese food. One meal included birds' nest soup, chop suey, squabs on lettuce, chicken chow mein, tea, ginger, and crystallized kumquats. She became adept at wielding chopsticks as though in preparation for life in Japan.

Exotic dishes added to the pleasure of times away from school, but more important to Elizabeth was the spiritual nourishment derived from Sunday worship and religious outreach. On weekdays after classes, she would return to her room feeling as if she needed "an internal bath from head to foot." Some of her professors seemed to go out of their way to ridicule faith in God or the Bible. In English and American literature classes, she charged, the teachers "picked out the risqué stories and questionable characters and agnostic ideas for us to consider."[29]

The most dangerous influence on campus, in Elizabeth's judgment, was that of Harry Emerson Fosdick, an outspoken critic of fundamentalist views such as those of I. M. Haldeman. Fosdick was pastor of nearby Park Avenue Baptist Church (later called Riverside Church) and professor of practical theology in Union Theological Seminary, which had reciprocal ties with Columbia University. Students enrolled for the master's degree at Teachers College could take some of their courses at the seminary. One of the most popular was Fosdick's course on "The Bible in Modern Preaching and Teaching."[30]

Elizabeth resolved to hear the "modernist" for herself. So great was the demand for his lectures that she had to apply for a permit to attend one class session and then wait several weeks for her turn. When the time came, she heard him talk about angels and, not surprisingly, deny their existence. "That serpent Fosdick has so many charmed," Elizabeth told Lizzie. "It's a wonder God doesn't strike him dead."[31]

The Final Stretch

In January, at the end of her first semester, Elizabeth faced the comprehensive exam required of M.A. candidates. For days she crammed, reading madly in poetry and novels, in writers' lives, in methods of teaching. She raced through Chaucer, Arnold's essays, Tennyson's poems, and on and on, her speed ever building. She skimmed the just-published *Galahad*, Edmund Wilson's amusing account of Greenwich Village Bohemia in the twenties.

The three-hour exam, Elizabeth reported afterwards, "included spelling, punctuation, grammar, composition, criticism, and just about every book you ever read or thought of reading up to the latest novels and plays."[32] She flunked. So did more than half the students who took the exam for the first time. Mercifully, the comprehensive was also given in April and in July, and students were allowed to take it up to three times. Three failures meant you were out.

Elizabeth was so much more interested in people and missions than in books and their contents that it is little wonder she failed the exam. The marvel is that she passed all her course work that first semester. As a consequence, a February letter from Teachers College stated that she had been accepted as a full graduate student, retroactive to September. "My standing has been pending," she explained to Lizzie, "and I've faced the possibility of being required to do one and a half years' work instead of one year's, since Judson is not A-1. However, they said they let my work at Louisville supplement my Judson studies."[33]

Her spring courses were Psychology of Adolescence, American Literature, English Literature in the 18th Century, English Literature, 1832-1880 (continuation of a fall course), and Voice and Diction. The Voice and Diction teacher, Azuba Julia Latham, was radically different from Mrs. George J. Sutterlin, her speech instructor at the Training School in Louisville. Professor Latham laughed at and "corrected" the Southerners' pronunciation of many words. After class Elizabeth would mockingly recite, "I am läughing like a cälf because I cän't see the gräss on this hälf of the yard."[34]

She took two noncredit electives, one in gymnastics and the other in Japanese History and Culture. The latter, taught by a graceful Japanese lady, included etiquette, tea ceremony, and flower arranging. Elizabeth cited this fascinating class as further evidence that God had brought her to the right place to prepare for service in Japan. These optional courses and various extracurricular activities were so enjoyable that the required subjects seemed a grind and a chore.

This circumstance affected her relationship with Ella J. Pierce, a WMU Training School graduate and Mars Hill College teacher who entered Teachers College at midterm. "She is most studious," Elizabeth said, "and wants to talk about Pope, Johnson, and all those dead celebrities at meal time when I want to forget and relax." To make matters worse, communication between the two was an ordeal; they often had to repeat themselves to be understood. Elizabeth slurred her speech, and Ella was slightly deaf. Ella also "jerked her words" and talked with her mouth full. "I nearly fling a fit," Elizabeth told her mother, "yet I can't afford to fling off a friend, especially a lonely one."[35]

Recalling the Training School rule against mentioning lessons at the dining table during exam periods, Elizabeth proposed a "Forget-it" club and enlisted several members. The club's one rule was that the members not mention school work when eating together. "It's funny," Elizabeth observed, "the more you study, the more crabbed and unsociable and solemn and long-faced you seem to become. Up here, you rarely hear a person laugh."[36]

As Elizabeth prepared for the comprehensive exam to be given April 30, she read feverishly once again, cruising through Dickens' *David Copperfield*, over eight hundred pages, and others like it. "My brain surprised me in being so well oiled, ready and responsive as I'd study, and keeping alert even late at night." During the exam, moreover, characters and plots were as easy to pluck from her memory as ripe grapes from a low-hanging vine. This time she passed. For days she "felt like a feather floating through the air."[37] In May she passed all her second-semester courses, feeling no less triumphant and elated than Charles Lindbergh, whose nonstop flight from New York to Paris that month was the talk of the world.

Not only Elizabeth, but her Southern Baptist friends were successful in their exams. She was convinced that the Lord gave special guidance to these pious women from small Southern schools because they strove to put him first. She also attributed her own success at Columbia, like her good grades as a child in Spartanburg, to her mother's faithful prayers.

During the week between exams and the graduation ceremony, Elizabeth observed classes at a high school and at Hunter College. To earn a little money, she looked after two first-graders at Horace Mann School, a nine-hundred-pupil school attached to Teachers College. Her duties were to feed the children some lunch and put them in the chauffeured car that took them home.

On June 1, 1927, wearing the cap and gown she had rented for two dollars, Elizabeth stood in line for the graduation procession. The line formed at 4:30 P.M., and commencement exercises began at 6:00 with playing of the overture from Rossini's "William Tell." The overture was followed by the grand march and an invocation given by the university chaplain. Eighteen thousand guests witnessed the conferring of degrees on 5,007 graduates, the largest class yet in Columbia's history. The names of the graduates, Elizabeth's among them, appeared in the *New York Times*.[38] Most degrees were conferred en masse, the M.A. graduates of the Teachers College standing as a body when their turn came. Afterwards, they picked up their diplomas at the college.

"I'd always declared I'd never be a teacher," Elizabeth reflected. "But this was a means to an end."[39] Her mission in Manhattan was to prepare successfully for her mission in Japan. The Master of Arts degree from a world-class university, supplemented by a Teachers College diploma certifying her competence as "Teacher of English," would be a passport to good-paying jobs overseas.

Though her days in Manhattan had been enriching, Elizabeth was glad to leave its wonks and wiseacres, its subways and skyscrapers, and return to the laid-back South. She was ready to swap a city that never slept for one that was dead by 9:00 P.M. After a stopover in Norfolk to visit friends from Settlement House days, she arrived in Spartanburg to a joyous reunion with Lizzie and Earle. Edward also made it home that summer, taking a breather from his work as a vagabond actor.

Elizabeth had a deeper appreciation for Lizzie, since her study of nineteenth-century literature had yielded new insights into her mother's early years. Now she could picture in vivid detail what life was like in her grandparents' home. "When I read the novels showing the ideas of society and the attitude toward certain types of labor," Elizabeth had written Lizzie, "I can sympathize with Grandfather in his unwillingness for you to marry Father, yet admire your spirit and see in you the modern girl of the time, in your attitude toward him and his work and your realization that it's not the work that makes the man."[40] She had written these words soon after reading *Vanity Fair*.

The summer at home passed quickly. The president of Converse College, Robert P. Pell, offered Elizabeth a one-year position as Instructor in Biblical Literature. He needed a replacement for Associate Professor Alene S. Grosché, who was on leave of absence.[41] Elizabeth accepted. Having spent her inheritance money, she needed the eighteen-hundred-dollar salary to pay her passage to Japan. There was no chance of appointment by the debt-laden Foreign Mission Board, now reeling from the disclosure that its respected treasurer, George N. Sanders, had swindled the Board out of $103,772.38.[42]

Elizabeth lived on the Converse campus and enjoyed the swimming pool, where she refurbished the Oklahoma tan that had faded in New York. Weekends she spent at home. Among the courses she taught were "Gospel of Luke" in the fall and "Gospel of John" in the spring, both required of seniors. As texts she used the books of Isaac N. Van Ness, corresponding secretary of the Baptist Sunday School Board. Van Ness was flattered. In future years he often sent Elizabeth literature and picture rolls for her work in Japan.[43]

8

"Woppess" at Sops Tickle

Newfoundland Hotel
St. Johns, N'fld.
June 7, 1925

Precious Mother,
We arrived here about 7:30 this morning looking like real immigrants with bags of all shapes and sizes. I believe I wrote you last in St. John's — I mean, I wrote in Halifax and spelled Nova Scotia wrong. Bound for me to. I really felt I should buy something there to

---

ELIZABETH WAS TWENTY-EIGHT, and Japan was still a half-world away. The Foreign Mission Board had turned her down yet again. Her future unclear, her mind unsettled, she read with more than passing interest an appeal in the *Student Volunteer Movement Bulletin* for summer missionaries in Newfoundland. Now a Canadian province, Newfoundland, including Labrador on the mainland, was then touted as "Britain's oldest colony - the world's new playground."[1]

The appeal came from the International Grenfell Association, whose founder and superintendent, Dr. Wilfred T. Grenfell, was a legend in his time. A man of boundless energy and courage, Grenfell had recently been knighted by King George V for a lifetime of service to hard-pressed fishers and loggers scattered along the bleak coasts of

Newfoundland. "Sir Wilf" had established hospitals, nursing stations, orphanages, schools, kindergartens, cooperatives, and fox farms. So inspiring was his well-publicized example of ministry that as many as 150 volunteers, mostly from America, came to Newfoundland each summer to assist in the work.

The volunteers were teachers, secretaries, agriculturalists, medical students, outdoor workers. They paid their own expenses, a minimum of $350 including room and board in private homes during their seven weeks of service. The Grenfell Association made the arrangements for their lodging and, in the case of teachers, furnished the books and other school supplies.[2]

References, a health certificate, and a photograph were required of each applicant, but there was no test of faith. The colony was predominantly Anglican, Methodist, and Roman Catholic. For the sake of good relations, volunteers were asked to observe the Sabbath strictly, avoid offending the sensibilities of the very conservative Methodists, and otherwise show respect for the local culture. Women were to refrain from smoking and from wearing knickerbockers. All were to eschew liquor, which Grenfell had long fought as the scourge of the land.[3]

Some volunteers, inevitably, proved to be failures. When one "spoiled youth" scorned his work as fit only for "wops," a derogatory term used of Italian laborers in the United States, Grenfell replied that in Newfoundland everyone was a wop and did his or her share of useful labor. The sobriquet took hold. "'Wop' is the name which the volunteers gave themselves," Grenfell wrote, "as a terse synonym for a worker willing to do anything, but not a past master at any particular job." The doctor later redefined the term as an acronym for "without pay."[4]

The majority of the wops—and "woppesses," as the women were called—came from well-off families and well-known colleges in the United States. Among them were two sons of John D. Rockefeller, Jr., Nelson and Laurance. The Rockefeller brothers later called the experience disillusioning, but many other alumni of this philanthropic venture looked back on it as so meaningful that they attended annual reunions and backed the Grenfell Association with their financial gifts.

To Elizabeth, the Newfoundland call was well-nigh irresistible. Money was no problem after teaching a year at Converse. Nine years had passed since she signed the Student Volunteer card, stating that "It is my purpose, if God permit, to become a foreign missionary." For six years she had tried without success to gain an appointment to Japan. "I thought that perhaps if I went as a volunteer summer worker to Newfoundland," she later explained, "I could fulfill my pledge, and then settle down to a normal life at home."[5] It was a plausible rationale.

Elizabeth applied to the Grenfell Staff Selection Committee in New York and was promptly accepted. She was one of a dozen volunteers who traveled together on the SS *Sylvia*, leaving New York June 2. During the five-day voyage blessed with cloudless skies and placid seas, the volunteers usually sat on the deck wrapped in sweaters and blankets against the chilly air.

New at ocean travel, Elizabeth was most curious about bathing facilities on the ship. About six o'clock the first morning a steward knocked on her door and shouted, "Bath ready, Madam!" She followed him to a bathroom where the tub was already filled with hot water. What a luxury! she thought—until she rinsed her face and tasted the brine.

The City of John the Baptist

On Thursday, June 7, the *Sylvia* passed through the steep-walled, narrow entrance to St. John's, the capital of Newfoundland and the most easterly city of the North American continent. Elizabeth and her friends were busy with eating breakfast, packing suitcases, having the immigration officer stamp their cards, tipping stewards to carry off heavy bags, chasing about looking for books they had misplaced. A Grenfell representative, Mr. L'miserie, met the twelve volunteers when they stepped off the gangplank. He had arranged for four of the group to go directly to Labrador on the mainland and for the eight working on the island—Elizabeth among them—to put up at the Newfoundland Hotel until Saturday. The hotel gave the volunteers a special rate of five dollars a day on the American plan, which included four sumptuous meals a day.

Sightseeing was high on their agenda. The band of eight walked along Water Street with its three- and four-story wood and brick buildings. They climbed Signal Hill and Cabot Tower, which rose five hundred feet above the snug harbor. "Down in the water," Elizabeth wrote, "bobbed lovely little sailboats, tiny tugs, and a few motorboats. As the fog cleared by fits and starts, we caught glimpses of the mountains beyond, the scant boggy green pasture for the sheep and cows, and the houses stuck on the rocky cliffs."[6]

There was plenty of daylight for sightseeing, since darkness descended around midnight and lifted about half past three. Even at eleven p.m. children were playing or carrying water from the spring. Elizabeth noticed that the inhabitants of St. John's were thin and rudely clad, as though followers of John the Baptist, the ascetic whose name the city bore. She was reminded that one objective of the volunteers was to help raise the standards of hygiene and nutrition and make people less susceptible to illness and disease, particularly tuberculosis, the chief cause of death in the land.

St. John's, with a population of forty thousand, was the only city of any size on the island. Outside the city, Elizabeth was told, nearly everyone lived in coves along the coast except for miners and prospectors. Often the only way to get from one hamlet to another was by a home-built motorboat on the open sea. This made consolidated schools impractical. Because the communities needing help were so numerous, the volunteers were expected to work singly, whatever the cost in unrelieved loneliness.

On Saturday the eight volunteers rushed to the docks with more bundles than ever, their trunks following in a crude wagon dragged by two horses. They boarded the *Prospero*, a poky mail steamer, for the final leg of their journey. Elizabeth's destination was Sops Arm, a logging and fishing community on the inlet by that name in White Bay. She was to live in a forester's home at Sops Tickle, an isolated cove a half-mile down the "tickle" or narrow passage of water between George's Island and the mainland. Her assignment was to teach weekday school in Sops Tickle and conduct a Sunday School in Sops Arm.

The 500-ton *Prospero* was to the 3,500-ton *Sylvia* what an outboard is to a luxury yacht. The *Sylvia* had comfortable deck chairs and spaces to walk, run, or play deck tennis. It offered spotless linens and table service, clean beds, and five meals a day, two being served on deck. The only deck chairs on the *Prospero* were six camp stools without backs; most passengers sat on a box or on the floor. One day Elizabeth rode in the stern with a sheep and two lambs and was rained on with soot from the smokestack. Her cabin was so tiny that only one person could dress at a time, doing so while the others pretended to sleep. As there was no place for the garments they took off, they piled them on top of the bedclothes. And Elizabeth's bed was "really a seat, springless and closely resembling the floor."[7]

Elizabeth and her friends were able to forget the crude accommodations in their enjoyment of the landscape, since the steamer crept along the shoreline. After each coarse meal, served on dirty tablecloths, they would rush to the deck lest they miss a glorious sight. The coast was "sometimes great piles of bare rocks in fantastic shapes, sometimes beautiful wooded slopes, sometimes a tiny hamlet tucked in a little cove, sometimes a single lighthouse perched high on some rocks."[8]

The ship glided past towering icebergs that Elizabeth studied with fascination. Sculptured by wind and sun, the bergs looked like camels with humps, like fish, like fairy castles, like "almost anything a lively imagination could picture them." Most were glistening white, others greenish blue. The water around the white ones looked nile green. Parts of one berg were transparent, as though hollow inside.[9]

The mail steamer stopped at many coves to "dump off packages, pigs, babies, and what not."[10] The stops varied from a few minutes to a few hours. At Hampden, a major settlement near the southern end of White Bay, the ship anchored long enough for Elizabeth to lunch with the hospital staff—mostly Scottish and Irish—and smack her lips over their plum pudding. It was her only tasty meal on the four-day trip.

Waiting at the Threshold

The *Prospero* arrived at Sops Arm Wednesday afternoon. As the water was too shallow for the steamer to dock, Elizabeth's trunk and three bags were lowered into a homemade boat, and she followed, climbing down a shaky rope ladder. A gentle rain was falling. A sweet-faced woman in the rowboat, a Mrs. Stark, asked Elizabeth if she were the teacher and told her that the Budden family would come in their boat to take her to Sops Tickle.

After climbing ashore, Elizabeth sat on her trunk in the rain and waved to her seven companions on the *Prospero*. Their assignments were farther up the coast. She watched with a sense of abandonment as the mail steamer disappeared, not to come again for two weeks. Mrs. Stark emerged from her house and urged Elizabeth to come out of the rain and cold and sit by her fire until the Buddens came.

Inside, Elizabeth found a roomful of prattling women and children. The focus of attention was a seventeen-month-old baby weighing thirty-six pounds. "The comments of the women were interesting," Elizabeth wrote. "One said it was an awful baby, one a wonderful baby, one a ridiculous baby. Well, it was all three."[11] The women declared there was a girl in another village who weighed 180 pounds and was only seven years old.

At length Mrs. Budden arrived, accompanied by a daughter. "There's no room for you here," she told Elizabeth, a greeting as welcome as a bee sting.[12] She had had no prior notice of the teacher's coming, Mrs. Budden claimed, but would try to work something out in a few days. Mrs. Stark then offered to keep Elizabeth until the Buddens had a place for her. The kind woman had a sick baby and two other small children, and she cooked for several working men besides her husband. Still, she took the stranger in and had her trunk moved to the community store.

The unexpected guest seemed to be a jinx. While helping Elizabeth up the steep stairs to her room, Mrs. Stark fell, reopening a wound on a finger. While making the room more comfortable, she knocked over the lamp and broke the glass chimney. Winnie the servant girl, trying to cook something for the guest, dropped the only two eggs in the house. Elizabeth saw them splatter on the floor.

Oddly, though, these accidents were greeted with merry laughs and smiles, and they worked to Elizabeth's favor. She played nurse by fixing Mrs. Stark's finger with some of her adhesive and mercurochrome. That night Winnie cut her own finger, another call for first aid. The ice broken, Elizabeth dried dishes, dressed and undressed a little girl, played with "forty-eleven" children in the village, visited and was visited. She began to feel at home in this halfway house.

Mrs. Stark was captivated by the American's "store-bought" dress and wished aloud for one just like it made with some cloth she had. So Elizabeth turned the dress wrong side out and cut another one by it. Mrs. Stark thought it beautiful, a "miracle dress." She warmly invited Elizabeth to stay with her as long as she wished.

Mr. Stark, "a little man with a twitching rabbit nose," was a merchant, an Anglican lay reader, and the village schoolmaster. He allowed Elizabeth to visit his classroom, where he "kept school" by walking up and down the aisle with a ruler in his hand. Children who raised their eyes from their book were whacked across the knuckles with the ruler. Elizabeth saw vividly how school teaching "should not be done."[13]

Most residents were engaged in logging and fishing. Elizabeth watched a woman and her near-blind father bring in a haul of cod fish they had caught early one morning. The pair cut up the fish and threw the livers into large barrels so that the sun could draw out the oil. The remainder of the fish they put into barrels of salt water, from which they would be taken after several days and placed on racks in the sun to dry.

The beautiful hills around Sops Arm reminded Elizabeth of Butler, Tennessee. So did the absence of plumbing and bathing facilities. Water was even more precious than at Watauga Academy, as there was no well or spring nearby. It was brought from some distance and placed in a barrel at the back door. This was primitive living indeed, but Elizabeth was now older and more tolerant of the "backward people" and "desolation" that had riled her in East Tennessee.

A Village with Four Buildings

Elizabeth spent three nights with the Starks. Saturday evening a band of men came from Sops Tickle, saying that everything was ready for the teacher. They rowed her and her baggage down the tickle, passing between hills and valleys wooded with silver birch and fir. Their destination was a rectangular six-room house where lived Mr. and Mrs. Budden, 16-year-old Effie Mary, 12-year-old Leander, 10-year-old Watson, 8-year-old George, 6-year-old Stella, 2-year-old Joyce, the 5-week-old baby of a sick woman in Sops Arm, the game warden, and a 19-year-old boy who worked at the lumber camp. In deference to Elizabeth, the game warden and the lumber-camp boy had moved out of their room to sleep the next seven weeks on the hard kitchen floor with their heads under the kitchen table.[14]

Elizabeth was touched by the efforts to make her comfortable. Her little room had a round feather bed with eight blankets on it, together with an immense bolster. On the wash stand were a bowl and pitcher, a refinement over the tin pan she had used at the Starks' house. Mrs. Budden and her sons had freshly papered the walls with brown oatmeal paper with a tiny rosebud border at the top (the other rooms in the house were papered with newsprint). Beautiful, homemade hooked rugs were not only scattered on the floor but hung on the walls for pictures and spread on the bed for cover. There was no chair in the room, however, but only the bed to sit on. Nor was there a closet, but only nails in the wall for hanging up clothes. Fortunately there was room for Elizabeth's wardrobe trunk, which had hangers and drawers. Her two suitcases went under the bed.

The walls and doors were so thin that Elizabeth could lie in her bed and talk to anyone in the house. Her ears picked up every little sound, such as brushing one's teeth. Other noises came from under the house, where lived three goats, five or six kids, two pigs, and a flock of chickens. The goats were her alarm clock, knocking their antlers on what was their ceiling and her floor. At this signal she would jump up, help chase the goats, and hold them while the children milked them. Then she would take her breakfast of warm goat's milk and boiled Irish potatoes, eating alone. Mrs. Budden always fed her separately, with special dishes and utensils, lest she be appalled at the table manners of the others.

The Budden residence was one of four buildings in the hamlet, all of unpainted wood. The two smaller buildings, the store and the toilet, hung over the edge of the water. Every community was said to have its own little store, stocking basic commodities brought in every two weeks on the mail steamer, and presumably every community had a toilet of sorts. The other building in Sops Tickle housed another Budden family—the water passage was known locally as Budden's Tickle[15]—and contained a workroom where the women carded the wool from their sheep, then spun and wove it. Another room served as the village school, doubling as a church on Sundays when there was someone to conduct services. The building's roof provided storage space for snowshoes awaiting use in winter.

Elizabeth taught nine children in the schoolroom, four from the home where she lived and five from the other. A tenth child she taught outside of school hours. As the pupils ranged in age from five to nineteen, the teacher had to hear eight or nine separate sets of lessons, always accompanied by the whir of the spinning wheel nearby. The younger children had to be kept quiet and amused and the older ones made to study instead of giggle and talk. They all sat on boxes or benches without backs, at crude desks their fathers had made.

Elizabeth spruced up the room with posters on the walls and colored butterflies suspended from the ceiling. This delighted the children, who said they had never had a teacher before who decorated the school. She also tacked up a blackboard, determined to be as effective as possible. Dr. Grenfell's oft-quoted description of the daring and resourceful North Sea fisherman also applied to Elizabeth: "Whatever they did, they did hard."[16]

A major challenge Elizabeth faced was the discrepancy between her speech and the children's. At first she tried to correct their pronunciation, unlike anything she had ever heard before. Its most distinctive difference was the *h* sound, which she explained this way: "You breathe hair but you have air and a at on your ead. You put fly hoil on you to keep flies hoff. You ride hin the boat of some hother person hif you have none hof your hown. . . . He is e and him is im and e lives hin han ouse."[17] But the pupils were clearly satisfied with their manner of talking, just as Elizabeth had been when corrected in speech class at Teachers College. "You are mistaken," they told her. Everybody knew that *h-a-t* was pronounced *at*. The teacher was just late in learning it.

One day Mrs. Budden showed Elizabeth some toothbrushes that the previous teacher had mailed to her children, one brush apiece with a tiny celluloid doll tied to each handle. "I would not think of letting them use them," the mother explained; "they must keep them nice in the wrapper since Miss ——— sent them."[18] To cope with such indifference to dental hygiene, Elizabeth devised a health chart on which her pupils earned black or gold marks. With this incentive, about half the children began brushing their teeth twice a day and the other half once a day. Elizabeth also enticed most of them to bathe all over once a week, something they had not done before. This meant a sponge bath, as there was no shower or tub.

Besides cleanliness, Elizabeth taught godliness with evangelistic fervor. Giving a Bible lesson daily, she led all the children to receive Christ as Savior except the five-year-old, whom she deemed too young for the decision. She wanted to have them baptized, but no clergy was available, and Elizabeth claimed no authority to administer the rite. This did not keep her from doing church. Every Sunday morning the women dressed up in hats and joined the children for worship in the schoolroom. Elizabeth delivered the sermon. Then after dinner, she and the children would pile into a little boat to be rowed over to Sops Arm, joining the children that Mrs. Stark had gathered in her house for Sunday School. Elizabeth would teach twenty to twenty-five children while the fathers and mothers listened outside. She taught them to sing "G-O-O-D," "Everybody Ought to Love Jesus," "Into My Heart," and other songs she had learned in her own childhood.[19]

After the first Sunday School session in Sops Arm, Elizabeth sat in Mrs. Stark's kitchen holding one of the babies. The outer door opened and in slipped three bashful girls with their hands behind their backs and their tongues seemingly paralyzed. There they stood, looking sheepishly at each other and then eyeing the teacher. Gathering up courage at last, they approached Elizabeth silently, and each one thrust out what was behind her back, a bunch of violets and plum blossoms. That made Elizabeth's day.

Fun and Failures

The most festive time for both communities was steamer day every two weeks. Everyone was agog, keen to know who got on, who got off, what mail and provisions everyone received, whether or not their mail-order shoes were the right fit. Elizabeth's main interest was the one or more letters that arrived from Lizzie each time with news of home. She in turn always had a long letter ready to send her mother, and rather than entrust it with the little post office in Sops Arm, she would board the steamer to mail it.

Apart from steamer day, the adults and young people seemed to have no entertainment and little fun. The teenage girls sat around doing handwork as though they were grandmothers, except when they were washing dishes or screaming at their younger siblings. Something needed to be done to brighten up their lives.

One evening Elizabeth was visiting at the neighboring Budden house. The mother was knitting socks; Dorothy, 19, and Lucy, 17, were crocheting; Sadie, 12, was rocking the cradle; Blanche, 10, was studying her lesson; Cecil, 8, was doing nothing; Leslie, 4, was seeking attention; Olive, just married, was holding her tiny baby. This seemed an appropriate time to make a proposal.

"Would you like to have a game night once a week?" Elizabeth asked.

"I don't know," someone replied.

Then Dorothy perked up and said, "Why don't we have a party?"

"What do you mean by a party?" Elizabeth asked. "Do the people come from all around here?"

"No, Miss, that's a picnic," Dorothy explained. "At a party there would just be us. We would play. That would be nice, for we don't know any games. We don't play any."[20]

So Elizabeth planned a Friday night party. The children pinned the tie on Buster Brown while blindfolded, played "Dave Wiggins is Dead," vied with one another in a cracker eating and whistling contest, and ran a potato race with knives. The next night, instead of quarreling, fussing, and crying, they played the games over again. Elizabeth felt that in her own small way she had influenced the culture to better the lives of the people—what Dr. Grenfell endeavored to do on a much grander scale.

A major irritation to Elizabeth was the shabby over-water toilet that served the community. It was so repugnant that she threatened to go home unless a new one was built. So the men went to work and finished the outhouse in mid-July. "I feel like singing a song out on the middle of the tickle," Elizabeth wrote, "standing right up in the boat."[21] Mabel Thorne, a volunteer on nearby Sops Island, likewise celebrated when her community built a toilet as a "monument" to her. Mabel donated $1.50 to the cause, and nearly everyone gave something in her honor. To further show their esteem for the teacher, the folks even painted the privy!

Elizabeth learned to handle a boat, or punt as it was called, so that she would not have to be rowed to and from Sops Arm. Her hands blistered, but soon she gained the confidence to take the children in the punt with her. In the long evenings when the water was calm, she would row to a nearby island, where all would gather flowers and stroll the shady paths. "The paddles made strange music," she wrote, "and the water burned in glistening balls of fire by the side of the boat."[22]

Once Elizabeth went out to an island with three boys to pick blackberries. The weather was inclement, but she had the protection of raincoat, rain hat, and galoshes. The berries, she discovered, were different from the ones in South Carolina. They were the size of the head of a black-headed pin, had a shine something like a muscadine, and grew down on the ground among the tiny leaves. "As you pick them," Elizabeth reported, "mosquitoes, sand flies, and nippers dine at your neck, eyes, cheeks, forehead, ears, feet, hands, so that you drop a good many you pick by stopping quite suddenly to scratch." One of the boys, Watson, cried out, "Jingles, the flies 'ave carried off me eyes and are coming back for the 'oles!"[23]

Elizabeth remembered the biblical plagues in Egypt, "when Pharaoh had his fit over the flies. . . . If it was the Newfoundland variety, I bet he did send for Moses in a hurry. They get in your hair and nibble your scalp, down your neck, under your clothes so that everyone gets cross."[24] To cope with these varmints, she made a queer costume for the beach that covered her head, neck, and arms. Even inside the house she wore a scarf over her hair and neck, for although her window was covered with both fine wire and mosquito netting, persistent black flies found their way in.

The plague struck again when Elizabeth tried to carry out a project sponsored by the Grenfell Association. To improve nutrition among the people, the volunteers were encouraged to teach them how to grow and eat spinach. Elizabeth had brought seeds from America, but making a garden was far from simple. The rocky soil was primeval, having never been cultivated. There were no gardening tools, forcing Elizabeth and the boys she enlisted to use axes to chop the ground. No sooner had they started removing stones than swarms of insects rose in anger and stung their faces. Their eyes swelled shut, they held hands and groped their way back to the house.

Despite that painful setback, Elizabeth doggedly worked on until the spinach was planted and a neat fence stood around the garden. The plants sprang up, making her proud and hopeful. Then one day the boys came shouting, "Oh, Miss, Miss! The 'ogs 'ave snouted up the garden!" Wild hogs had broken down the fence around the garden and rooted up the plants.[25]

Another project that collapsed was one concocted by Elizabeth on her own: teaching the children to swim. They protested at first, saying "there is poison in the water until August." When August arrived, ushering in the last week of her stay, Elizabeth helped them rig up some bathing suits. "I gaily led the way in," she wrote, "but in seconds was out, my blood almost turned into jelly by that iceberg-chilled water." Two men sauntering by reported seeing a shark nearby, further convincing Elizabeth that her venture had been unwise.[26]

On the closing day of school Elizabeth directed a program in which the pupils showed off what they had learned. The three mothers were present, showing great pride in their children. After the program, three girls pattered in dressed up as cats and distributed whistles, balloons, and pencils to the children. Elizabeth gave prizes for outstanding work and presented little remembrances to the mothers and the cats.

Elizabeth would have enjoyed seeing the long, long days change to long, long nights and the dog sleds bringing the mail over the snow. But her stint was over, and her money was running low. Knowing that the children would have a government teacher during the winter months made it less difficult to say goodbye. As a twentieth-century person in a nineteenth-century environment, the volunteer had made a worthy contribution as teacher, preacher, gardener, recreational director, and nurse, and the people seemed to appreciate what she had done. She had gained for herself a bundle of memories and eight wanted pounds.

On the evening of August 8 Elizabeth boarded the *Prospero* with Mabel Thorne, who had spent the last night and day in Sops Tickle. Both were given a rousing send-off, though the hour was late because the steamer waited for the moon to rise before sailing. The *Prospero* was so packed that Elizabeth slept in the dining room. But sleep she could, relieved to put behind the hazards and frustrations of pioneer life, comforted by the thought of going home.[27]

After a day at St. Anthony, site of the Grenfell Association headquarters and its newly opened hospital, the steamer returned to St. John's. There Elizabeth and Mabel transferred to another ship and cruised down the St. Lawrence River to Quebec and Montreal, from which Elizabeth traveled by train to Spartanburg and a big welcome home from her first stint abroad.

Gideon's Fleece

Elizabeth looked for work in Spartanburg but found nothing appealing. With the boom of the twenties about to give way to the bust of the thirties, jobs were scarce, especially for women. There was little choice but to mark time on her life journey, doing volunteer work as a YWCA secretary and a trainer of black Sunday School teachers. In her home church, she had charge of the junior department in Sunday School and taught the Business Girls' Bible Class.[28] Unknown to Elizabeth at the time, both groups later would provide generous financial support for her work in Japan.

Her schedule allowed time for serious reflection. Was she frittering away her life with these volunteer activities? Was she merely collecting experiences as others collected stamps? Had the two months in Newfoundland really fulfilled her student volunteer pledge? Could that stint have been a divinely planned orientation to a full career overseas? What was God's will for the present?

Increasingly, Elizabeth sensed that the time had come to go to Japan. The feeling made little or no sense, for Newfoundland and the subsequent months of unemployment had exhausted her savings. To strike out now seemed reckless to the point of madness. Was her mind coming unhinged? The only earthly rationale for going to Japan now was George Bouldin's standing offer of assistance. Bouldin had laid down one condition: that she be absolutely certain God wanted her there. So before heading for the distant land of her dreams, Elizabeth needed proof that her inner sense of direction was God's leading and not a mere hankering of her own.

"Like Gideon of old," she was to tell the Bouldins, "I asked for a sign. If he wanted me to go, would he furnish the necessary money? I asked that money for the expenses across be the 'Gideon's fleece.'"[29] Elizabeth recalled that the Old Testament hero, unsure of God's leading, had laid out a wool fleece overnight on a threshing floor. The next morning, when the surrounding ground was wet with dew, the fleece, inexplicably, was still dry. Gideon had his proof.

And Elizabeth had hers. As if by a Bible-time miracle, the money she had requested came flooding in. Missionary societies she had never heard of sent checks through the mail. Friends and acquaintances, among them a crippled woman who hobbled to the door, brought gifts to the Watkins home. In time the contributions, all modest, added up to $150. Elizabeth asked the agent at the railroad station whether he could find her passage to Japan for that amount. The agent could. The wanna-be missionary had divined the divine will in the most practical of ways.

Elizabeth completed her summer duties at a church camp in Charleston and began packing the $37.50 trunk she had bought in Norfolk. She obtained a passport valid for two years and renewable for another two. Friends and relatives feted her with parties and showers. The farewell service at Southside Church was more solemn than previous ones that sent her to nearer destinations. In Japan, a Mrs. Matthews declared, Elizabeth might be "eaten up by cannibals."[30]

9

Welcome Mat in Japan

Seinan Gakuin
Sept. 15, 1921

Dearest mother
You have been so good to write I
did enjoy the letter written from Aunt
Annie's that came yesterday. Thank you.

T HE SEVEN-THOUSAND-TON *LONDON MARU* pitched and rolled as it plowed through the rough waters of the northern Pacific. Elizabeth was miserably sick, unable to hold her head up or use her eyes without getting dizzy. She picked over—or ignored—the Western-style meals that mannerly stewards brought to her side. Four days out of Vancouver, when the landlubber began to lose her queasiness and get her sea legs at last, a merciless typhoon lashed the Japanese freighter as though a Jonah were aboard.[1]

Elizabeth languished in her cabin six of the fifteen days at sea. Having a surfeit of time for prayer, she asked repeatedly for employment in Japan. On the morning of August 21, surprisingly, God seemed to say, "Stop praying that prayer." Why stop? Elizabeth wondered; the prayer seemed legitimate. Then just before noon a telegram was placed in her hand. It read: "Position secured meet you Yokohama Bouldin."[2]

IMPERIAL GOVERNMENT TELEGRAPHS. (Delivery Form)

George Bouldin had recently been named acting president of Seinan Gakuin, the Baptist boys' school in Fukuoka. He had scrounged the yen equivalent of eight hundred dollars—the annual salary of a single missionary—to employ a much-needed English teacher. Elizabeth had the job.

The next morning the *London Maru* passed through the Uraga Channel into Tokyo Bay. Mount Fuji glistened in the distance, framed against a bright blue sky. Small boats glided over the smooth waters on either side of the oceangoing vessel. The atmosphere on board was fresh and crisp, the officers sporting immaculate white uniforms. The passengers were nervous and excited, all the more as Yokohama drew near and they strained to see the pier where they would dock. One Japanese youth was about to meet the girl he would marry and take back to America. Two Japanese boys from New Jersey would set foot in their ancestral land for the first time.

A Japanese student told Elizabeth that he wanted her to meet his brother. "There he is," the student cried, pointing to a figure on the pier. Look as hard as she could, Elizabeth could see only a woman where he was pointing. The student explained that the person wearing straw hat, shirt waist, long skirt, and geta (wooden clogs) was indeed his brother.[3]

One man in the crowd Elizabeth could not miss. George Bouldin, six feet three inches tall, towered above the Japanese like a Jeff among Mutts. He was less rawboned than a few years before, when a physician at Battle Creek Sanitarium in Michigan had put him on six quarts of milk a day until he had gained twenty-five pounds.[4] His imperious air was unchanged.

George Washington Bouldin was born on a 350-acre farm in Jackson County, Alabama, in his mother's eighteen-foot-square bedroom built of hewed cedar logs. Among his thirteen siblings were Benjamin Franklin Bouldin, attorney; Thomas Jefferson Bouldin, physician; and Virgil Bouldin, whose more modest name gained wide recognition during his twenty-one years as an associate justice of the Alabama Supreme Court. Not to be outdone in the sibling rivalry, George adorned his own name with the plumage of a doctor of divinity degree from Howard College in Birmingham.[5]

Dr. Bouldin, as Elizabeth always called him, took charge of her and her luggage with the efficiency that was his trademark. Soon the two were aboard a narrow-gauge train puffing its way towards Gotemba, a resort town near the base of Mount Fuji. From Gotemba Station they took a Ford taxi to the Bouldins' summer house two miles away. Elizabeth's trunk would arrive at the station the next day and be promptly delivered to the house for a charge of ten sen, equivalent in American money to five cents.[6]

Missionaries on Vacation

When the taxi shuddered to a halt and Elizabeth clambered out, George's wife Margaret Alice, called Maggie, rushed out as though to welcome a long-absent child. Close on Maggie's heels was Cecile

Lancaster, whose advice to earn an M.A. degree had jump-started Elizabeth's preparation for freelancing in Japan. So enthusiastic was the reception that all the stress, the setbacks, the seasickness—everything Elizabeth had endured to reach this day now had its reward. To her Training School sisters she wrote: "At last Cinderella has her wish!"[7]

Waiting inside the house was Maggie's mother, Priscilla Jane Krotger Lee, who had lived with the Bouldins the past dozen years. Still vigorous in her seventies, Jane Lee had a reputation for serving up the finest in Tennessee cooking. The Bouldins and other missionaries called her Mama-san, and that with genuine affection, although the Japanese applied this term to a woman in charge of a *bā* (bar) or *kafē* (café)—two kinds of drinking places in Japan.[8]

Also inside were Southern Baptist missionary Carrie Hooker Chiles Rowe and her five-year-old Mary Elizabeth, who, Elizabeth noted, "wears Japanese shoes like a native."[9] Like Cecile, the mother and daughter were temporary houseguests of the Bouldins. Their husband and father, John Rowe, had died of pneumonia in Gotemba only two weeks before at the age of fifty-three. The community was still in shock.

Rowe had been laid to rest in the Foreigners' Cemetery at Yokohama, next to the tiny grave of Mary Janette Bouldin, who had died twenty years before. Since losing her only child, Maggie had lavished her mother-love on all who needed it, Japanese and foreigners alike. Hooker and Mary Elizabeth Rowe now felt the soothing warmth of her glowing heart. Elizabeth sensed it too. Maggie became her "Japan mama" and an intimate friend for life.

Brought up a Cumberland Presbyterian, Maggie had submitted to Baptist immersion two weeks before her marriage to George Bouldin. Acquaintances at the time described her as "high-toned" and "self-made." Elizabeth found her good-natured and full of fun, with a never-failing twinkle in her charming blue eyes. "She is a good psychologist," Elizabeth observed, "who keeps everyone happy and comfortable around her, never letting the atmosphere become in the least bit strained."[10]

George, undisputed head of the house, became a surrogate father to Elizabeth and won her lasting respect. "Dr. Bouldin has a charming sense of humor," Elizabeth said. "He seems full up to the neck with jokes as well as with common sense." She noted that he never let his scholarly pursuits interfere with personal relationships, always cultivating friendships and freely sharing his fine collection of books. "He insists on not only exactness," Elizabeth added, "but honesty, uprightness, and fairness."[11]

To Elizabeth, George and Maggie were the ideal couple, as congenial as any she had known. Both were musical, outgoing, hardworking. In contrast to her lanky husband, however, Maggie was plump, so that when she wore red, an audacious color in old Japan, her appearance hinted at one of the round, red post boxes strategically placed throughout the country. Japanese friends playfully referred to the Bouldins as "the telephone pole and the post box."[12]

After a hot bath, Elizabeth was treated to Mama-san's baked chicken, dressing, rice, gravy, corn, tomatoes, eggplant, bread and butter, preserves, and watermelon. Her weight down to 102 pounds, good home cooking was just what she needed. After supper, Norman and Fannie Williamson dropped by to meet the newcomer, bringing with them five-year-old Norman, Jr., called Sonny Boy. Elizabeth had stared at the Williamsons with envy and admiration when they sat on the stage at the Baptist convention in Memphis. Now they greeted her as an equal, as a colleague-to-be at Seinan Gakuin.

Why were these missionaries clustered in Gotemba? Why had their mission meeting taken place here? Except for Harvey and Lucile Clarke, assigned to student ministries in Tokyo, sixty miles northeast, all the Southern Baptist missionaries lived and worked in southwestern Japan, hundreds of miles away. The majority, however, owned or habitually rented summer houses in Gotemba or in Karuizawa, another resort ninety miles northwest of Tokyo.

Gotemba was cool and surrounded by beauty. Clematis, pinks, thistles, and ferns adorned its sweeping hills. Mount Fuji loomed large, that majestic cone soaring into the sky from a base sixty-three miles in circumference, the most sacred and celebrated peak in Japan. The town attracted missionaries of several denominations with their children, generating a Christian fellowship varied and rich.

Ninooka, the foreigners' section of town, boasted a swimming pool, tennis courts, a chapel, a club with guest rooms and a dining room, an open pavilion where community picnics were held, and two dozen privately owned houses on half-acre lots. Soft spring water was piped to every house. The land itself belonged to the national government, but the rent for each householder was a modest two dollars per year.[13]

The Bouldins' two-story house was of high-grade *hinoki*, or Japanese cypress, a whitish wood used for constructing shrines and fine homes. The furniture, mostly homemade and unpainted, reminded Elizabeth of furniture she had seen at church camps in the States. The house had sliding walls and sliding glass windows designed to admit an abundance of sunshine and mountain air. And the view of Fuji was picture-postcard perfect, since George had taken the lead in developing Ninooka and had been first in line to choose a lot.

Karuizawa, the resort northwest of the capital, was higher and cooler than Gotemba, and its summer population was larger and more cosmopolitan. Missionaries of every denomination competed with diplomats and business people for available space. Visitors flocked in for the bustling conferences and the fancy parties known as pink teas. An American-style drug store sold ice cream and soda drinks. "Karuizawa is . . . everything good," one missionary said. "It sends you back to your field more gentle, more kind, more human, more Christian."[14]

But some missionaries thought Karuizawa too formal, too snobbish, too aristocratic. Emperor Akihito and Empress Michiko, for example, both vacationed there in their youth, first meeting on the tennis courts. In 1920 a band of discontented missionaries had established a foreign settlement at Lake Nojiri, sixty-five miles beyond Karuizawa in the Japan Alps. Nojiri was an ideal place for sailing in the afternoon breeze, and for nonsailors as well, it was a haven for unpretentious, wear-anything living. This informality would have been to Elizabeth's liking, since she complained of having to dress up merely to eat a meal in the club at Gotemba. Nojiri was to become the favorite vacation spot for Southern Baptist missionaries after World War II.

Whether patrons of Gotemba, Karuizawa, Nojiri, or some other retreat, most missionaries believed that an annual vacation away from the sweltering cities was essential to physical and mental fitness. Very few felt guilty about leaving their work during the hot summer months.

Even Elizabeth, hyperactive though she was, acknowledged that unbroken work in an alien culture was a ticket to shattered health.

After several days with the Bouldins in Gotemba, Elizabeth visited Karuizawa, where she lodged with Franklin and Daisy Ray, Southern Baptist missionaries assigned to Hiroshima. This was the Daisy Ray whose dowdy attire and emotional speech at Judson College had disgusted a sixteen-year-old freshman—now her guest. The two women became close friends, and even bedfellows later when Daisy came to Fukuoka for a New Year's conference. After five days of hikes and picnics in the crisp mountain air, Elizabeth returned to Tokyo with Naomi Schell, a Training School sister, as companion and guide.

Appointed to Japan in 1921, Naomi Schell had taught at the girls' school in Kokura with growing disenchantment, which had been Elizabeth's own experience at Watauga Academy. Now she faced a new and exciting challenge. The Japan Mission in session at Gotemba had approved her request to do full-time "social-evangelistic work" in Tobata, a slum-ridden factory town adjacent to Kokura.[15]

Elizabeth and Naomi, soul mates by virtue of their common devotion to social work, made the most of their time together in Tokyo. After checking into the YWCA, they visited three or four settlement houses to see how the Japanese cared for the needy in this showcase capital of four million people. At least twelve of Tokyo's settlements were Christian institutions, including two affiliated with Northern Baptists. Scurrying about the city, largely rebuilt since the devastating earthquake of 1923, Elizabeth marveled at the wide boulevards, massive granite-stone buildings, and gleaming subway, its turnstiles adapted from the ones she had often pushed in New York City.[16]

Sunday morning, Elizabeth and Naomi attended Sugamo Church, known to foreigners as Second Baptist Church. Kimono-clad greeters handed them cushions and fans for their comfort. "My first Japanese sermon," Elizabeth reported tersely. "Recognized 15 words!"[17]

Sunday evening, they attended Koishikawa Church, or First Baptist, on the same compound as the Clarke residence. Elizabeth gushed over Lucile, to whom she had given a rubber apron at the WMU shower in Norfolk. She met warm-hearted Harvey and two of their six children, Lucile and Walter. Harvey was "cordial," the children "very attractive."[18]

To the Work in the Field

In late August and early September, as was their custom, the missionaries closed up their summer homes and returned to their fields of service. By prior arrangement, Elizabeth was to rejoin the Bouldins in Fukuoka. After a Monday tour of fabulous Meiji Shrine, she and Naomi Schell boarded a sleeping car at Tokyo Central Station for the long ride to southwestern Japan. On the same car were missionary Lolita Hannah, the music teacher at the girls' school who had been appointed at age twenty-one; her sister Lillian, a contract teacher at Canadian Academy in Kobe; and Florence Walne, the MK Elizabeth had come to know at the Training School. "Florence put me to bed," she told Lizzie.[19]

The train shuddered through scores of tunnels, its cars inhaling smoke and soot, and the steam locomotive's whistle wailed through the night. But Elizabeth, weary from a string of novel days and talk-filled nights, slept well in her snug lower berth. The next morning she and her companions ate a ham-and-eggs breakfast in the diner while the "boy-san" made up their berths.

In late afternoon the train pulled into Shimonoseki, the port city at the southwestern tip of the main island of Honshū. Passengers going on to Kokura, Fukuoka, and other points on the island of Kyūshū had to transfer to a ferry. Not until 1942, during World War II, was a railroad tunnel completed under the mile-wide Kammon Strait.

Florence Walne, who lived in Shimonoseki with her parents, kept Elizabeth overnight. Her mother Claudia looked pretty and relaxed, only slightly aged since the Walnes' 1921-22 furlough in Louisville. But Ernest was broken and tired, suffering from overwork and distraught over the death of John Rowe.

Unlike their younger colleagues, the venerable Walnes, in Japan since 1892, habitually spent their summers at home. It was a comfortable place, high on a hill fanned with breezes from the sea. Next door, at a lower level, stood the Baptist publishing house that Ernest directed. It was this year—1929—that the business set an all-time publishing record of 250,000 books and 1,750,000 tracts, most items bearing the prominent name of Toyohiko Kagawa.[20] For Ernest, however, this achievement was no greater than the stress it inflicted. The next year he would spend time in a sanitarium and in six years he would be dead.

The next morning Elizabeth and Ernest Walne took the ferry to Moji Port, then boarded a Fukuoka-bound express. He got off at Kokura to assist the girls' school in the wake of its president's death, but the Williamsons, aboard the same train, took charge of "Miss Watkins" and kept her overnight in their Fukuoka home. Being passed around for protection, she decided, was more pleasant that being passed around for inspection, as had happened in Memphis.

The Williamsons occupied one of two missionary residences on the boys' school campus, wood-and-stucco houses that were two-story and Western-style except for the servants' quarters. One residence was vacant, because Kelsey and Maude Dozier had returned to the States on furlough after Kelsey had resigned as school president, relinquishing his duties to George.

After a night with the Williamsons, Elizabeth moved in with the Bouldins at their waterfront home in Jigyō, one mile east of the campus. Her bedroom window framed a splendid view of Hakata Bay with assorted boats on the water and wooded mountains on two sides. Best of all, the Bouldins' beach—smooth, sandy, safe, secluded—was so close that Elizabeth and Maggie could be swimming and frolicking in the surf within minutes after the thought. Elizabeth remembered having to ride a clanging street car one hour each way in order to enjoy the beach at Norfolk.

The luxury of a private beach was short-lived, however. Within days the Bouldins moved to the campus residence that would ever be known as "the Dozier house." Six Japanese workmen, their bare backs glistening with sweat, loaded the furniture and trunks on hand carts and pushed them through the streets. The men seemed jolly even while carrying heavy loads up and down stairs, working in rhythm with the loud choruses they sang. It was the habit of laborers to sing in turn and in unison to bolster their morale.

Elizabeth's new bedroom, which overlooked the campus rather than the sea, was equipped with a red brick fireplace, a cold-water lavatory, and a hanging closet with built-in shelves. The furniture—double bed, desk, dresser with oval mirror, rattan chair, rocker—was in good repair, all of it rented from the Doziers except for the bed. Most pleasing to Elizabeth, sunshine streamed into the room from two sides, through three large windows and two little ones. She could nap or sunbathe on the window seat and dream of lying on the high back porch of her childhood home.

On cold nights Elizabeth slept with foot warmers and a hot water bottle under a crazy quilt comfort that Lizzie had made. Only occasionally did she have a coal grate fire in the room, since warm air filled the house from the potbelly stove in the dining room below. Elizabeth liked to sit by that stove to dry her hair or chatter with the others. In winter it vied with the dinner table as the hub of social life in the home.

Elizabeth's favorite spot outside the house was a palm tree where she often sat while writing her weekly missile to Lizzie. The palm was surrounded by tall, ivy-wrapped pines, and a red maple stood nearby, overlooking a flower bed with Indian blanket, Joseph's coat, carnations, cannas, and others that Lizzie could have identified had she been present. Elizabeth used that spot often, for the winter was unusually mild. "Dr. Bouldin says it's a case of 'tempering the winds to the shorn lamb,'" she wrote, "the lamb being I."[21]

Another place Elizabeth frequented was Momoji Beach, five minutes away. Cluttered with tea houses and bathers in the summer, it now was deserted and serene. Elizabeth would count the many colors in the rolling waves, revel in the distant hills, and find gorgeous shells at her feet, until "intoxicated with the loveliness" all around.[22]

Between the campus and the beach lived the Training School classmate who had turned Elizabeth's heart toward Japan: Phebe Lawton, now Mrs. Faucette. By coincidence "Elizabeth" was her middle name, as it was Cecile Lancaster's and Naomi Schell's. In 1926 Phebe had resigned from the Foreign Mission Board to marry Thomas Frederick Faucette, who had come to Fukuoka in 1925 as a YMCA-sponsored teacher in a government school.

Of Methodist background, Thomas had joined Seinan Gakuin Baptist Church, but he was the wrong man for Phebe. Said to be loose in morals, he mistreated her and their only child Thomas Taneo, born in 1927. Thomas remembers that he and his mother were forced to live upstairs in the house, and that once when he was out on the balcony, his father, working in the yard below, threw dirt at him. Things were so bad that Phebe considered drowning herself in the sea nearby, but could not do so because of Tommy. "I am worse off than a cow," she moaned.[23]

To a distressed Phebe, Elizabeth was a godsend. They talked endlessly while eating or sewing, while visiting historic sites or attending combination tea parties and chrysanthemum shows. Phebe was likewise a blessing to Elizabeth, for she had the leisure to serve as mentor and guide, to help her get used to being treated as though an extraterrestrial. Tommy, as he was called then, sometimes went along, invariably drawing oohs and ahs, and sometimes stayed at home with the maid.

Elizabeth found shopping in Fukuoka as convenient as in Norfolk. Buses to town ran every five minutes or so. Street cars, attached to overhead wires that sparked, ran about twice as often, but they were slower. Whether bus or trolley, the fare was less than two cents, though more for greater distances. To Elizabeth, the major difference was that dogs were allowed on the buses but not on the trollies. On one bus she counted twenty humans and three canines, one of the latter being "immense."

The day came when Elizabeth boarded a street car on her own and became so immersed in study that she rode past her stop. Her impromptu gestures and faltering words to the conductor must have conveyed her plight, for he stopped the car, got off, hailed a trolley going in the opposite direction, put Elizabeth on it, and told the other conductor not to collect any fare. "Wasn't that courtesy for you!" she exclaimed.[24]

Walking on the streets could be unnerving, as there were no sidewalks. Pedestrians mingled with buses, street cars, automobiles, bicycles, and hand carts without number. No matter how vigorous the horn-blowing, some pedestrians made no effort to yield the right-of-way. Children played in the streets as though in a park. Fortunately, the drivers were well trained: the examination for a license was so demanding that the majority of applicants failed.[25]

Fukuoka, an old castle town that had merged with the still older city of Hakata, was home to two hundred thousand people (one million less than at present). Fukuoka was and is a prosperous industrial center, famed for its high-grade silk textiles and its lifelike Hakata dolls. The city's name means Prosperity Hill.

The department stores were large and attractive, surging with men and women in roughly equal number. The most stylish *depāto* had roomy elevators that lifted shoppers to a roof garden, which offered a tea room, a well-equipped children's playground, and a panoramic view of the city and its neighboring mountains and sea. Japan was more modern than Newfoundland, Elizabeth pointed out, and contrary to Mrs. Matthews' fears, cannibals were nowhere to be seen.[26]

Most of the items Elizabeth shopped for were available in the department stores or the myriad of specialty shops run by snappy "Yankees of the East." The exceptions were a sprinkling of ten-cent-store items: Western-style combs, hairpins, and little safety pins. Elizabeth had these articles sent from home, along with her preferred brand of toothpaste, Ipana. She paid a ten-yen (five-cent) handling fee on each foreign package but never had to pay any duty except on some children's toys from Montgomery Ward. Many of her clothes she made herself, and others Mama-san made for her, both copying the latest fashions in the *Pictorial Review*.[27]

The Bustling Bouldin Place

The Bouldin household included one other single, Effie Evelene Baker. Five years older than Elizabeth, Effie was an energetic, ambitious Texan who had put herself through high school and college by working and studying alternate years. She was on furlough in the States until September, when she returned to Fukuoka brandishing an M.A. from Teachers College in New York. Effie was "thoughtful, gentle, spiritual, and a lover of beauty," Elizabeth rhapsodized. She could "paint, draw, write poetry, speak Japanese, lead the boys well, play tennis well, talk interestingly, sew, and I don't know what all else."[28]

The versatile Effie excelled Elizabeth even in vigor. Besides classroom teaching, she conducted several Bible classes, directed plays, trained students for English-speaking contests, taught pep songs to the baseball team, practiced with the glee club, and played for two chapels a day—one in the college and one in the middle school. She visited for her church—Seinan Gakuin Church—and attended all its meetings.

The five members of the Bouldin household—George, Maggie, Mama-san, Effie, and Elizabeth—shared the expense of running it. They equally divided the cost of goods and services that benefitted all, such as fuel for the downstairs stove and the salary for the maid. Coal for the fireplace in one's bedroom was an individual expense.

The maid lived in the servants' quarters with her parents. Unlike them, she was a Christian, an active member of Maggie's Sunday School class and YWA (Young Woman's Auxiliary). The primary school graduate spoke no English but seemed to understand a little, nodding or shaking her head when Elizabeth spoke to her.

Lacking a washing machine, the household used a commercial laundry, which picked up and delivered seventy-two pieces of clothing and linens each week. As for cooking, Mama-san reigned supreme, adept at pleasing the taste buds of all. Maggie and Effie occasionally prepared dishes with an artistic flair after the Japanese fashion, and the maid's mother was on call when there were many mouths to feed. Elizabeth kept her distance from the kitchen stove and let the others vie in fattening her up.

Every day Maggie made sure that the two skinny ones, George and Elizabeth, drank both eggnog and Ovaltine (a malted milk drink). Fortified with these supplements and the consistently hearty meals, Elizabeth weighed 111 pounds at the end of nine months in Japan, a gain of one pound a month.

Though not eager to cook, Elizabeth did her share of household chores. She often served tea to Effie's English classes or to Maggie's YWA girls when they came for a cooking and sewing class. Soon she had classes of her own, and all three teachers helped one another with the serving of refreshments and the playing of games. The classes met all over the house and yard with one exception: George allowed no meetings in his bedroom.[29]

The Bouldins had a tin-lined bathtub, about as large as the enameled one in Elizabeth's Spartanburg home and equipped with hot and cold running water. The household bathed Western style, washing inside the tub instead of beside it. "This is bath night," Elizabeth wrote Lizzie one Tuesday. "Everyone is through but Mrs. Bouldin, and she takes only a minute or two."[30]

The members of the household passed around an English newspaper, the *Japan Advertiser*, mailed daily from Tokyo, and the two new books George received each month through a book club. George also took some Japanese newspapers and read them avidly, to Elizabeth's envy. She shared her *Literary Digest*, a gift from her brother Earle. This prestigious weekly, with 1,400,000 subscribers worldwide, was useful for teaching English.[31]

The Bouldins had a telephone (number 3170), on a party line with the Williamsons. They had no radio, which could have picked up broadcasts from the government-run NHK (there were no commercial stations in Japan until after World War II). Maggie did not want a radio, she said laughingly, "because it would be too tantalizing to have one and have no time to enjoy it." So many guests swarmed in and out, that when Elizabeth had some time to herself, she could hardly think for the chatter resounding through the house.[32]

Although the house was Western-style, the Bouldins enforced the same strict policy on footgear that applied to Japanese-style homes. What was worn outside, whether sandals, geta, boots, or shoes, was forbidden inside. The Bouldins' policy made practical sense. Any kind of footwear could track in mud or filth, and Japanese leather shoes had hard heels and soles that could scratch the wooden floors. In the genkan (entrance hall), guests changed to the indoor footwear laid out for them, either zori (straw sandals) or slippers (scuffs with no upper around the heel). Foreign guests who were squeamish about shucking their shoes in public could pull on the soft cloth covers reserved for their use.

George and Maggie Bouldin had an endless procession of dinner guests. They entertained—in groups of up to thirty—the school's trustees and supporters, the sixty-odd teachers and their families, and the senior class. "In Japanese culture," George told Elizabeth, "entertaining is a primary means of influencing others."[33] True, but an overflowing house also brought him pleasure, perhaps because he grew up in a family of enormous size.

The meals served were Western-style, whether for "hollow inter-mediate boys" or wealthy patrons, and everyone ate with knife, fork, and spoon. Though bereft of chopsticks, however, the guests were no less Japanese in conduct. As was their custom, they loudly sucked anything liquid through their gold- and silver-lined teeth. "By the chorus," Elizabeth commented on one occasion, "everyone must have thought the dinner delicious." After eating, each guest would wield a toothpick with one hand behind the other hand. This done, all would play games and laugh until sore.[34]

The two Baptist pastors in the city, Elizabeth wrote in admiration, "are among the quickest and most brainy men we have anything to do with. They show up brilliantly in the games, as well as elsewhere." Kiyoki Yuya, thirty-nine-year-old son of a samurai, was pastor of Seinan Gakuin Baptist Church, which met in the school. Kamori Shimose, forty-two, was pastor of Fukuoka Baptist Church, closer to downtown. Yuya had studied at the Baptist seminary in Louisville, Shimose at the University of Chicago divinity school. Both men spoke English elegantly, but Shimose, unlike Yuya, wore only Japanese dress.[35]

Elizabeth applied for membership in Fukuoka Church, to which the Bouldins belonged. When her letter of transfer arrived from Southside Baptist in Spartanburg, Pastor Shimose flourished the document as though it were a presidential citation. There was a return slip to be signed by the church clerk; Shimose insisted on signing it himself. After Sunday morning worship the letter was read publicly, and Elizabeth was voted in. Then she was made to stand up front while greetings were read, after which a deacon extended "the right hand of fellowship"—a Western-style handshake.

The college faculty honored Elizabeth with a welcome dinner at the Chamber of Commerce. There were large dinner napkins, and white-coated waiters served fine Western food. Pastor Yuya, who doubled as a professor in the theological department, delivered a formal greeting in English, expressing sentiments Elizabeth would never forget. "If we had only a few beans to eat," Yuya told her, "we would divide them with you. If we had only a torn old quilt to sleep under, we would give you a piece of it."[36]

Though mildly embarrassed, Elizabeth was pleased that the Japanese made so much of her coming. They seemed to appreciate her not being under the Foreign Mission Board or other supporting agency, but "working day by day for my living just as they did."[37] They made her feel truly wanted.

The missionaries for their part treated Elizabeth as a member of the Japan Mission, including her in their activities as though she had been appointed by the Board. One apparent reason is that the Mission was desperate for new personnel. Of the twelve missionaries appointed to Japan in 1921, when the Board was still euphoric over the Seventy-five Million Campaign, only Effie Baker and Naomi Schell remained. The Mission had only twenty members, the same as in 1920.

They were spread as thin as the islands over the broad Pacific. Norman Williamson, reluctantly filling a need for teachers in Fukuoka, still bore responsibilities as a field missionary in Kumamoto. Cecile Lancaster had been teaching in Fukuoka three days a week besides her duties in Kokura. John Rowe's death was attributed to overwork. So eager was the Japan Mission for reinforcements that it afterwards told the Foreign Mission Board, "We will accept the plain garden variety missionary."[38] It was a time when Elizabeth was certain to find the welcome mat out.

"This is the first time in ten years I have felt really settled and absolutely satisfied," she told Lizzie. "All restlessness is gone. The feeling I must move on that has gnawed at me since 1920 has gone."[39] Elizabeth had toiled in six different places during her wilderness journey, ever on the lookout for an opening to the promised land. This year the Jordan had parted. She had reached her Canaan at last.

10

Teacher and Student

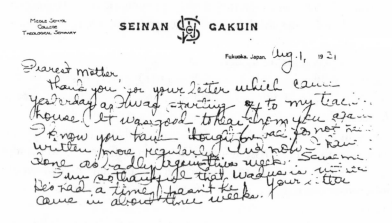

WHEN ELIZABETH BEGAN TEACHING AT SEINAN GAKUIN in 1929, the school occupied ten acres of flat land surrounded by a gray stone wall. A street through the center divided the five-year middle school from the four-year "higher school" or college. The middle school campus centered on a three-story brick building with administrative offices and a chapel seating eight hundred students. The other buildings on both campuses—classrooms, dormitories, gymnasiums— were cheap wooden structures. There were two athletic fields, both grassless, and several tennis courts, one of cement. Gnarled, windblown pine trees overhung the sandy paths.

Enrollment in the middle school (grades seven to eleven) was 401, and in the college (grades twelve to fifteen), 231.[1] The college had three departments: literary, commercial, and theological, the last a tiny seminary with eight students. Several of its theological graduates had done further study at Southern Baptist Seminary in Louisville. A few graduates of the other departments had succeeded in entering Tokyo Imperial University or Kyūshū Imperial University in Fukuoka. This was no small achievement, considering the fierce competition and high attrition rate at each level of education. The term "examination hell" was already entrenched in the Japanese language.

The major appeal of Christian schools like Seinan Gakuin was their ability to provide excellent instruction and teacher-training in the field of English. They utilized missionaries who were not only well-trained and highly motivated but were native speakers of the language they taught. Such instruction was in great demand. "The teaching of English," wrote James E. Wood, Jr., "has been more readily accepted without serious controversy in Japan than in any other mission field."[2] A mastery of this universal language opened the door to many coveted positions in business and government.

Like other middle and higher schools, Seinan Gakuin also offered its students a wide range of extracurricular activities. Among the sports were fencing, archery, swimming, tennis, rugby, basketball, volley ball, and baseball. Cultural opportunities included string orchestra, glee club, Japanese music club, English and Japanese speaking societies, two school magazines, and a newspaper. The participants in each activity formed a club or fraternity, which often took precedence over class work. The clubs of whatever specialty fostered the development of a greater sensitivity to personal relationships, especially the intricate relations between juniors and seniors in the hierarchical society of Japan.[3]

As a Christian school, Seinan Gakuin also sponsored a YMCA, two BYPUs (Baptist Young People's Unions), and a Gethsemane Band. Members of the Gethsemane Band, named after the garden where Jesus prayed before his arrest and crucifixion, devoted themselves to prayers for their non-Christian classmates. All students were required to attend chapel daily and take two hours of Bible weekly, and dormitory students had to attend church each Sunday. Many also joined voluntary Bible classes, particularly English Bible classes taught by the missionaries.

Maggie Bouldin, Effie Baker, and Elizabeth each conducted three Bible classes in their home, offering a separate one for each of Seinan's nine grades. Elizabeth's classes, meeting on three different afternoons, included one of middle school students and two of college students. Intent on evangelism through these classes, she distributed mimeographed invitations to gain new recruits.

Sensei (Teacher) in Seinan

Watkins *Sensei*, as she was customarily addressed, taught English at various levels in Seinan depending on the need. "I am crazy about my work," she told Lizzie. "It has in it the elements of teaching that I enjoy, and almost none of the phases I detest."[4] Most of her classes were oral English, which required less time for grading than English composition, and she was free from the administrative duties that had encumbered her at Watauga Academy.

The middle school boys needed all the help they could get in oral English. Hardly able to distinguish the *l* and *r* sounds, for example, they pronounced *play* and *pray* the same. Even those who could read and write the language remarkably well for their age balked at conversation. "It scares them for you to speak to them in English," Elizabeth wrote, "although they may be reading Shakespeare's *Hamlet*."[5]

At the college level Elizabeth used material from the *Literary Digest*, since "the boys scorn anything babyish."[6] Some of these students were fluent in conversation, especially those in the English Speaking Society that Effie had helped organize six years before. The members would switch from Japanese to English when their meetings began, and back again when the meetings ended, just as the students at Watauga had switched back and forth between standard English and their mountain dialect.

Elizabeth helped the English Speaking Society rehearse a play called "The Rising of the Moon," one of two plays the members presented on a Saturday evening. The boys not only had excellent memories, she discovered, but they proved to be artists in decorating the stage and naturals in acting their parts. The performance lasted from six o'clock to eleven—five hours of unbroken English.

All the students seemed disciplined and polite. Upon entering chapel at eight in the morning, they bowed. When the chord was played for the first hymn, they stood, bowed in unison, then sang with vigor. When chapel ended they stood and bowed yet again. In the classrooms the students would stand and bow to the teacher at the beginning and again at the close of each lesson, obligating Elizabeth to bow in return.

These regimented Japanese in brass-button uniforms were spirited and fun-loving like schoolboys anywhere. In a class of sixty-eight, Elizabeth asked one student to come to the front. As he was walking up the aisle someone thrust out a foot to trip him. Another time she assigned a poem for the class to memorize by the next session. At the beginning of that session the class president asked to speak. "We thought you wanted us to continue the previous lesson," he told her, "so none of us has prepared the poem." Like students Elizabeth had taught in Tennessee, these balky boys were "adept at playing dumb."[7]

Occasionally a boy she called on in class would stand rigid like a telephone pole and say no more than the pole would say in response to her questions. Yet discipline was never a problem. Sassing or threatening the teacher was unheard of, and Elizabeth found that she could maintain order by one simple act: she wrote on the blackboard the name of anyone who talked or was inattentive or who explained in Japanese to the one called on to respond to her question in English. The name on the board worked magic, since Japanese culture instilled in the young an inhibiting sense of shame.

According to a story told among the school's alumni, however, one or more unnamed boys in Elizabeth's conversation class snitched her black grade book (called "devil's book" in Japanese). She caught the culprits and gave them a zero.[8]

"She was a strict teacher," recalled Toraji Murakami. "She kept notes on her students and knew each one well."[9] Elizabeth helped prepare Murakami for Kyūshū Imperial University and for his later roles as teacher and then chancellor at Seinan Gakuin. Before his death in 1996 the school had become a prestigious coeducational university with ten thousand students.

Elizabeth's spoken English posed a formidable challenge to the Japanese. Her enunciation of many words was slurred. But her lively and varied teaching methods more than offset this handicap. They contrasted with the lecture method used by most Japanese teachers, who expected the students to take notes, ask no questions, and feed back the information verbatim on a final exam. In most classes, rote memory, not creativity, was what counted.

The word *shiken* (examination) had an ominous sound like the proverbial "fire, sword, famine, or earthquake." It terrified the students, and rightly so, for they studied very little during the term, then crammed madly, trying to learn a half year's work in a few days. Elizabeth spared her students this ordeal; it was her practice to grade daily and not give final exams.[10]

One day a group of sixteen English teachers visited one of Elizabeth's middle school classes. These Japanese men and women were curious to observe the methods of an instructor who used only English in the classroom. Elizabeth had knots in her stomach when she started the lesson, not knowing what response she would get from her boys, themselves pale with fright and uncommonly quiet. To break the ice, she led some games such as "Birds Fly" and "Where Do You Live?" Then she used flash cards for vocabulary drill. Soon the students were at their ease, even volunteering to answer questions under the visitors' gaze.

Elizabeth applied to Japan's Ministry of Education for a permanent teacher's license. Though not required for teaching in Seinan Gakuin, government recognition would confirm that she was fully qualified to teach at the college level or in any lower grade. One requirement for the license was an examination from the college physician. On the appointed day this gentleman came to the school in a black ricksha, examined Elizabeth in Maggie's presence, and pronounced her fit. Also in her favor was the M.A. from Columbia University and strong recommendations from Seinan Gakuin, whose own prestige stood to benefit from Elizabeth's success. In the fall of 1930, one year after making application, she was granted the permanent license. The fee was seven yen.[11]

On March 11, 1930, graduation day at Seinan, Elizabeth slipped into a dark blue dress with pleating around the hips, which was her closest match to the formal black attire expected at the ceremonies in the middle school chapel. The commencement exercises were identical in many ways to those in public secondary schools. As required by the government, there were the singing of the national anthem and the solemn, ritualized reading of the Imperial Rescript on Education. Speeches were delivered by President Bouldin and by representatives of the undergraduates, the graduates, and the prefectural governor. Diplomas were presented to 149 graduates, some of whom also received special awards and gifts. One boy had not been absent for the full nine years—five years of middle school and four of college.

Yet the program was distinctly religious, from the processional "Onward Christian Soldiers" to the closing hymn "God Be With You 'Till We Meet Again." Scripture reading and prayer had a prominent place. As at every commencement in the school's history, the students sang "Jesus Savior Pilot Me," one of their favorite hymns. Elizabeth exulted in the forceful Christian witness of which she was a part.[12]

Beginning with the new school year in April 1930, Elizabeth's weekly schedule included ten hours of classes in the college and six hours in the middle school. She used Bible books such as Ruth and Esther as texts for upperclassmen. But her first-year middle-school students, those "tiny, darling boys," she taught entirely by the oral method. They were "virtual infants," she said, "among them a cripple on crutches, a dwarf boy, a stammerer, and one about half blind. I found I could get their mouths open easier than I could get them shut."[13]

Teacher off Campus

George Bouldin asked Elizabeth to take over an English Bible class he taught at Fukuoka Baptist Church during the Sunday School hour. Called Truth Seekers, the class was designed to draw young men to the church. Elizabeth assumed the task with characteristic zeal. She ordered pennants, pins, and posters for the class and gave to each student a New Testament with English and Japanese versions in parallel columns. With twenty-five dollars sent her by Royal Ambassador boys in South Carolina, she started a lending library of Japanese-language books on the Bible and the Christian faith.[14] Often she would type out questions on the lesson, using carbon paper to make copies for the students.

A Japanese girl whose family name was Oda asked to be admitted to the Truth Seekers class. Her request was odd. The Japanese educational system segregated boys and girls above the primary level, and churches generally followed suit. In worship services, men and women sat on opposite sides of the auditorium, like the military cadets and Judson girls at the college church in Marion, Alabama.

Oda was no ordinary woman. A graduate of the Methodist girls' school in Fukuoka, she was one of five female students permitted to attend classes with the twenty-five hundred males at Kyūshū Imperial University. Women had won a few such concessions during the 1920s, an era marked by democracy, Westernization, and movements for women's rights. In one indication of change, in November 1929, for the first time ever, the emperor of Japan received in audience a woman: Evangeline Booth, flamboyant but able commander of the Salvation Army in the United States and a daughter of the army's founder, William Booth.[15] In the same month the Truth Seekers class voted to admit Oda.

No doubt about it, Oda made an unforgettable impact on the class. Not only did her proper English set a high standard for the boys—she learned "like lightning"—but her graceful form caressed their eyes. One Sunday she would wear a colorful kimono, and the next a black velvet dress with felt hat. By contrast, the class's only other female, Watkins *Sensei*, looked drab.

The boys themselves were a colorful bunch. One, said Elizabeth, "looks like the picture of the young John the Baptist and has as attractive a voice as face."[16] Some who belonged to the college harmonica club enlivened the class with their sweet music. They would accompany the singing of the class song, "Thy Word Will I Hide in My Heart," and other favorite hymns.

Elizabeth took her class on picnics. "I had a hard time trying to talk to the students as we walked along," she wrote. "They would walk a few steps behind me. If I stopped to let them catch up, they would stop. It was so hard to carry on a conversation with someone behind you."[17] Japanese etiquette taught that teachers should precede their pupils, that the pupils must never step on their teacher's shadow. Elizabeth noticed that wives deferred to their husbands in the same way and more, the husbands arriving at church several minutes ahead of their wives.

She often prayed for wisdom to answer the many questions posed by the students. They would ask: "Can I smoke cigarettes and be a Christian?" Her answer was that a smoker could not be the best kind of Christian. Smoking was prohibited on campus, and Elizabeth used anti-cigarette posters from America to discourage the practice off campus. "How can I find God?" was the query she welcomed the most. Elizabeth gave careful thought to strategies for leading her students to faith in Christ.[18]

Just before Christmas, a traditional time for baptisms, three of the Bible-class boys were immersed in the unheated baptistry at Fukuoka Church. They wore white blouses and sashes and black skirts to their ankles, preferring their native garb to the white baptismal robes usually worn by women and girls. Elizabeth, snug in her woolen "long drawers—long sleeve unions," winced at seeing the three converts dipped in frigid water. Afterwards she was told of the converts at Seinan Gakuin Church, who stood on the beach in a cold wind while singing "There Is a Fountain Filled with Blood," then were immersed in the sea.[19]

Elizabeth helped prepare for the annual fund-raising bazaar at Maizuru Kindergarten, where Maggie was superintendent. She embroidered pot holders and tea towels as her contribution to the hundreds of items to be offered for sale. She washed the kindergarten windows with Bon Ami and wrapped crepe paper around frames to be used for booths. When the big day arrived, she helped Effie play a Victrola phonograph and scurried about the crowd trying to be useful. All went well, and that evening Maggie lavishly thanked her two helpers before slumping into a chair exhausted. "Bazaar," Maggie sighed, "is spelled b-o-t-h-e-r."[20] As pronounced by the Japanese, the two English words sound alike.

In the fall of 1929, Elizabeth's church hosted the annual convention of Japan's WMU. About fifty women attended, some with babies and small children. Elizabeth was deeply touched when a choir of YWA girls sang "Just As I Am," the hymn that was sung when she made her profession of faith at age ten. Another highlight of the meeting was the decision to sponsor the settlement work Naomi Schell had started in Tobata. Elizabeth was impressed at how the Japanese women would rise all over the church to speak their minds about this and other matters.

Elizabeth was asked to write a program for the WMU magazine, complete with songs and prayer topics. The next year she was invited to speak to the local Baptist women on "Glimpses of WMU Work in America." Such opportunities pleased her greatly. "The Japanese Christian women in general far surpass the American ones in giving and praying," Elizabeth bragged to Lizzie. "They think it nothing to stay at a WMU meeting for two or three hours."[21]

Student of the "Dreadful" Language

While serving as a teacher at school and church, Elizabeth slowly adapted to the strange new environment. She was a child again, carefully listening and observing, daringly testing the unknown, learning from her painful blunders.

Unfortunately, she did not have a child's ear for the Japanese language. Nor did her previous experience with other foreign languages—Latin, French, and German—prepare her for learning one radically different from the others and far more difficult. But she had to try. It was a matter of survival to have at least an elementary command of the "devil's tongue" and to be able to recognize the most common Chinese characters among the thousands used to write this "macaroni language."

Elizabeth took private lessons from Chiyo Mizumachi, president of Japan's WMU since its beginning in 1920 and wife of the college dean. The eldest daughter of a mayor, Mrs. Mizumachi was grace itself, as polished as the finest lacquer. She had lovely clothes and a sweet face and manner. Florence Walne described her as "a charming little woman, very quiet and modest."[22] Her executive skills were akin to those of Berta Spooner, Elizabeth's erstwhile boss in Oklahoma.

Three times a week Mrs. Mizumachi—*Sensei* to Elizabeth—would come to the entrance hall of the Bouldins' house, step out of her dressy geta into soft straw zori, and go up to Elizabeth's bedroom for a two-hour lesson. When they were finished, the pupil would race to the entrance and rearrange the teacher's geta for easy access. She always placed the geta so that *Sensei* would not run the least risk of getting dirt on her "little white-mittened feet."

Sensei would have a lesson written out in English for Elizabeth to read aloud in Japanese translation. The teacher would ask questions, and the pupil would stumble through her answers. Even while they were enjoying cocoa and chocolate steam pudding or other refreshments, *Sensei* would keep asking questions. She seemed to have unlimited patience and an ever ready sense of humor, laughing heartily at her pupil's mistakes.

Learning at a snail's pace tried Elizabeth's own patience to the extreme. "What I do learn leaks out so fast!" she exclaimed. Her experience was not unusual. George Bouldin told her, "You have to learn every word and forget it ten times before you know it." She had recognized fifteen words in a Japanese sermon soon after coming to Japan, and in March she recognized a hundred. Yet more was needed than countable words. "I can't understand one whole sentence in the sermons," Elizabeth groaned.[23]

Some of her students told her soothingly that Japanese grammar was more difficult than English grammar and that they themselves did not understand it. That was little consolation. Elizabeth took refuge in the thought that if only she had the opportunity to attend language school, as most missionaries did, she would progress as rapidly as anyone else.

When walking alone on the streets, Elizabeth would look for the objects whose Japanese names she was trying to fix in her mind. Whenever she saw them—chickens, puppies, articles in the shops, whatever—she would call their names together with suitable adjectives. In many foreign countries she could have enlarged her vocabulary by reading the store signs with the aid of a dictionary. But not in Japan. She had no idea how to look up words, a frustration she never tired of airing. The Chinese characters might as well have been Egyptian hieroglyphics.

Studying the language on her strolls made Elizabeth less conscious of being watched. Not for one minute was she free from curious stares. People would turn around to gaze at the creature from another world. Windows would fly open and several pairs of eyes would peep out. Sometimes a troop of children would follow her for some distance. Elizabeth wanted to hang a sign around her neck that read, "Please don't look at me," but that would have made folks stare all the more.[24]

Elizabeth was amazed to learn that most Japanese, though the best of friends, called each other by their family name. The surname was followed with a term of respect, usually *Sensei* for a professional such as teacher, pastor, doctor, or lawyer. For most people the term was *San*, meaning Mr., Mrs., or Miss. Even school children went by their surnames. In the case of married couples, the man would call his wife by her given name, but she would call him "Honorable Husband."[25]

The language of prayer, Elizabeth further discovered, was entirely different from conversation, and the language of public speaking was different from the language of letter writing. After making a stab at using Japanese in a GA or YWA group, she would sit crestfallen, like Elijah, then skip the prayer and go on to the sewing or other activity.[26]

Elizabeth's errors sometimes left her mortified. She confused sound-alike words such as *kami* (God) and *kame* (turtle), *sumi* (charcoal) and *tsumi* (sin). She guessed wrong at what others were saying to her. When struck with a volley of talk, she would respond alternately with "Thank you" and "Don't mention it," hoping one would fit. Once Elizabeth thought a woman was thanking her for a Christmas present. "Don't mention it," Elizabeth said. She learned afterwards that the woman had said, "Please come to see me."[27]

One Saturday she was out visiting to enlist new pupils for a Sunday afternoon *kodomo-kai* (children's meeting). As she approached some children in the street and invited them to the meeting, several fled and those who remained were visibly frightened. Misunderstanding her *kai*, they thought she was trying to "buy" children.

Once when shopping alone, Elizabeth bought some material that seemed just right for a Sunday dress. Afterwards she wished she had known enough Japanese to talk with the clerk about her purchase. "Got home to be told it was underclothes material," she wrote to Lizzie. "So I'll appear on Sunday in Japanese underclothes!"[28]

1. Lizzie Bomar Watkins, mother of Elizabeth Watkins, was one of ten children born to John Earle and Louisa Bomar of Spartanburg, South Carolina. The Bomars were a prominent, well-to-do family.

2. Lizzie posed as a student at Richmond Female Institute in Virginia. She graduated from the Baptist school in 1887, when she was twenty-one.

3. Lizzie was active in many organizations, but especially in her Baptist church, where she taught Sunday School classes and led mission groups.

4. Eddie Watkins, Elizabeth's father, pursued Lizzie Bomar for five years before they were married in 1895. He was a loyal Presbyterian.

5. Eddie Watkins posed in front of his Camden Grocery House in Camden, South Carolina (circa 1899).

6. Lizzie gave birth to a girl April 21, 1900. The child was named after Eddie's mother, Elizabeth Taylor Watkins.

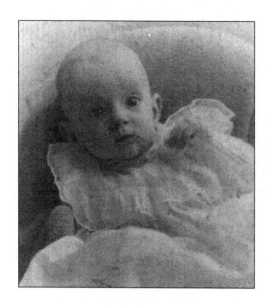

7. Baby Elizabeth was adored by her parents and her many relatives.

8. At three years of age, Elizabeth was fond of dolls and pretty clothes. She later designed and made her own clothes.

9. A bright but mischievous child, Elizabeth went to the Baptist church with her mother while her father attended the Presbyterian church.

10. The Watkins family moved to Spartanburg in 1904 and built this roomy house on Irwin Avenue.

11. Elizabeth took great pride in her brothers Earle (left) and Edward (right), especially after their father's death in 1909.

12. Earle labeled this snapshot, "Sis at sweet sixteen." At that age Elizabeth graduated from high school and entered Judson College in Alabama. In her senior year at college she felt called to foreign missions.

13. Elizabeth graduated from the Woman's Missionary Union Training School in Louisville at the age of twenty-two. She applied to the Foreign Mission Board for an appointment to Japan but was turned down on grounds that she was "handicapped somewhat with youth."

14. Employed by the Home Mission Board, Elizabeth taught at Watauga Academy, a mountain mission school in Butler, Tennessee. This was the administration building.

15. Elizabeth lived in Farthing Hall, the girls' dormitory.

16. Elizabeth went to Japan on her own in 1929 and supported herself by teaching English. In her free time she served as principal of the Garden of Love, a Baptist kindergarten in an outcast village.

17. Elizabeth led the Garden of Love graduation ceremony in 1935.

The Seventh English Speaking Meeting at the Kokura Baptist Church. 1932. 10. 1

18. Southern Baptist missionaries in Japan utilized Elizabeth's skills as an English teacher. Foreigners seen in this photo are, from left to right, Kelsey Dozier, Elizabeth Watkins, Naomi Schell, Lolita Hannah, Delia Burke (Maude Dozier's mother), Maude Dozier, and Cecile Lancaster.

19. Elizabeth lived in this 450-square-foot house on the campus of Seinan Gakuin, the Baptist boys' school. George Bouldin, standing in the doorway, had built the house as his "Detached Palace."

20. Wrongly accused of entertaining men in her home at night, Elizabeth persuaded Lizzie to come and live with her. Mother and daughter posed in front of their "palace."

21. Inside the "palace" Lizzie taught English Bible classes and private pupils, hugging the coal-burning stove in winter. Her students revered her. Lizzie and Elizabeth were both forced out of Japan during World War II.

22. After her belated appointment by the Foreign Mission Board in 1948, Elizabeth was director of the Tobata Good Will Center, which offered social and religious services.

23. When Elizabeth left the Good Will Center in 1952, the kindergarten mothers had her dressed as "a Japanese bride, wig and all."

24. Central Japan Station members donned *yukata* for their "fun night" performance at the 1958 mission meeting. Faces visible on stage, from left to right, are those of A. E. (Bud) Spencer, Ramona Mercer, Betty Masaki, Audrey Fontnote, James Satterwhite, Frances Horton, Gladys Nelson, Doris Spencer, Calvin Parker, and Elizabeth Watkins.

25. Elizabeth was noted for her wit and humor, but she could also be somber.

26. Members of the Central Japan Station posed at a meeting in 1962. From left to right, front row: Ramona Mercer, Harriett Parker, Martha Sherer, Helen Sherer, Luke Gillespie, Bee Gillespie, Elizabeth Watkins; second row: Louise Medling, Asano Hoshizaki, Mary Lou Emanuel, Grace Emanuel, Wayne Emanuel, Reiji Hoshizaki; back row: Bill Medling, Calvin Parker, Dewey Mercer, A. L. Gillespie, Robert Sherer.

27. In Shikoku, Elizabeth encouraged pastors such as Toshio Odori (right rear) and trained many young people. Ichirō Odori (front row, second from left) became pastor of Seinan Gakuin Baptist Church.

28. Elizabeth was proud of Yawatahama Baptist Church, the last church she planted in Shikoku.

29. On July 3, 1970, faculty and alumni of Seinan Gakuin gave a "sayonara party" for Elizabeth. Former governor Katsuji Sugimoto, seated to her left, helped her win a decoration from the emperor.

30. Unwilling to retire, Elizabeth ministered to internationals in Utah and other western states until her death in 1983. Her remains were buried in Oakwood Cemetery, Spartanburg.

Student of Confusing Customs

Elizabeth also made a valiant effort to learn the peculiar customs of Japan. After several embarrassments stemming from her ignorance of proper behavior, she started going once a week to a professional teacher of etiquette. The teacher was understanding and made the lessons fun, but Elizabeth, unaccustomed to sitting on tatami, sometimes felt like "a cow down on the floor."[29]

She gradually learned how to conduct herself in a Japanese home. "When maid brings tea," her faded notes read, "touch fingers to floor. Bow slightly. To pick up cup, extend both hands, thumbs along index fingers. Right hand slips under the cup, left along the side of it."[30]

Surprisingly, the Japanese often served her coffee instead of green tea, and Elizabeth could not bring herself to decline it as she would in a foreign home. "Now I really enjoy it sometimes," she confessed after five months in the country. "Who'd have thought my 'black poison' would ever be anything but something to be endured as medicine!"[31]

Many of the customs, she noted, relate to the changing of the seasons and the people's instinctive attachment to nature. Her letters contain vivid descriptions of the Chrysanthemum Festival, the Dolls' Festival, and other festive occasions. The most conspicuous holiday was New Year's, when the houses and shops were gaily decorated with bamboo and oranges festooned in front, along with attractive arrangements of rice straw and pine. Bamboo is a symbol of long life, Elizabeth learned, and oranges are a symbol of plenty. She observed that the whole city—indeed the whole nation—was cleaner than at any other time of the year.[32]

At Seinan Gakuin, as at most other schools, the students and teachers gathered on January 1 for a service of celebration. This was followed by a faculty tea party, at which Elizabeth and her colleagues each received a box of cake with New Year's greetings. Afterwards they ate a Japanese meal together and engaged in friendly banter.

During the New Year's season nearly everyone would put on their best clothes and call on friends and acquaintances. Many dropped by the Bouldins' home, intoning the prescribed greetings and leaving their visiting cards in a little tray on a table in the entrance hall. The visitors would tarry in the yard to enjoy the gorgeous chrysanthemums, pink roses, and white Chinese lilies. Elizabeth thought the setting was ideal for launching a new year. Ripe oranges hung in nearby trees, giant pines laughed in the wind, and the waves at the beach rolled and boomed.

February 11 was Kigensetsu, a national holiday that celebrated the legendary founding of the empire in 660 B.C. It was claimed that Emperor Jimmu, a great-great-grandson of the sun goddess, ascended the throne on February 11 of that year. While most Japanese worshiped at a Shinto shrine, Elizabeth and Effie used the occasion to visit Naomi Schell at her home in Tobata. For Elizabeth, it turned out to be the first opportunity to bathe Japanese style.

Naomi's bathtub, made of wood, was so deep that the water came up to one's neck. The water was heated directly by a fire underneath. Elizabeth bathed from a small pan beside the tub, rinsed off the soap, then stepped into the tub to soak and relax. The water was not drained from the tub until everyone in the house had used it. Elizabeth explained that "they don't think it dirty water at all."[33]

She learned from her friends that to the Japanese, hot water up to the neck was but one of two ingredients required for a bath to be fully satisfying. The other ingredient was companionship. It was a venerable tradition for men, women, and children to tub together. The incursion of Westerners in the nineteenth century had forced the Japanese to segregate their public bathhouses, with the exception of many hot-spring resorts, but this did not extinguish their love of crowds and dread of loneliness. Under segregation, men enjoyed the companionship of men, and women of women. Smaller boys usually bathed with their mothers.

"I hope never to go in a public bath," Elizabeth told her mother.[34] Shortly thereafter, Phebe Faucette led her into the sulphurous, medicinal waters of Futsukaichi Spa, near Fukuoka, introducing her to an elegant pleasure that the Japanese had cherished for centuries. Elizabeth was to experience it countless times during the years ahead.

Elizabeth attended her first funeral in Japan when the mother of one of Seinan's teachers died. Having no black outfit but confident her dark blue silk dress would do, she accompanied Effie to the rites at a

Buddhist temple noted for its lavish display of gold. The pair deposited a fancy envelope containing "incense money" at the reception desk, watched by men in black arm bands, then joined the mourners seated on tatami near an altar bearing the ashes of the deceased. The chanting of eight priests in colorful robes, the reading of condolences from the various groups connected with the family, and the lavish burning of incense reminded Elizabeth of a Greek funeral she had attended in Norfolk, Virginia. One striking difference was that everyone in attendance received two gifts from the stricken family—a furoshiki and a package of funeral tea.[35]

Elizabeth also attended the funeral of the little boy of one of Seinan's janitors. After the Christian service at the school, the mourners walked out through the sandy pine grove to the crematory. "To me that is a horrible thing," Elizabeth wrote. ". . . My heart ached for the sobbing mother as the fire began to crackle."[36] No one could have convinced her in the gloom of that day that she too, by her own choice, would be reduced to ashes after her death.

The first wedding Elizabeth attended in Japan turned her thoughts inward. Would she herself ever be a bride? On her thirtieth birthday, she could imagine her brother Earle saying, "Old enough to get married, eh Sis?" All she needed was a proper man. "I wouldn't mind so terribly being married in Japan to a Baptist preacher," she wrote, "but anything else appears as most unattractive to me."[37] There were no unattached men in the Japan Mission at the time, and Phebe's calamitous marriage outside the organization served as a red flag.

With so many new experiences crashing upon her, Elizabeth suffered a mild case of what a generation later was termed "culture shock." The malady itself is ancient and universal. Elizabeth was a *gaijin*, a foreigner, a self-conscious outsider overwhelmed with new situations and unfamiliar demands. But she was adapting well, and her natural curiosity and sociability would take her far beneath the surface of a culture often thought inscrutable. Elizabeth, teacher and student, had come to stay.

11

To the Top of Mount Fuji

At Mrs. Bouldin's
Ninooka, Solemba
July 11, 1930

Precious Mother,
Here we are in the mountains, and right glad I am. It had become very hot in Fukuoka, the sun steaming the earth after the rainy season. Here the cold mountain water and bracing air are refreshing. I have enjoyed a long sleep since lunch. We arrived at nine this morning after 26 hours of traveling. Mrs. Bouldin, the maid, and I — the others are coming later. I am eager to begin studying as soon as possible. Tuesday, though, we hope to go to Yokohama to see Florence.

THE MONTH OF JUNE ushered in the rainy season, the several weeks of gloomy, sultry days that pleased the farmers but depressed nearly everyone else. The air was so humid that leather shoes sprouted whiskers and clothbound books turned a musty gray. Elizabeth's pep seemed to drain out in sticky perspiration, whether she was drilling her middle school students in English conversation or making peach ice cream for her Bible class boys. Mosquitoes swarmed, reviving memories of her troubles with the huge biters in Newfoundland. George Bouldin kindly bought her a mosquito net and put it up in her room. Mama-san endured the heat of the kitchen to can strawberry preserves, since it was the only time of the year when big, juicy strawberries could be had for a cent and a half a box.[1]

The summer style in dress burst out like a vast field of daisies. Policemen and students in military schools changed to white uniforms on June 1. Many girls and young women started wearing Western-style dresses, which were cooler and cheaper than summer kimonos. Elizabeth saw some "wonderful creations" in the way of clothes on both women and men whenever she left the campus.

Typically, a man wore a light-figured kimono with open throat. The garment was secured with a sash wrapped around his hips and tied in a bow at the back. His feet were bare except for geta. A stiff, American-style straw hat was perched incongruously on his head. Often a big pleated skirt reaching to the ankles was worn over the kimono, giving the effect of shirt waist and skirt. Elizabeth also noticed a few men in American-style white flannel or cotton suits, their feet properly covered with socks and leather shoes.

Little boys and girls commonly played around their homes in their birthday suits, and some of the grownups wore little more. Even on the open streets Elizabeth saw women nude to the waist, their only covering a rough cloth wrapped as a skirt from the waist to the lower legs. She saw men wearing only a loincloth of great brevity. "You wonder where modesty ends," Elizabeth commented, "and sensible comfort begins."[2]

She had been shocked her first month in Fukuoka when she turned a street corner and met a brown man in loincloth coming in her direction. But the novelty of nudity was wearing off now. While she was conducting an afternoon Sunday School in a nearby mining village, for instance, big boys strolled about her with not even a string around their sleek bodies. In summer, stripping was as natural as fanning.

On the train, Elizabeth told Lizzie, it was "nothing to see a nice looking man in a business suit suddenly stand up in the aisle, strip off his foreign style clothes, and put on his native kimono, going to sleep in a little while with his big bare feet decorating the car seat."[3] Although most travelers exposed no more than their BVDs, Elizabeth said, the loincloth was the only thing never removed in public. She wondered whether she were too prudish and whether Americans in general were burdened with a false modesty.

After the first week in July the rainy season lifted, exposing the earth to a scorching sun. School classes, Bible classes, and most clubs

observed a summer recess. After a last flurry of activity—grading
composition books, judging English-speaking contests—the missionaries were free to go to the mountains for cool water and bracing air.
George helped Elizabeth prepare for the trip to Gotemba. Before
breakfast one morning he bought her a Japanese-style suitcase, actually
a large straw basket, and brought it home in his arms through the
streets. After Elizabeth had packed the suitcase, he roped it, helpful
"father" that he was.[4]

Maggie, Elizabeth, and the maid went ahead of George, Mama-
san, and Effie. For Elizabeth, the twenty-six hours on a gritty train
were anything but boring. At each stop vendors walked up and down
the station platform crying their wares, offering *bentō* (box lunch),
sandwiches, ice cream, tea, coffee, milk, fruit, newspapers, and
books. Seemingly under a physical strain, these hawkers carried their
merchandise on heavy trays suspended from their necks. Unlike their
counterparts in America, they remained outside the cars, the passengers buying through the windows.

The consumers of the merchandise nonchalantly dumped their
garbage on the floor, the more fastidious among them aiming it under
their seats. At regular intervals an attendant would saunter through the
car cleaning up the mess. He would first pick up the bottles and other
reusable containers with a pair of tongs, then use a pair of short
brooms, one in each hand, to sweep up the apple peelings and crab
bones and all the other rubbish.

The contrast between the ugly clutter inside the train and the scenic
views on either side was stark. Elizabeth feasted her eyes on the
passing sights of rural Japan, one giant garden with none of the land
wasted. Small, irrigated rice paddies stretched in terraces all along the
way. Each paddy was flat but at a different level from the adjoining
ones, and all were separated from one another by little dikes made of
mud or stone and grass to hold the water in. The tufted rice plants
were a tender green, having been transplanted only a few days before.

Earlier, in Fukuoka, Elizabeth had watched the process of trans-
planting rice seedlings from the nursery beds to the flooded fields. The
farmers would stick the plants into the ooze in rhythm with their
unaffected singing. When they had completed a field, always in a
remarkably short time, the plants would be standing in perfect rows,

each plant equidistant from the others and all bending gracefully in the same direction. The artistic sense of the Japanese seemed inborn.

Through the train windows Elizabeth saw rural folks drawing water from a well, leading a buffalo home from plowing, weeding and fertilizing the flooded rice plants, spreading matting out on the ground preparatory to sunning grain. In the evening she caught glimpses of people inside their homes stretched on the floor or sitting on their feet at a low table or desk. The homes were wide open, the paper doors thrown back. Electric lights flickered everywhere, even from thatched-roof farmhouses and small hamlet shacks.

In Paradise Again

All of Japan, her promised land, was a fascinating world to Elizabeth. In its midst was a paradise: Gotemba. This summer she looked forward to enjoying Gotemba far more than was possible the year before, when her stay was tantalizingly brief.

Mount Fuji charmed her daily, at times in a haunting way. It was a phantom mountain, hiding its countenance behind a shroud of dark clouds, dimly appearing as an enormous ghost, unreal and mysterious, and then popping out as a reddish-brown peak with clouds rolling about its base and snow glistening from the crevices near the summit. In the course of a single day its face would change spectacularly as the sun moved across the sky from dawn to dusk. Silhouetted against the scarlet sunset, Fuji seemed even more gigantic. Elizabeth could well understand why "its name is one of the first words that every Japanese baby hears from its mother's lips; the first picture of anything he sees, and also the first sketch he makes."[5]

On clear days the sun streamed in on Elizabeth's bed, a perfect place for sunbathing after lunch. The house was so high up that no one could see in the windows. Elizabeth would experience a delightful cleansing with the sun beating first on one side and then on the other of "bare me," only her head in the shade. This was her way of "storing up red corpuscles to last all winter."[6] She also used the time to memorize Japanese—except, of course, on Sundays.

Some of the foreign residents always had an umbrella over their heads when outside in the sun, but not Elizabeth. Wearing her russet bathing suit and yellow cap, she would dive into the concrete-lined swimming pool several times a day. While acquiring a wanted tan, however, she got freckled worse than ever.[7]

Accompanying her sunbathing and her swimming was background music of the sweetest kind. The birds in the surrounding trees were tireless in their singing. Bush warblers, mockingbirds, nightingales, and trilling bob whites joined in the chorus, a welcome change from the Fukuoka sounds of clanging trollies and tooting taxis. Elizabeth also enjoyed the chirping crickets and other summer insects. She was impressed that the Japanese would buy a cicada for two sen (one cent) and keep it in a wire cage to hear it sing, as Americans did a canary.

Dr. and Mrs. R. E. Chambers, Southern Baptist missionaries to China, were spending the summer in Gotemba to recruit his health. One night Chambers had an attack of some kind, and his wife rushed him to St. Luke's Hospital in Tokyo, leaving their three children at the Bouldin house. Since Maggie was busy with cooking and housekeeping, Elizabeth took charge of the children, ages three to eight. She fixed cots for them in her room and dressed, fed, and amused them. The two younger ones she helped bathe. When she was scrubbing five-year-old Harris's face, he resisted and asked, "What kind of soap is that?"

"Perfectly nice soap," Elizabeth replied. "I brought it from your house."

"But it's laundry soap, isn't it? Mother says laundry soap burns, and it does!"[8]

Elizabeth's goof as a substitute mother in no way diminished her infatuation with the missionary children at Gotemba. Despite their varied roots in England, Scotland, America, China, and Japan, the children behaved like siblings who took genuine pleasure in one another. Some of them never saw any foreigners outside their own family from one summer to the next. Others would leave home at the age of ten or eleven to attend boarding schools, usually the Canadian Academy in Kōbe or the American School in Tokyo or Shanghai. They all formed lasting friendships at Gotemba. To their elders' delight, these gifted youngsters also became a troupe, staging costume concerts and other entertainments.

They could also play pranks. One Sunday a group of them persuaded their parents to let them go home after Sunday School, skipping the church's worship service. On the way they happened upon a snake. Two of the boys killed the snake, then carefully placed it coiled up in a chair shaded by the firs, pines, and spruces between the chapel and the club. When church was over, Elizabeth wrote, "along came the most dignified of the English ladies here. She has a single eye glass. Her head is at such an angle, I fear if she had no umbrella, it would rain down her nose. Her neck looks incapable of bending." This was the random victim who started to seat herself in the rigged chair, noticing the snake just in time. Her shriek echoed through the hills, and the boys chuckled over their stunt for days.[9]

A Full and Merry House

In mid-July more escapees from steaming Kyūshū arrived in Gotemba and were shoehorned into the Bouldin house. Now on the roster, besides Maggie, Elizabeth, and the maid, were George, Mama-san, Effie Baker, Naomi Schell, Lolita Hannah, Cecile Lancaster, Hooker Rowe with daughter Mary Elizabeth, and two Japanese students. To accommodate so many at once, the Bouldins built an extra room for the two students, put the maid on an enclosed upper porch, divided two rooms into four by using sliding screens, and made double-decker bunks for themselves in a narrow room. Maggie again proved herself a wonder at keeping so many people happy under one roof.

Mama-san took over the kitchen, and all palates were pleased. Elizabeth ate large helpings of carrots, potatoes, vine-ripe tomatoes, red figs, Japanese grapefruit, fine-textured watermelon, and brown bread with *mizuami*, a kind of syrup. She paid the Bouldins six dollars a month for food, while lodging was free.[10]

One week in August was set aside for the annual mission meeting, the first since Elizabeth's arrival in Japan. The Southern Baptist missionaries who came to Gotemba for only this week lodged in the foreigners' club, a stone's throw from the Bouldin house behind a grove of evergreens. All the participants took their noon meals at the club.

The meetings were held daily in the chapel. The missionaries invited Elizabeth to lead a morning devotional and gave her the privilege of speaking on the floor during business sessions. Most important, they passed a resolution unanimously requesting the Foreign Mission Board to grant her regular missionary status.[11]

On Tuesday evening that week, the Northern Baptist missionaries at Gotemba joined their Southern counterparts for a social. Mama-san fried five chickens, and others prepared beans, potatoes, tomatoes, corn bread, and ice cream. After supper the group played "hilarious" games. Elizabeth was enamored with Clara Converse, a Northern Baptist missionary in Japan since 1890. Feeble and nearly deaf, Miss Converse told fascinating stories about the pioneer years of culture clashes and ricksha crashes.[12]

Most weeks at Gotemba Elizabeth studied Japanese two hours each morning with a professional tutor from Tokyo, Kako *Sensei*. She went to the teacher's house just across a hill. Kako *Sensei* was superb as both a person and a teacher. Elizabeth resolved to make thorough preparation for each lesson in order to get the most for her money, but despite the good intentions, she usually ended up cramming in bed before breakfast. With so many competing activities like tennis and swimming, and with so much chatter in the house, studying Japanese required the spirit of a martyr. Another distraction was George's personal library. Elizabeth delved into novels by H. G. Wells, Sinclair Lewis, and Thomas Hardy, often reading herself to sleep at night.

Although on vacation, Elizabeth taught a Sunday School class of eight girls, all missionary children, and an English Bible class for Japanese young people. She could no more decline these opportunities than she could turn down a slice of watermelon. The English Bible class suffered a heavy turnover, for students came and went during the summer. In search of new members, Elizabeth visited the summer villas of counts and barons and other aristocrats, villas with lovely grounds, handsome dogs, and bevies of servants. She delivered hand-painted cards on which she had written invitations to the class, but the response was almost nil.[13]

The Once-in-a-Lifetime Climb

On Thursday and Friday, August 14-15, Elizabeth climbed Mount Fuji in a party of seven. Her fellow climbers were George and Maggie; Lolita Hannah; Grace Bears, a Lutheran missionary; Yasushi Kusakari, a Seinan college student; and a Japanese man from the community who served as guide and burden bearer. Mama-san prudently stayed at home, as did Cecile Lancaster, who had made the climb in 1923 with Professor W. O. Carver and others. Cecile respected the adage that one is a fool not to climb Fuji and one is a fool to climb it twice. George, an alpinist, had been up it four times, but Maggie, like Elizabeth, had never been before.[14]

Elizabeth was confident. Eleven years earlier she had climbed North Carolina's Mount Mitchell, at 6,684 feet the highest peak east of the Rockies. Fuji's altitude, however, was far greater: 12,365 feet by popular reckoning—a figure easily remembered by 12 months and 365 days—and two dozen feet more according to standard reference works. But the climb would not be strenuous, her companions told Elizabeth, since they would ride horseback much of the way.

The party travelled fifteen miles by taxi to a gateway at the mountain's base, where they engaged their horses. No sooner was Elizabeth astride her steed than the others began calling her the Queen of Sheba. They thought her the perfect adornment for her even-tempered, redheaded mount. Her blouse was rose and white, knickers grey, stockings and shoes brown. A varicolored silk scarf flew from her seven-cent rice-straw hat.

Each horse was gently led by a man walking at the animal's head and holding the bridle close to his own head. This left the riders free to stretch or rest their muscles, turn to chat with those behind, or drink in the surrounding beauty. The spruce and firs vied in loveliness with those in North Carolina. Myriads of ferns grew along the path with mountain flowers dotted about. Moss-covered logs lay here and there, and above them in the trees hung festoons of moss similar to the old man's beards in the trees near Charleston, South Carolina.

The party ate their supper at a stop seventy-five hundred feet above sea level. The sunlit clouds below looked like fairies' dresses of

rose and pearl grey and crimson. Above was the blue, blue sky, and
the towering mountain yet to be conquered. After disposing of their
fried chicken bones, tomato skins, and sandwich crumbs, the climbers
mounted their steeds and pressed on, passing the timber line and losing
the pleasant company of vegetation.

From the base of Mount Fuji to the summit there were ten main
stops, or stations, with tea houses and stone lodging huts, and there
were some halfway stops also. The Bouldin party paused at most of the
stations to rest the horses and the Japanese guide. The burly guide
climbed all the way on foot, carrying their food and bedding on his
back.

Except for Maggie, they had engaged their horses only to the fifth
station. Elizabeth for one was glad to dismount at this point and start
walking. It made her self-conscious to see the Japanese climbing all the
way on foot, whether college students doing it for sport or religious
pilgrims resolved to worship at the shrine on the summit. Most discon-
certing, old people were carrying still older people on their backs.

Elizabeth had not walked far before she had second thoughts. The
air was so thin she could hardly breathe. She stumbled through the
deepening dusk, straining to pull herself up the bare rocky path to the
sixth station. Then swallowing her pride, she hired another horse and
rode in company with Maggie to the eighth station, where they would
spend a short night. Both women were draped in army blankets as they
sat in their saddles, for a mere sweater did not suffice against the cold.

The eighth station, about a mile from the summit, was as far as the
horses could go. From this vantage the panoramic view was stunning.
The guide called the names of some twenty towns whose lights twin-
kled at them from a great sea of clouds. He pointed out Tokyo in the
far distance, which appeared as a single glare. Even more awesome
were the spangling stars hovering overhead, never before so close and
bright.

Inside the station's one-room lodge, many climbers were sleeping
on the floor between thick futons. A few men were hunched around the
open fire in a large square hole in the center of the floor, over which
swung a kettle of boiling water. Elizabeth tore off her leggings and
shoes and crept up to the fire to thaw her cold toes. Then she wrapped
her own blanket around her over her clothes, slipped between two

futons, and rested her head on a hard Japanese pillow. Heavy breathing all around stirred the air.

No sooner had she lain down, it seemed, than Elizabeth was awakened by the movements of people getting up. The time was two-thirty. There was no need to dress except to tie on her hat, fasten her shoes and leggings, and seize the stout mountain stick she had purchased at the foot of the mountain. She and her companions ate a snack of chicken and sandwiches, then strode out into the frosty three o'clock air against a field of lingering snow.

Elizabeth toiled up the path as though she had been climbing all night. Every few feet she had to stop and rest, only to shudder from the cold that penetrated her sweater and blanket. The moisture in her nose turned into icicles that rattled when she tried to breathe—a horrid feeling. Kusakari, the Seinan student, asked to take her on his back. She refused, but allowed him to "pull and push me along."

The slow-paced Bouldin party had hoped to reach the top before sunrise, but they were still on the slope when that glorious moment arrived. They stopped and faced to the east as the great ball burst into view, a sight never to be forgotten. Pilgrims clad in white clapped their hands and chanted prayers. Most climbers stood in place until the sunlight swept over the fields and villages far below.

When the Bouldin party reached the summit, the four women—Elizabeth, Maggie, Lolita, and Grace—piled down on cots and covered themselves with futons. After resting awhile, they walked around the crater, looking down into the centuries-old cavity from different sides. Part of the crater's wall was ice, with a light sprinkling of crumbled rock. Other parts looked like solid rock, brown or reddish or black. Steam was spouting up in various places, and the air reeked with sickening, sulphurous fumes.

Soon it was time to descend. The route down the mountain was on a different side, the path steeper and shorter. No tree was to be seen, no flower or blade of grass, just miles of volcanic ash. With each step they sank halfway to their knees in the cinders. Still, they took great strides, almost running down the slope.

They came to a tea house where lava sleds were available to rent. After some haggling over the price, Maggie and Lolita decided to ride. Each crouched in her flat-bottomed sled, bracing her feet against the turned-up edge in front and folding her knees under her chin. Men who seemed to run on air pulled and guided the sleds with cords. Elizabeth, following on foot, could hardly stop laughing at "fat Mrs. Bouldin, with her scarf flapping off from behind, doubled up in that little tin tub!"[15]

Farther down the slope, they found a horse carriage to rent. There was just enough room for six people, with three seated on each side facing one another. As the horse pulled the springless carriage over the volcanic rocks, the guide walking, the passengers swayed back and forth laughing. At a lower elevation, back in the world of trees and wild flowers, they boarded a taxi for the remaining distance home. Mama-san welcomed her charges with a steaming hot bath, a fried chicken dinner served in bed, and pampering for the next two days.

The Fuji adventure has a sad footnote. The Japan Mission had asked Elizabeth to have a physical examination so that it could forward a medical report to the Foreign Mission Board with its recommendation that she be appointed. So after the Fuji trip, as prearranged, she went to the Seventh Day Adventist Hospital in Tokyo, accompanied by Hooker Rowe. The examining physician thought Elizabeth had a leaking heart and might be getting a goiter. This diagnosis went into her permanent file at the Board.[16]

Elizabeth knew she had pushed herself to the limit in making the strenuous climb and had been ill at the summit. So the physical exam, as a means to missionary appointment, was untimely. A follow-up exam a month later showed no heart problem or thyroid disorder, but the negative report held sway for years to come.

Toward the end of August the air was turning cold and—as Elizabeth later put it—"tickling my bones, reminding them of the joy of snuggling between blankets." Vacation time was up. The rushing winds and rattling windows were nudging the Bouldin household to pack their things and return to their Kyūshū home.[17]

12

Faith Missionary at Work

THE QUIET RETURN OF THE BOULDIN HOUSEHOLD to Fukuoka was followed by the heralded return of the Dozier family—Kelsey, Maude, and Maude's mother, Delia T. Burke. A crowd of about 250 was at the train station to welcome the Doziers back from their furlough in the States. The celebrated family stayed briefly with the Williamsons before starting a year's residence in Shimonoseki, replacing the furloughing Walnes. While in Fukuoka, Kelsey eagerly shared with Elizabeth a story about her uncle Paul Bomar in Alabama. "He slipped me five dollars," Kelsey said, "and told me to buy whatever book I wanted."[1]

The Doziers retrieved the furnishings they had left in the house taken over by the Bouldins. There was "quite a tearing up of the place," Elizabeth said. Out went a mattress here, a bookcase there, chairs, desks, and miscellaneous pieces. Effie Baker was not much affected because all her furniture was her own, but nothing was left in Elizabeth's room except the bed and the built-in closet with shelves. Fortunately, Maggie and Effie had some spare furniture to lend.

That month Elizabeth's financial security was disturbed no less than her snug bedroom. George Bouldin had explained from the outset that only one year's salary was available from Seinan Gakuin. Over a period of many years, Foreign Mission Board appropriations for the school had been budgeted at two yen to the dollar. In reality, the dollar was worth a fraction more. So each time the Mission converted dollars to yen, it realized a small budget excess, which went into an exchange fund for special needs. This was the fund George had exhausted in employing Elizabeth. Now teaching without pay, she learned from Maggie that some of the Japanese teachers had asked Dr. Bouldin to reduce their own meager salaries and pass on the savings to Elizabeth. She was humbled by their concern but glad that George had refused.[2]

The truth is, Elizabeth's income had sagged but not ceased. She was earning a little from private pupils, and gifts came sporadically from abroad. Her cousin Mary Bomar Wallace had sent a donation during the summer, and friends such as Nonie Gravett led their mission groups to send her offerings. The most generous check came from six of the business women she had taught in the Billy Sunday Bible Class at Southside Church in Spartanburg. Their gift of one hundred dollars paid her room and board for four months.[3]

In 1931 Elizabeth began teaching part-time in Fukuoka's government school for girls. Her salary was only fifty yen a year, but every morsel helped. That same year she struck gold when Mary B. Rhodes of Memphis sent a year's salary—eight hundred dollars—in a lump sum. Mrs. Rhodes, whose husband ran a successful furniture business, had learned of the freelance and her financial straits through the WMU secretary, Kathleen Mallory. The eight hundred dollars lasted two years, reminding Elizabeth of the Old Testament widow's jug of oil that did not fail until the drought had ended.[4]

Harriett Ellis Levering, a WMU leader in Baltimore and widow of the banker-philanthropist Eugene Levering, Jr., heard about Elizabeth from the Bouldins and sent her additional money. Still other donors, some of them nameless, helped keep her bank account in the black. Even so, unlike the other Americans in Fukuoka, Elizabeth had no substantial salary from a board or an institution. After her first year at Seinan Gakuin, she was once again a "Woppess"—worker without pay.

The Japan Mission Year Book, followed by the *Japan Christian Year Book* as it was called after 1931, listed her as an "independent missionary." In popular terminology, she was a "faith missionary." The latter nomenclature was applied both to independents and to members of "faith missions," those nondenominational and interdenominational foreign missionary agencies "whose governing concept is to look to God alone for financial support."[5] Missionaries sponsored by these agencies generally had to raise their own support, as did independents. Those who adhered to the faith principle strictly never appealed for money directly.

Elizabeth thought both terms—"independent" and "faith"—misleading. She freely acknowledged her dependence "on God and on other missionaries and Japanese believers" with whom she worked. She pointed out that "all missionaries are on faith."[6] True, but "faith missionary" was a meaningful designation for those like Elizabeth who had to pray about their financial needs as a matter of course. She was one of those, however, who had no scruples about "shaking the bushes" to get her prayers answered.

If Elizabeth's faith and her many contacts virtually guaranteed an adequate income, her place at the Bouldin table ensured a more than adequate diet. In early 1931 her weight was 117 pounds, up from 111 the previous spring and from 102 when she arrived in Japan. The next year she asked Lizzie to send her a small corset, size thirty-four, because "my hips are big & stomach sticks out."[7]

Elizabeth told of the day when she was swelled not only with food but with pride. In September 1931 Charles and Anne Lindbergh stopped over in Fukuoka on a tour of the Orient, landing their pontoon-equipped *Sirius* in the local seadrome. They were welcomed by George Bouldin, representing the Chamber of Commerce as interpreter and host. George brought the Lindberghs to his house in the afternoon. The members of the household shook their hands and joined them in the living room for lemonade, ice cream, and cake. Adding to the excitement, the yard swarmed with school boys and reporters clattering about Colonel and Mrs. "Lindy."[8]

Afterwards, Elizabeth playfully accused George of being "a tiny bit stuck up" over hosting the famous couple. He had looked patrician in his white trousers, dark jacket, and fancy straw hat. She too gloried in the presence of these and other dignitaries who passed through Fukuoka from time to time, but paradoxical though it may seem, Elizabeth was most at home in the company of "nobodies." As iron filings are drawn to a magnet, she was drawn to the world's needy and neglected, and she found them almost at her doorstep.

The Dregs of Society

Premodern Japan was a caste society, rigidly divided into four hereditary classes. These classes were—in descending order of respectability—samurai, farmers, artisans, and merchants. The samurai enjoyed the highest rank because they held the power of the sword. The merchants were relegated to the bottom tier because they handled the filthy lucre disdained by the samurai and trafficked in goods they did not produce.

Not everyone fell into these four classes. The priests and nobles stood above or beyond caste. The pariahs, called *eta* (full of filth) or *himin* (nonhuman), groveled in the cellar below caste. These untouchables were street sweepers, garbage collectors, grave tenders, beggars. Some were butchers or tanners, occupations considered defiling in a Buddhist society because of their association with the slaughter of animals. All the outcasts were regulated by law as to where they could live and even what they could wear.[9]

In 1871 the Meiji government, having replaced the feudal regime three years before, issued the Edict of Emancipation that legally abolished the derogatory names of *eta* and *himin* and freed the outcasts from the cruel restrictions. But the deeply embedded prejudices and social sanctions against them could not be removed by decree. The "new commoners," as they were designated, remained objects of discrimination, especially in marriage and employment. Though not physically distinguishable from other Japanese, their official family registers and home addresses made it virtually impossible—and frightfully dangerous—to conceal their identity as descendants of the *eta* and *himin*.[10]

In 1930, about one million outcasts lived in some five thousand hamlets and ghettos in various parts of the country. One of these ghettos, Jigyōhama, touched on Hakata Bay between the Seinan Gakuin campus and the former Bouldin residence in Jigyō. It was no less segregated and scorned than a neighborhood of blacks in the American South of the time. The residents—some eighty families—were ridden with class hatred, inferiority complexes, and loathsome diseases. Their clothes were grimy, their houses decayed.[11]

These unfortunates eked out a living by working twelve-hour days. They made salt from salt water, peddled dried fish and seaweed, pushed flower carts through the city, hired themselves out for hard labor. Often small children were left to fend for themselves. Thefts and murders were frequent; the police called Jigyōhama the worst part of the city. Maggie Bouldin told of a young man she taught there who was stabbed in a fight and lay at the point of death. "My poor reckless, wild boy," she cried.[12]

In 1929, when Maggie first took a shortcut through the outcast village, children shouted *gaijin* (foreigner) and threw rocks at her feet. Her response was to bring roses from her garden and give them to the children. In 1930 she began Sunday afternoon children's meetings in the village hall, a fifteen-minute walk from her campus home. Filthy kids, some displaying ugly skin blemishes on stark naked bodies, gathered around her little portable organ and learned to sing Christian songs. They listened to Bible stories they had never heard before, their sore eyes wide with delight.

Before long, however, a gang of unruly boys started disrupting the meetings. They would throw rocks and sand through the windows or rush in and scare the smaller children. Maggie, tactful as usual, calmly invited the bullies to her house. "We dreaded their coming," Elizabeth said, "expecting they would tear things up."[13]

They came in full force, seventeen strong. Surprise of surprises, these ragamuffins had washed their faces! Maggie put out individual tea tables and used her best china, serving tea, doughnuts, and fruit. The boys were "perfect gentlemen," Elizabeth said.[14] To keep them that way, Maggie persuaded three college students to organize them into a volleyball team. So successful was her strategy that anyone could walk through the outcast village without fear of being stoned.

Encouraged by Maggie, teachers at her Maizuru Kindergarten started a Monday night sewing club for older girls in the village. Elizabeth tagged along each week to help teach knitting and sewing to the twenty-five who attended. The club meetings were distinctly Christian, always including Bible lessons and hymns.

Determined to do yet more, Maggie set out to open a kindergarten in the village. The headmen gave her permission to use the public hall for this venture also. The only hurdle was obtaining funds to renovate and furnish the bare hall. Elizabeth wrote to her former Sunday School class in New York City and obtained a gift of one hundred dollars. This sufficed to replace the dirty, worn matting with a good wooden floor and equip the ramshackle building as a kindergarten classroom. The new kindergarten was named Ai no Sono, or Garden of Love. Tuition was set at two sen (one cent) per day to cover the cost of paper, crayons, and other supplies. Thirty-five children were enrolled.[15]

On April 14, 1931, about fifty mothers and fathers crowded into the hall to watch the opening ceremony. The children, "once so dirty as not to be recognizable," were dressed in their best holiday clothes. Some of the boys wore new suits with brass buttons down the front and standard kindergarten caps—black with a tassel dangling on one side. One girl had a handkerchief pinned to the front of her dress. "It was interesting," Elizabeth wrote, "to see how poor people in shabby clothing would use their meager means to make their children look nice."[16]

Maggie went all out for the Garden of Love. She persuaded a large corporation to make available a free playground for the kindergarten. She wheedled a dentist into donating sixty toothbrushes. To cope with the rampant trachoma in the village, she enlisted a doctor to examine the eyes of the children and adults alike and to treat the infected ones. Each afternoon the village hall became a crowded clinic.[17]

Despite the risks to her own health, Elizabeth plunged into the work with Maggie. She was not surprised to get head lice and athlete's foot, nor even the dreaded trachoma that infected both eyes in October 1931. It happened, Elizabeth conjectured, because the children would run to meet her and stick their germ-laden hands into her pocket where her handkerchief was, and she would wipe her eyes with the handkerchief. The symptoms of trachoma were inflammation, tearing, pus, and pain.

The Japanese teachers Maggie had enlisted were also infected, but they recovered within a month or so. Elizabeth's symptoms persisted for more than a year. There were times when she was unable to determine a flower's color or to distinguish the features of a person walking toward her on the street. She sat for as much as six hours a day by the kitchen stove, putting hot applications on her eyes. "I would know what penance to give bad people to do," she told Maggie, "if I were a Catholic priest."[18]

For twelve months, Elizabeth went to the village clinic almost daily, paying the doctor two yen per visit. Her patience exhausted, she wisely submitted to three weeks of specialized treatments at a well-equipped hospital. The expense was greater, and the trip each day required two hours of her time as well as carfare. But she was cured, making it all worthwhile. Admonished to wear glasses all the time to prevent eye strain, Elizabeth bought a pair of reddish brown horn rims that looked nice with her hair.[19]

Her bout with trachoma was a burdensome trial, but Elizabeth never wavered in her commitment to the outcast village. To the contrary, she gave herself without stint. Over the next several years she saw her pupils become indistinguishable from other pupils in the public schools, where formerly they had been harassed. Two sixth-grade boys whom she pointed to Christ entered Seinan Gakuin's middle school. The village so changed for the better that she did not hesitate to walk there alone at night. The only time she was frightened was when some dogs growled at her menacingly. Elizabeth was wearing a new coat sent from America, and the village dogs, she realized, were eyeing its fur collar.

Diamonds among the Coal Mines

Elizabeth's work with outcasts had much in common with the ministries she conducted in two coal-mining villages near Fukuoka. The craggy miners in Meinohama and Takinoyama were not despised or ostracized, but in terms of poverty and dirt they were little better off than outcasts. They too lived in hovels and wore grimy clothes. Elizabeth looked upon their chubby-cheeked children as diamonds in the rough.

Each Sunday afternoon she walked the two miles to Takinoyama, accompanied by several college and seminary students and some girls from Seinan Gakuin Church. These volunteers conducted a graded Sunday School. Elizabeth was unable to teach, her Japanese inadequate, but she could certainly draw a crowd. Children would rush out of their houses to stare at the foreigner, then walk behind her chanting, "A six-footer from India." They would run past her in order to turn around and walk towards her for a longer look. Sometimes the children excitedly called out their parents to behold the strange creature. "I felt like an elephant come to town," Elizabeth said.[20]

Each week her helpers carried a portable pump organ, a song chart, some little Bible picture cards, and Sunday School papers. The classes met out of doors, in an open space between the rows and rows of coal miners' shacks. When it rained, the children squatted under umbrellas in the rising muddy water, their Bibles on their laps. Heat and cold they ignored.

The girls wanted to make foreign dresses for summer wear. After much urging from their mothers, Elizabeth agreed to help, telling the girls to bring old newspapers with which to make their patterns. Each week she sat on the straw matting floor of a borrowed room, where she oversaw the cutting and sewing and agonized over fittings. The smiles of the children in their new dresses were ample reward for her labors.

One Saturday afternoon when she went to Takinoyama for a children's story hour, Elizabeth passed a large barber shop that was crowded with little girls. How she wished for a camera! It happened to be the appointed day for younger girls to have their hair cut and their necks shaved. The older girls, who usually wore their hair in one or two plaits, were not involved in the hair-cutting rite.

In 1931 the Sunday School at Takinoyama moved into the village hall, and Elizabeth added a kindergarten class. The Bouldins' maid helped with this group, bringing skills acquired from years of working with Maggie. She and Elizabeth laid a grass mat on the theater's bare stage for the preschoolers to sit on. They also put up a white curtain made of unbleached goods to separate the kindergarten class from the rest of the Sunday School that met on the theater's floor.

The kindergarten class began with twenty-seven tots and soon had forty. The children, "as good as gold," allowed Elizabeth to lift them up onto the high platform and off again when their class was over. They had to be held over their own clogs so they could stick their toes into the thongs. "If I happened to hold one over the wrong shoes," Elizabeth said, "he would draw his legs up under him so that he looked legless."[21]

There was visiting in Fukuoka at the time a Fact Finding Commission representing the Laymen's Foreign Missions Inquiry, a program subsidized by John D. Rockefeller, Jr. All the members of this interdenominational group, which included Northern Baptists though not Southern Baptists, went to the mining village to observe the Sunday School and its new kindergarten. One member called it "some of the most interesting work" they had seen in Japan.[22]

During the Bible story, which was under scrutiny by the distinguished visitors from abroad, one "wee thing" decided to go to the toilet. She was having trouble getting into her high rubber boots at the edge of the matting, so Elizabeth picked her up and put her in the boots. When the girl returned from the toilet, Elizabeth lifted her out of the boots. Almost at once the girl had to go again, and Elizabeth repeated the ritual. Then, no sooner was the child back and seated than she wanted her to go yet again. Elizabeth refused, sensing that it was only a game with the child. "I became hard and heartless," she wrote, "for I was entertaining the crowd nearby much against my wishes."[23]

Life in a Japanese Home

Professor Itō of Seinan Gakuin arranged for Elizabeth to spend a week with his aunt and her husband, the Okamuras. He wanted her to experience life in a Japanese home. After her Japanese lesson one Monday morning in July 1932, Elizabeth walked with Itō to the aunt's home. Having dealt with low-class pagans in her rugged field work, she would now get to know some high-class "heathens."

Mr. Okamura, a retired Army officer who had fought in the Sino-Japanese and Russo-Japanese wars, was tottery but jolly. Mrs. Okamura was kindness personified. They were served by a pretty live-in maid, who ate meals with her employers as though a member of the family.

Twice a day, before eating breakfast or supper, the old man was down on his knees before the family altar crooning his prayers. Elizabeth was deeply moved by the tapping of the bell, the beating of the little drum, the smell of the burning incense. She admired the "reverence, regularity, and spirit" of his worship. "He really puts me to shame," she told Lizzie. "You hear much of the poor benighted heathen, but except for the fact they don't have Jesus as Savior, there's no truth in it."[24]

In the front room hung two mottoes in Chinese. Professor Itō, who dropped by each day to see if any interpreting was necessary, translated the mottos as "A true heart moves heaven" and "Generous toward others, sincere of heart." It was increasingly clear to Elizabeth why Lottie Moon in China had despised the term "heathen."

The guest was ushered to the best room in the house, the one in the back where the sliding doors opened on a little garden with a pool full of goldfish, an old mossy stump, and a hanging urn. The room had no bed. After supper the maid would take from the closet two silk futons, a linen sheet, and a pillow, and arrange them on the tatami floor. Elizabeth slept restfully each night, retiring around nine o'clock and rising at six.

Each morning she washed her face in cold water from a tin pan, then knelt on a cushion before a tiny dressing table that suggested the miniature furniture in a dollhouse. By now Elizabeth was inured to sitting Japanese style. She was no longer bothered with crunching knees and straining muscles as in her first year in Japan.

The food was outstanding for its fine quality, wise selection, and delicious flavor. One meal consisted of sea bream soup, rice and wheat blended, broiled eel, raw cucumbers chopped up with some other vegetable, lovely ripe tomatoes, and plum preserves. Another meal included egg plant and boiled fish, cooked cucumbers, raw fish, cabbage pickle, radish pickle, rice and wheat, grapefruit and raisins chopped together.

After supper Elizabeth sometimes watched her host while he trained his chrysanthemums. In each pot was a wire that Okamura bent to the shape he wanted the plant, and as the plant grew, he tied it to the wire with strips of rice straw. To keep the bugs away, he put moth balls in each pot. Elizabeth seized the opportunity to learn from a master.

During her stay in the Okamura home, the community observed the annual cleaning day designated by city health officials. The members of each household took up their tatami mats, stood the mats out in the sun, changed the paper under the mats, and scrubbed every available surface in the house. Then they stood around nervously while officials inspected the house so thoroughly as to look under the matting and in the closets. If any dirt was found, or worse, if there were signs of mice, the household was ordered to clean again. So it is little wonder that the people worked hard on cleaning day except when they stopped for morning and afternoon tea.

There were awkward aspects to Elizabeth's visit with the Okamuras. Her language teacher at Gotemba, Kako *Sensei*, had told her that the Japanese had contempt for a woman who would sleep during the day. This had not deterred Elizabeth from taking her customary nap after lunch at the Bouldins' house, but what should she do in a Japanese home? If she forewent the nap, she would doze off toward the end of the day, and that too might incur the Okamuras' scorn. So with a *shikata ga nai* ("can't be helped") mind-set, she laid out her bedding after lunch each day and fell asleep as though in her own home.

There was another dilemma. If she stayed in her room to read or to write letters, the Okamuras might think her unfriendly and queer. If she went to the front room and sat at the wicker table in one of the comfortable chairs, they would begin to entertain her. Mrs. Okamura would show her dozens of old Japanese prints by famous artists. Elizabeth, unable to express her thoughts, would feel like a dumb brute.

Such quandaries notwithstanding, the week-long visit was satisfying throughout. The peace and quiet in that home, the simple beauty and kindness, were just what Elizabeth needed at the time. The Okamuras "were the salvation and the making of me," she told Lizzie, "truly a gift from God."[25] It was the first summer she spent in Fukuoka rather than in Gotemba with the Bouldins.

The Festival of the Dead

One Saturday Elizabeth noticed many children on the streets holding tiny paper lanterns suspended from bamboo sticks. In front of almost every home was hung a large round lantern with the family name and family crest painted on it. Inside could be seen more lanterns, delicate and hand-painted. It was August 13, the first day of the Bon Festival, the festival of the dead. The spirits of the dead were believed to come back home and stay three days. Places were set for them at the dining tables.

Like Christmas in the Western countries, it was a season when the trains were packed with people going home to be with their families. Presents were exchanged as at New Years', thus transferring a good portion of the summer bonuses to the pockets of hustling merchants. For Elizabeth, this year's observance was one of the more poignant episodes of her life.

The climactic day of the festival was Monday, August 15, when the spirits were sent back to their resting places. At seven that evening, Elizabeth walked to the nearby beach with two Japanese women. The beach was a little Coney Island in the summer, with tea houses, merchandise stalls, ferris wheel, swings, and a place for fireworks in the evenings. There were also diving boards, slides into the water, and a boathouse with twenty-four boats to rent. Elizabeth enjoyed watching people stroll on the boardwalk out over the water or just mill about as they waited for the entertainment to begin.[26]

As at a signal the spectators formed a huge circle on the sand, many rows deep. Some forty women trooped out of one of the beach houses to perform the traditional Bon dances. They wore kimonos with yellow sashes, white head bands with silver stars, long black and silver aprons from waist to feet, and the usual wooden geta. Their kimonos had a blue background and white figures, the flowing sleeves held back by red cords. On each hand was fastened a pink feather pompon, and one hand held a tiny fan.

An oldish woman in somber dress stood in the center of the troupe with a drummer and six or seven flutists. She sang as they played, and the other women danced with graceful gestures, repeatedly joining in the singing with a refrain that sounded like *Haiyohai*. Caught up in the fervor, Elizabeth yearned to dance with them.

About eleven o'clock a procession formed of people carrying miniature boats made of boards, bamboo, and rice straw, and fitted with white cloth sails. The boats represented the spirits of loved ones, the smaller ones indicating that the loved one had died as a child. On the sails of each boat the name of the deceased was painted in large Chinese characters. The masts were rows of hooks from which hung paper lanterns of various shapes and colors. Each boat was also adorned with paper flowers and contained food, toys, or other things the deceased person liked.

The members of each family gathered around their boat at water's edge and gave it their last loving touches. Then the men waded out into the sea to launch it. Some swam out into deep water, helping their frail craft fight against the rolling waves. But the wind was so strong and the waves so merciless that the lanterns blew out and the boats turned over in the brine.

From behind the crowd on shore, sky rockets began to go off. With a sobbing, sucking intake of breath, one rocket after another shot out over the sea to help light the little boats. Elizabeth saw a brave young man in a rowboat striving to pull a string of the little spirit boats safely over the waves. Wailing chants and tinkling notes from silver bells arose from spectators on the beach.

Elizabeth felt warm streams running down her cheeks as she watched helpless little capsized boats washing back on the shore. The melancholy scene brought to mind the fate of the souls represented by the boats—souls in the dark night, unable to get to God. A friend told Elizabeth that the sight was much lovelier when the waters were calm, but that the souls would go safely on to their resting place even though the boats lost out to the waves. "I'm glad I saw the stormy departure," Elizabeth wrote, "for it was more striking and full of meaning to me."[27] The missionary trudged home deep in thought.

13

Fire on the Campus

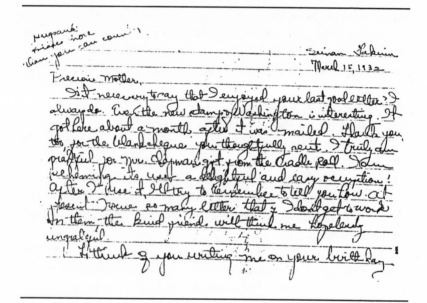

IT WAS MONDAY EVENING, March 14, 1932. Unlike most evenings, the atmosphere in the Bouldin home was that of a library where quiet is enforced. Elizabeth was sitting at the dining room table working on final grades. Effie and Mama-san were in the living room reading. George and Maggie were out of town, he for a funeral and she for a committee meeting. At half past eight the phone rang. Effie picked up the receiver and heard a voice shout, "The seminary dorm is on fire!"[1]

Effie had no sooner hung up the phone than the neighborhood fire bell started ringing furiously. In a surge of panic, she and Elizabeth dashed out into the cold, sleety night in their house slippers, notified Fannie Williamson next door—Norman Williamson also was away—

then ran to the seminary dorm, a two-story wooden structure only a stone's throw away. Flames were leaping from a room over the kitchen.

Effie rushed into the building to help fight the fire. Her action was no mindless outburst of Texas bravado; she had been steeled for this moment ever since her uninsured home and everything in it had burned when she was twelve, leaving the family destitute.[2] But the students cried *abunai* ("it's dangerous") and urged her out. They had formed a bucket brigade to carry water from the bathroom up to the blaze. Still determined to do her part, Effie ran to get a water hose. Elizabeth, feeling useless, returned home for her hat, coat, and overshoes, then made her way over tree roots to join the growing horde of spectators.

The telephones were open all over the city, with switchboard operators telling inquirers that Seinan Gakuin was the site of the fire. The NHK radio station also was reporting the news. Concerned citizens—Seinan alumni and students, parents and pastors, business representatives—were swarming to the campus along with the curious and seekers of thrills.

Meanwhile, volunteer firemen had arrived and were tearing away the burning wall, fearlessly climbing the walls and roof. Japanese firefighters were noted for their acrobatic feats, every brigade showing off its stunts each New Year's as though a Barnum and Bailey's circus. The volunteers were soon joined by the professionals, who arrived in clanging wagons equipped with hook and ladder, hose and pump.

It amazed Elizabeth that no one was removing belongings from the other rooms of the dorm. The students seemed confident that the fire would be confined to the one room ablaze. And it turned out that they were right, for as the firemen tore away the burning parts, the building gradually ceased to smoke.

Elizabeth hurried back to the house to report the fire under control. Mama-san had stayed behind, muttering that she could be of no help. She was warning the maid, who had been washing her long thick hair when the fire bell sounded, not to go outside and get chilled. The maid's mother was in a tremble, since her husband had helped fight the fire.

Elizabeth had returned none too soon, for someone was needed to receive the stream of visitors who came to the president's home to express their concern. They presented their calling cards at the door with low bows and words of sympathy, and Elizabeth took the cards one by one to Mama-san. A few teachers came inside and stood around as though at a wake.

At length a delegation of firemen with bobbing lanterns came to assure the family there was nothing to worry about. By then George and Maggie had both returned, though separately, and the whole household was together once more. Maggie was in agony, however, her fingers smashed. The accident occurred after some of the teachers' wives saw her in a taxi and began running after the car. She had the driver to stop and pick them up, and in the excitement of the moment, the car door was slammed shut on her fingers. Stoic that she was, Maggie laughed and chatted with the visiting women till the last one was gone. The next morning she went to the doctor in excruciating pain.

That day George visited seventeen fire stations in the city and surrounding towns that had responded to the alarm. He presented each station with a fancy gift envelope stuffed with cash, a gesture customary and obligatory in Japan. The expenditure was far less, George pointed out, than the thousands of dollars it would have cost had not the firemen saved the building from total loss.

Simmering Strife

For all the excitement it aroused, the fire that damaged the seminary dormitory was relatively minor in its effects. Something far more destructive to Seinan Gakuin was simmering at the time: strife among the missionaries who controlled the school. A little background is necessary to understand the friction that was about to blaze up and sweep through the campus like a firestorm.

Ever since New Testament times, missionary colleagues have hotly disputed issues both weighty and trite. At times, as in the case of Paul and Barnabas, they have resolved the conflict by going their separate ways. At times they have grudgingly stayed together, letting their disagreements smolder, sometimes flaring up but more often lingering as embers of malice and resentment. When they have been forced to live together under one roof, contentions have been especially sharp. In one notable case, Narcissa Whitman deeply resented having to share her home in Oregon Territory with a missionary who chewed tobacco.[3]

The Southern Baptist missionaries in Japan were no exception to this pattern. When the Bouldins, Doziers, and Rowes arrived in 1906, for instance, the three couples lived five months in "a two-story structure with thin walls and floors that gave little chance for secrets or quiet."[4] Naturally they got on one another's nerves, at a time when they were under stress to learn the language and adapt to the alien culture. As a general rule, the Foreign Mission Board provided construction or rental funds with a view to separate housing for each family, but budgetary limitations and other problems forced some awkward doubling up from time to time.

Single women stood last in line for housing, for they were normally expected to live with a married couple. In some cases this arrangement was not unpleasant. Lolita Hannah and Mary Walters, who lived with the Walnes, became a part of the family and consistently called the Walnes "Father" and "Mother." Lolita later published a glowing tribute to her Japan parents and corresponded with them as long as they lived.[5]

As for Elizabeth, there is no evidence of any tension or disagreement between her and the Bouldins during the three years she lived with them. To the contrary, there was full mutual acceptance, and she remained close to the Bouldins as long as they lived. Several other women who lived with the Bouldins proved to be George's staunchest supporters against his critics.

Even so, placing singles with families was a risky policy, as illustrated by a flare-up at the Rowe home in Kokura. One evening after supper, Cecile Lancaster told Hooker Rowe she could no longer eat the kind of meals they were having, that she had to have green vegetables every day.

"I'll have you know," said Hooker, "it's not easy to look after a house and meals to suit everybody."

John Rowe spoke a calming word.

Hooker flared at her husband. "Oh, you always take up for 'little sister.'"

Emboldened, Cecile spoke on. "Also, please do not throw out my mail before I open it."

Hooker's eyes flashed with anger. "You never read those old Sunday School papers. They pile up for months and the girls can't clean up at all."[6]

Such incidents usually faded into oblivion, but some could do permanent harm. One of the damaging episodes began with Sarah Frances Fulghum, a single missionary who moved in with the Bouldins in 1919, after completing a year of language study in Tokyo. Mamasan quickly sized up the newcomer and told Maggie, "That woman means trouble." Maggie ignored the warning, pouring on Frances the selfless love for which she was noted. One day she received a high-voltage shock. "My dear," said Frances, "you are losing your husband. You must liven up and do something about yourself."

Frances claimed that George was taking an undue interest in her. As though being stalked, she appealed to the other men of the Mission for help. When later asked if a twenty-nine-year-old woman—a strong and assertive woman—couldn't have managed things for herself, she retorted, "No, he insulted my personality. I had to have protection."

To what extent George was guilty of harassment, if at all, lies buried in the murky past. One rumor had him waving at Frances as he passed by her bedroom door—a picayune offense. His strongest claim to innocence was the loyal support of the other single women who lived in his home. "Of all the things he may have been," one wrote, "he was not a womanizer. A wolf doesn't change, and no one I knew ever heard of any such tendencies on his part." The people who believed the accusation, she added, were those who disliked George.[7]

Elizabeth agreed with this assessment. Dr. Bouldin took the place of the revered father she had missed since the age of nine, and he could do no wrong. But others saw George as imperious, haughty, arrogant. He could seem even traitorous, often siding with the Japanese against his American colleagues. The Mission was of two minds about him.

Maggie, bearing the brunt of the nasty squabble, suffered a complete breakdown. In 1920 the Bouldins were granted medical leave so that she could obtain treatment at Battle Creek Sanitarium in Michigan. After their departure Frances lived in a house by herself, the only single missionary to do so. A gifted educator and vocalist, she became principal of Maizuru Kindergarten and founder-director of Seinan's glee club.

Frances fell in love with Nobuaki Uehara, a medical student in one of her English classes. He called her "my little fool" and she called him "my big fool." In 1927, on her thirty-seventh birthday, Frances announced her engagement to twenty-three-year-old Nobuaki. Her colleagues, particularly the embarrassed single women, tried in vain to dissuade her. After finessing her way through a barrage of criticism, Frances resigned from the Foreign Mission Board and married Nobuaki in June 1928, one year before he finished medical school.

In 1930, pregnant with her first child, Frances came to the Bouldins' for an extended visit. She was "feeling rotten." Maggie took her in and "nursed her back to a measure of strength" over the next couple of weeks. Such mercy and kindness impressed Elizabeth deeply. "Mrs. Bouldin's first name is 'helpfulness,'" she wrote, "and the second is 'unselfishness.'"[8]

Hooker Rowe, however, chided Maggie for taking care of Frances. "You, of all people," Hooker said, "after what she did to you!"

Maggie flared like lightning. "Don't you mention that," she said. "For years I hated her and now it's gone from my heart and I won't let anyone bring it back."[9]

But scandals have a life of their own. Though everyone in the Mission frowned on Frances' entanglement with a student, not everyone discounted her earlier charges against George Bouldin. His vulnerability had increased since 1925, when three young couples resigned in protest against his policies as Mission treasurer. Citing his "flagrant disregard" of Mission actions, the "gang of six" said they would not truckle to such a man. Although the Mission overwhelmingly backed George in that conflict, the rift between him and the other male members had since become a yawning chasm.[10]

In the spring of 1932, one week before the dormitory fire, George submitted his resignation as president of Seinan Gakuin effective July 10. On that date he would complete three years at the helm, George explained, and the school was mature enough to have a Japanese president. But there was a more compelling, unstated reason for his action: the missionary trustees were after his scalp.

George was at odds with the trustees over two issues. One was Sunday baseball, which Kelsey Dozier, backed by his trustees, had strictly prohibited. Having no heart for imposing blue laws on the Japanese, George had deftly worked out a compromise with the baseball team to allow it to compete in the intercollegiate tournament finals that were always held on a Sunday.

The controversy weighed heavily on Elizabeth. No less scrupulous about Sabbath observance than Kelsey Dozier, she had never played tennis or studied Japanese on that holy day, nor had she prepared school lessons, even when under intense pressure at Columbia University. Nevertheless, her support for Bouldin did not waver. In her eyes he was a genuine Christian who understood the Japanese, put their interests first, and rightly enjoyed their admiration and support.

In later years Elizabeth praised Bouldin as a God-given constraint on her dogmatism. She would make a statement and he would ask, "Are you sure that is correct?" She would answer, "Certainly," whereupon he would say, "Suppose we look it up." To her chagrin, one of his reference works would show her mistaken. "After this continued for some time," Elizabeth recalled, "I was convinced that the other fellow could be right and I wrong. God thus supplied one of my great needs."[11]

Besides the Sabbath issue, what alienated George from his trustees was his tolerance for the movement called Asakai ("morning meeting"). Elizabeth described Asakai as "a fervent, emotional, spiritual movement, a desire for the apostolic form of Christianity."[12] It was a reaction against the cold formalism and bland preaching that she often decried. Whatever its merits, Asakai, as is often true of such movements, proved divisive and disruptive. Many of its adherents were voted out of their churches as schismatics or heretics. But Elizabeth saw them rather as ardent, Spirit-led Christians who had the courage of their convictions.

Asakai raised its head even within Fukuoka Church, where Pastor Shimose and the majority of members took a vehement stand against it. Ten young people, whom Elizabeth called the backbone of the church, were forced to leave, as were some of their sympathizers. "Their faith means so much to them," Elizabeth wrote, "that they are willing to suffer for it. Our Sunday School lost practically every teacher."[13]

Kelsey Dozier was appalled at Elizabeth's stance. He chided the Foreign Mission Board's T. B. Ray for encouraging her to come to Japan even though she could not be formally appointed. "Indeed another wreck will be registered if we are not mistaken," Kelsey wrote. "She has done good work as an English teacher we hear, but lacks balance in religious matters." Ray concurred: "She is a good girl, but I am afraid she has just that lack you mention in your letter."[14]

Elizabeth's enchantment with the Asakai movement may have contributed to the perception that George was too sympathetic towards it. The truth is, he looked upon the movement with far less favor than she did. His refusal to take a stand against it was grounded in his ecumenical spirit, his tolerance of diversity in Christian faith. This set him apart from his more rigid Southern Baptist colleagues, who feared the movement would spread like kudzu and do great harm.

On this issue George lost the support of Ernest Walne, the Mission's elder statesman. Walne had no quarrel with George's imperious ways, for he himself often treated younger missionaries as children and ignored Mission rules.[15] But Asakai he saw as a threat to all the Baptist work. The withdrawal of Walne's powerful support sealed George's fate.

Five male members of the Mission—Clarke, Dozier, Ray, Walne, and Williamson—formally accused George of having an "improper attitude" toward Asakai and recommended that he "sever his connection with the school and move to Kumamoto."[16] The trustees, dominated by the same men, not only accepted George's resignation from the presidency but declined his request to stay on as dean of the seminary.

Once again Maggie reeled from the attacks on her husband. George placed her in a sanitarium for two months of rest and carefully weighed his options. Defiant as expected, he announced that the Bouldins would not move to Kumamoto but would withdraw to their private home in Gotemba.

In June, the Seinan students went on strike to protest their president's resignation. "The boys fought to the last to keep Dr. Bouldin," Elizabeth wrote, "begging him not to leave, but he comforted them by saying that Gotemba is not so far away but what it was possible to return."[17] The students resolved to continue fighting the trustees throughout the summer vacation and until the action was reversed.

Elizabeth attended the meeting of the faculty, parents, and alumni at which the trustees formally reported their decision and introduced Matsuta Hara as acting president. Hara, dean of Seinan Jo Gakuin, had been brought in temporarily after Dean Mizumachi had declined the post of president. "One after another the parents and graduates leaped to their feet," Elizabeth reported, "and demanded explanations of why Dr. Bouldin was asked to leave, declaring they wanted no other president. They got no answer from the trustees other than the oft-repeated statement that no reasons would be given."[18]

Some indignant parents freely spoke their minds: "You, preachers, pastors, acting so! You haven't the spirit of Jesus! We thought Seinan was a school of love but we see no love. You are thinking only of your own selfish interests. We were mistaken when we sent our children here."[19]

Sitting before them, taking the heat, were Chairman Genroku Ozaki, Kelsey Dozier, Norman Williamson, Dean Mizumachi, and Acting President Hara. Waiting at the Williamson residence were two other trustees, Franklin Ray and Harvey Clarke. Elizabeth asked the latter two for explanations but was rebuffed.

Distressed at the turn of events, Elizabeth skipped the faculty's farewell party for the Bouldins. The welcome meeting for Hara she also ignored. Granted, Hara had always been kind and gracious to Elizabeth when she visited Seinan Jo Gakuin. So had his wife, a charming, talented, and devout woman whose father had become an outcast in order to minister to outcasts. Mr. Hara, taking a bold Christian stand, had married into the tainted family despite harsh criticism from his own family and friends. Recently he had included Elizabeth on a tour of Korea with Cecile Lancaster and their senior class of fifty girls. Now, however, Elizabeth was disappointed in her hero. She felt he was "selling himself to the foreigners, taking a job that other self-respecting Japanese had refused."[20]

Life without the Bouldins

George, Maggie, and Mama-san left for Gotemba Saturday night, July 9. The railway station swarmed with well-wishers, Elizabeth among them, from Seinan Gakuin, churches, kindergartens, WMUs, YWAs, and the community at large. Many had come to see off Effie Baker as well, who had chosen to leave with the Bouldins. She was to sail for America later in the month, resign from the Foreign Mission Board, and marry a high school principal in Texas who had waited twelve years for her consent.

The Bouldins had made a whirlwind exodus from the house, leaving furniture and several packed boxes along with throwaway stuff. That night Elizabeth went to work straightening up. The next day she followed her usual schedule: morning services at Fukuoka Church, afternoon Sunday School at the Takinoyama mining village, hospital visitation, evening Bible class. Two women who sat by her in morning worship kept whispering the names of the stations the Bouldins would likely be passing at that particular time. Several friends gave her the "you-must-be-very-lonely stuff."[21]

On Monday Elizabeth began her visit in the Okamura home as described in the previous chapter. The next week she was back in her familiar setting, except for the people around her. The Bouldins' maid and her mother left because Elizabeth could not pay their salaries by herself. But the maid's father, to provide security, continued to sleep in the servants' quarters at night.

Besides the Bouldins and Effie Baker, Elizabeth had to give up her devoted friend Phebe. Thomas Faucette packed his wife and five-year-old son off to Los Angeles, threatening to do something drastic to her if they did not leave. He never saw them again and never sent them a penny. One of Phebe's sisters paid for her and Tommy's bus fare from Los Angeles to St. Petersburg, Florida, where their parents lived. Thomas later obtained a divorce in Reno. Phebe never remarried. Tommy graduated from college and seminary and became a pastor.[22]

Virtually abandoned, Elizabeth had no lack of sympathy from the Japanese, in whose eyes living alone was a dreadful fate. Some offered comfort by appealing to her own Christian faith. A teacher told her,

"There are two of you in the house, aren't there—Jesus and you." A card from a freshman read: "You are not alone. The great God is with you."[23]

Elizabeth had thought it would be impossible to be cook, maid, washerwoman, homemaker, teacher, and student, all at the same time. "But by careful planning," she reported, "preparing vegetables at night and cooking three things at the same time over the coke in the wee Japanese stove while I have my [Japanese] lesson or teach in college, I manage to do my work and eat on time and keep thing tidy. I am kept so busy I rarely have time to muse on being lonely."[24]

Food was cheap enough. She could get a mess of spinach or a long cucumber for a fourth of a cent. Also cheap were string beans, potatoes, egg plants, tomatoes, bamboo shoots, and fruit. She would buy fruit when it was fully ripe and thus reduced to one-half or one-third price. When she ate apples she saved the peelings to make apple butter, with which she mixed peanuts or boiled custard to make a tasty dessert. Occasionally she bought sweet potatoes from an old man who had a stand on a corner near the school. Baked in the jackets, the potatoes were steaming hot and very tasty.

School activities that autumn were almost normal, even though the strike committee continued to meet and explore ways to get the Bouldins back. Their efforts would be in vain. But Elizabeth was relieved to know that Maggie, who had "feared for her reason," was much improved. She and George were conducting a Sunday School and various clubs for the rural children and youth at Gotemba.[25] At year's end they would resign from the Foreign Mission Board.

Unbearable Heat

Now it was Elizabeth's time to face tribulation. The Bouldins had been within their rights to share their Fukuoka home with her as long as they were assigned there. But when they vacated the house, as demanded by the Mission, Elizabeth was expected to move out also. She had no permission to live there.

Elizabeth claimed squatter's rights. She had faithfully worked with the Mission and the school for three years. Why should she be stripped of an entitlement she had clearly earned? She was little different from a contract teacher, for whom housing was always provided. And why should she be dislodged from a house that no missionary needed or wanted? Two other Mission residences in Fukuoka were unoccupied at the time. "Why is an empty house," she cried out in consternation, "better than a house used day and night as Jesus' house?"[26]

The Mission never served an eviction notice, but the missionaries were snippety and made her feel unwanted. They seemed as cold as the thin air atop Mount Fuji. Her supportive friends Florence Walne and Lolita Hannah had returned to America, where they stayed and later took husbands. Among those still on the field, only Cecile Lancaster seemed warm and understanding. Elizabeth's next door neighbor, Norman Williamson, frowned on her presence as though she were the lingering daughter of a hated, overthrown shogun.

Hungry for companionship, Elizabeth invited a friend named Minohara to live with her. A Christian and musician, Miss Minohara regularly assisted in the work at Takinoyama, and often, since Effie's departure, played for chapel services at the school. She was willing to help Elizabeth with household chores and serve as a language assistant.

There was a formidable obstacle to this arrangement. Minohara's father had been angry with her ever since her conversion to Christianity, and he still forbade her to attend church. She had often gone to Pastor Shimose for counseling, and several friends were upholding her in their prayers. Minohara saw Elizabeth's invitation as an opportunity to break with her parents and devote herself to Christian service. She sent word to Elizabeth through Shimose that her parents were moving back to the country on Sunday, September 18, and that she would join her the day before.

Chō Shimose, the pastor's wife, knowing that Minohara would be unable to bring bedding from home, assembled an attractive set for her, including a padded bathrobe. On Saturday, September 17, Toshi Fujita, a seminary student, helped Elizabeth buy Japanese foods that Minohara might like. Then they went by her house and found her at the foot of the tall stone steps looking sad and pale. She said she would come at seven that night.

Elizabeth returned and admired the room, formerly Mama-san's, that she had made as attractive as possible for her new house mate. She had washed the dresser and closet shelves, put in new towels and washcloths, made a bed spread of cretonne, covered a pillow, made a dresser scarf, moved up the white silk curtain from the study, hung her prettiest pictures on the wall, put some of her dolls and vases and books in the book stand on the desk.

All was ready for Minohara, and Elizabeth could scarcely wait for seven o'clock to come. The time came and went. In the big empty house she kept the lights burning a bright welcome and listened hard for footsteps. She could almost hear her excited heart beating as the time dragged by. A little after ten, Pastor Shimose appeared with a burden on his back, the bedding his wife had prepared. He kindly took the heavy load upstairs to Minohara's room. Toshi Fujita had come with him. The two men soon left, saying that since it was so late, Minohara probably would not come until morning. Had her father locked her in? they all wondered.

The next morning Elizabeth rose early and began to watch the gate. She stayed home from church to await her friend. Minohara still did not appear. At one o'clock Toshi came by to accompany Elizabeth to the afternoon Sunday School at Takinoyama, and they decided to go by the Minoharas' house first. En route they were told that at eight that morning the daughter had been seen in a car with her parents leaving for the country.

The mystery quickly unraveled. After church that morning Norman Williamson had called a meeting of the two school deans to oppose Minohara's move to the Mission residence. It came out that he had sent word to Minohara previously that Elizabeth had no right to invite her. Elizabeth was incensed to learn this, since Norman had given no inkling of what he was up to. She had asked him to tell her any time she did something out of line.

Upon returning home from Takinoyama, Elizabeth consulted with Dean Mizumachi. A deacon in the Seinan Gakuin Church and "a man of prayer,"[27] he was a graduate of Tokyo Imperial University who had polished his English at the University of Louisville in Kentucky. Elizabeth had established a good relationship with the dean, both as a Seinan teacher and as his wife's student in Japanese. She could pour out her heart to this gentleman, confident that both her words and her feelings were well understood.

Mizumachi told Elizabeth that he had asked Pastor Shimose to talk to Williamson and request him to show her more kindness. The American missionaries set a terrible example for the Japanese with their fussing and hatred, he said, and it would be better without them, since they were a bad influence. As for Elizabeth, it was regrettable that no funds were available for a salary, but he wanted her to continue teaching and cooperating with the school. The dean's words were a soothing balm.

That night Norman and Fannie Williamson came to Elizabeth's front door, his face as stern as that of a judge throwing the book at a felon. Norman told her that the night before, after ten, she had received a man into the house. Whether a student or somebody else, he didn't know or care. Since she was receiving men into the house any and all hours of the night, she was making a bad reputation for the Mission house. He did not want that kind of girl on the campus.

Elizabeth explained that Pastor Shimose and Toshi Fujita had come. Norman said he didn't care who it was. Elizabeth stared at him for a moment, her emotions ricocheting between anger and resentment and disbelief. Hadn't he known his own pastor's voice? Hadn't he seen Toshi, one of his own students? Norman was implacable. He said he was washing his hands of her and would exercise his authority to the limit in protecting the Mission property.

The whole thing was incredulous, shocking. Elizabeth had made prudence her rule of thumb. During the summer she had not let the students come even in groups. After school had started again, she had let them come for Bible classes or conferences, but never after dark. Yet she was accused of receiving men into the house any and all hours of the night! The oft-touted romance of missions seemed like a cruel joke.

Elizabeth told Norman that if he did not want her in the big house, she would move to the Bouldins' cabin, having received permission from them in a letter. This was a small house George had built for his own use several years before when he was commuting from Kokura, an arrangement that allowed Maggie to serve as president of Seinan Jo Gakuin while the Rowes were on medical furlough. After moving to Fukuoka, the Bouldins had made the cabin available to seminary students too poor to afford the dormitory.

In the eyes of his critics, however, George's cabin was a monument to his arrogance and free-wheeling ways. Without going through channels, he had used personal savings to build a private house on property owned by the school, which in turn belonged to the Mission and ultimately to the Foreign Mission Board. So when Elizabeth suggested to Williamson that she could move to the Bouldin cabin, she was only turning up the heat in an already scorching encounter.

"Indeed you shall not!" Norman snapped. "The Bouldins are gone. The cabin is no longer theirs!" However legally correct his position, he sounded more like a scowling Kabuki actor than a missionary who made sweet music on his violin and taught seminary students how to sing. Even Kelsey Dozier thought him "very sensitive."[28] Elizabeth thought him churlish. She despised his "sourpuss face." "I could cheerfully have burned his house down," she recalled, "I hated him so."[29]

Soon afterwards, however, the Williamsons turned friendly, possibly nudged by their pastor at Mizumachi's request. Fannie brought peppers from her garden and some marshmallows, as if to confirm that she was still a Training School sister. She also invited Elizabeth to a surprise birthday party for Carolyn Mae Teague, a distinguished Methodist missionary from Alabama who was to receive the same imperial award as Elizabeth.[30]

Norman too was all sweetness and light, exuding the cordiality of a good neighbor. But Elizabeth was not mollified; the wound in her psyche still festered. "When I hear his loud hymn singing at family prayers every morning," she told Lizzie, "I want to spit! I know you'll be hurt and shocked at me, but I'm just telling you the truth. A girl's reputation is precious."[31]

There was no way she could keep the lid on her cauldron of resentment. Not only was her reputation impugned, but she would not have Minohara as her associate. They had planned to have clubs and meetings for girls and women at night and for children during the day. Minohara was also going to help with the kindergarten at the outcast village, playing the organ and teaching children how to play it.

Before leaving Fukuoka, Maggie Bouldin had given Elizabeth the outcast village record book. "Please carry on," she had said. Elizabeth did not feel qualified to assume this burden. Maggie could pour out her heart in Japanese and people would listen, they loved her so. Elizabeth could hardly communicate, making it imperative to have someone of Minohara's caliber at her side. Now her hopes had been dashed to the ground.

After Minohara returned to Fukuoka with her parents, Elizabeth was able to see her from time to time. But the twenty-five-year-old college graduate was firmly in her parents' grip. "Tonight," wrote Elizabeth on December 5, "my friend Miss Minohara is being married. It's to a man she has never once seen. It's at a shrine with all the heathen trimmings. Oh, I did want to interfere, to snatch her away! And the poor child did look so miserable. It was her heathen parents' doing. They hatched it up and made the arrangements without consulting her."[32] Later, because Minohara often fell ill trying to do farm work with her mother-in-law, she was allowed to assist Elizabeth once again.

At Thanksgiving time, four months after the Bouldins' removal from Fukuoka, Edwin and Mary Ellen Dozier arrived in Japan. Invited by the Mission, they came under sponsorship of the Virginia WMU, since the debt-burdened Foreign Mission Board had a moratorium on new appointments. In December, while Edwin and Mary Ellen were in Kokura visiting his parents Kelsey and Maude, the Mission's executive committee assigned them to the Fukuoka house where Elizabeth was staying and where Edwin had grown up.

Elizabeth inquired about living with the younger Doziers as she had lived with the Bouldins. Norman Williamson informed her that newlyweds ought to live alone and that the Doziers wanted it that way. His stringent mood no longer in evidence, Norman gave her permission to move to the Bouldin cabin—with strings attached. "Mr. Williamson says if I do," Elizabeth reported, "since it is very near the seminary I can have no girls to visit me there. I feel that it would be unbearable not to have girls or young women in my home. . . . I can't get too chummy with the young men. . . . Always have to hold myself in dignified reserve. So the girl friends are necessary."[33]

Still, Elizabeth had little choice but to move to the cabin. And she had to move at once, because she had accepted an invitation to spend the Christmas holidays with the Bouldins in Gotemba and would not be back before the Doziers were ready for the Mission residence. The Williamsons put themselves at her service. The day before she left, they gave her both dinner and supper. Norman, meltingly helpful, went to the post office and bank for her, paid some bills, retrieved her shoes from the repair shop, tied up her luggage. As though trying to mend their strained relationship, the next morning he brought over a steaming hot breakfast at six, accompanied her to the station, and put her on the train. Though not purged of resentment against her neighbor, Elizabeth was grateful indeed, having worked all night readying the big house for the Doziers.

At Gotemba, seated by a warm stove and facing Mount Fuji, she watched dark clouds roll around the snow-covered dome and hide it from sight. Her 1930 trek up the mountain came to mind as though a word from God. Up above the clouds and mist, she remembered, the undimmed sunshine had turned those same dark clouds into a boundless sea of the most gorgeous colors she had ever seen. On the darkest days, she was reminded, the sun is still there—radiant, caressing, warm.

14

Princess in the Palace

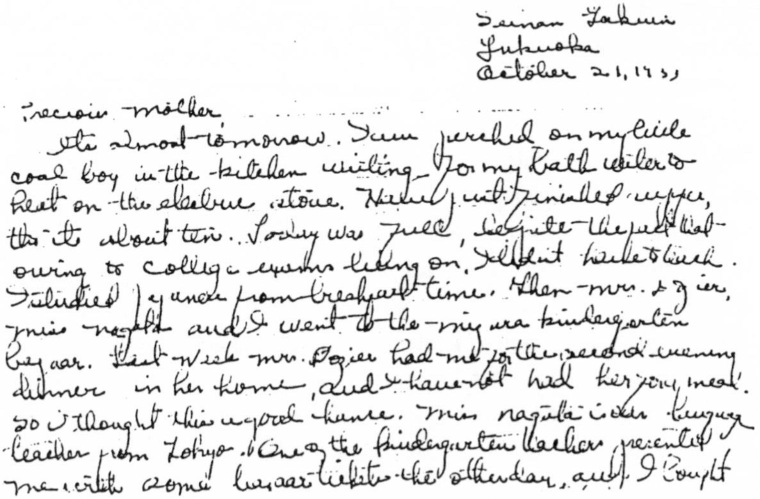
Seinan Gakuin
Fukuoka
October 21, 1933

Precious Mother,
It's almost tomorrow. I am perched on my little coal box in the kitchen waiting for my bath water to heat on the electric stove. Haven't yet finished supper, tho' it's about ten. Today was full, despite the fact that owing to college exams being on, I didn't have to teach. I studied Japanese from breakfast time. Then Mrs. Dozier, Miss Nagata and I went to the Miyura kindergarten bazaar. Last week Mrs. Dozier had me for the second evening dinner in her home, and I have not had her for a meal. So I thought this a good chance. Miss Nagata is our language teacher from Tokyo. One of the kindergarten teachers presented me with some bazaar tickets the other day, and I bought

RETURNING TO FUKUOKA, Elizabeth set to work making her new home livable. She had moved in hurriedly before the Gotemba trip and had left the place a mess. Now she cleaned and decorated until each room bore her personal touch. She made the most of furnishings she had purchased from the Bouldins, Effie Baker, and local shops.

The Bouldin cabin, as it was aptly called, measured 12.7 tsubo (452 square feet) and cost one thousand dollars to build. By contrast, the Mission residence Elizabeth had vacated was 47.67 tsubo (1,696 square feet), not including the servants' quarters of 13.25 tsubo, and cost eight thousand dollars.[1] In a house smaller than the servants' quarters of her previous home, she would save a lot of steps.

George Bouldin liked to call the little house his "Detached Palace," after the detached palace built in Tokyo for the crown prince. "I am keeping the name," Elizabeth wrote, "for that is what I want it to be. Am I not a child of the King of kings? Is a princess's home not a palace?"[2] The cabin-palace on the college campus was to be her home for the next eight years. She purchased fire insurance of five hundred yen on the house and five hundred yen on her furniture and books.

The front door opened directly into the living room. To the right, under the two front windows, was a built-in window seat. In the corner beyond stood a lady's desk, a blue picture of Mount Fuji hanging above it. Against the far outside wall rested Elizabeth's steamer trunk, covered in green and topped with her long Newfoundland pillow. Beyond it was a heating stove in front of a broad fireplace. The coal box was squeezed into a corner nook.

Also in the living room were a rocker, a wicker chair, a carved chair made of black hardwood, and a center table on which rested a green lamp, the gift of Elizabeth's Bible class boys. A blue and tan wool rug covered the floor. The room's two inside walls were lined with book shelves holding Bibles, hymnals, and many volumes of short stories, poems, and other literary works.

Since the living room doubled as a classroom, a huge blackboard stood behind a curtain that covered some of the book shelves. Elizabeth unveiled it when needed. She changed the room around depending on the guests, bringing in folding chairs, ferns, and special decorations.

"When students came for a party," Elizabeth wrote, "if there were twenty-one in all, by using even the coal scuttle as a chair, everyone could sit down, but if there were twenty-two of us, they had to keep playing games that required someone to stand."[3]

Besides the living room, the house had two narrow bedrooms, a kitchenette, and a bathroom. There were times in the winter when icicles stood in the bathroom all day, since a passageway separated it from the rest of the house. It would warm up a little when bath water was heated in the Japanese-style stone tub.

Elizabeth bought a hammock for forty cents and strung it between two pine trees in the yard. She liked to read or write letters while gently swaying. With seeds Lizzie had sent, she raised a crop of "flower children," calling them Rose, Daisy, Violet, Pet (petunia), and Jerry (geranium). After supper each evening Elizabeth drew buckets of water to keep them healthy. When insects began to attack her rose bushes at night, she started tying up the bushes each evening with strips from an old sheet, turning her yard into a "goblin land."

With little time to shop or cook, and no refrigerator or instant foods, Elizabeth asked the school if she could take her meals at the seminary dormitory. The school said no, but it allowed her to purchase the meals and eat them at her house. Three times a day Elizabeth found a tray at her door brought by Mrs. Arita, the dormitory matron. There would be rice and fish, potatoes and other vegetables. If Elizabeth was away when the meal arrived, as often happened, she would eat it cold when she returned.

Some of the Lutheran and Methodist missionaries expressed concern. "You can't do it," they said. "No American ever has. If you continue to try to live on Japanese food, you will go home an invalid."[4] But Elizabeth liked the convenience of the arrangement, and she stayed well, maintaining her weight of 120 pounds. The unsavory meals were more nourishing than she realized. By fall, however, she craved Western food far more than she had craved Southern fried chicken in New York.

Elizabeth knew that the Williamsons had dessert twice a day, something her Japanese meals never included. "I put my pride in my pocket," she told Lizzie, "took my foot in my hand, and went over to ask Mrs. W. if she would have an extra portion made for me, promising her two yen a month for it."[5] Fannie said she would. The desserts usually had custard or something else made with eggs and milk, two ingredients lacking in the Japanese diet. The dessert often contained nuts, a delicacy. At noon four days a week Elizabeth would go to Fannie's kitchen door, hand in yesterday's saucer, and in exchange get a delicious concoction. What the Williamsons thought about the deal, she never knew.

As superintendent of the Garden of Love kindergarten, Elizabeth oversaw its first graduation, held in March 1933. She cleaned up the village hall and decorated it with flower stands and ferns from her house, potted plants borrowed from the middle school dormitory, and cut flowers from the college campus. Standing before distinguished guests and parents in her formal dress—she now had a black one—the superintendent handed out diplomas to thirteen graduates, each of whom stepped forward and bowed politely. The mothers beamed with pride.

At Seinan Gakuin the graduation exercises that month were overshadowed by the heralded installation of Yoshio Mizumachi as the school's president. Previously he had declined the position. "He and his wife and mother protested against it," Elizabeth wrote to Lizzie, "but the trustees were unanimous. His wife said he finally agreed for the sake of the school, there being insufficient money to get someone else."[6] The debt-burdened Foreign Mission Board had greatly reduced its subsidies to Seinan. In April, nevertheless, the school put Elizabeth on salary again, paying her forty yen per month. Edwin Dozier had urged this action upon learning that Elizabeth was teaching without pay except for an annual Christmas gift.[7]

Mizumachi recommended Elizabeth to the College of Commerce in Moji, which sought a part-time English conversation teacher for the first- and second-year students. Beginning in May, she taught there several hours each Tuesday. One of her pupils, Masaichi Ono, later an executive with Idemitsu Kōsan, a leading oil company, remembered her as cheerful and smart-looking, but clothed in plain hand-sewn dresses that clashed with the finery worn by other foreigners on the streets of this international port.

Ono happened to be in the teachers' room one winter day when Elizabeth warmed some rice cakes on the heating stove and ate them for her lunch. He shared his discovery with his classmates, who thought it incredible that a foreigner would eat rice cakes. During one class session, Ono said, when the students took turns calling out the English names of pictures in their readers, one boy roared out the Japanese term *hikōsen* instead of "airship." The teacher's eyes grew big and round. When the laughter had subsided, she said smilingly, "Mr. I——, afterwards I want you to teach me Japanese."[8]

On her first visit to Moji a representative of the Mitsui Bank invited her to teach English to its employees one hour a week. The bank paid her more for one hour—sixty yen monthly—than did the Moji school or Seinan Gakuin for several hours' work. Elizabeth boasted of "three paying jobs."

Lizzie Comes to Stay

Financial security, however desirable, was no substitute for the physical and emotional security formerly provided by the Bouldins. Since being wrenched from their protective, loving arms, Elizabeth had found life precarious and at times frightening. A teacher of boys, she strained to exercise the utmost caution in entertaining them in her home, ever mindful of the scandalous behavior of Frances Fulghum and the false accusation from Norman Williamson. To avoid suspicion, she sought to be circumspect in the most innocent of contacts.

Adding to her discomfort, Elizabeth had a terrifying run-in with a burglar one night, catching him by surprise when she returned to her house from a class. While she ran for help, he escaped. Lying about the house were burnt matches the intruder had used while searching in the dark for money. What if the palace had burst into flames! This traumatic experience haunted Elizabeth for weeks.

With little hope that the Bouldins would return to Fukuoka, Elizabeth pined increasingly for her mother. What a comfort her presence would be! The nostalgic words of a poem—"Make me a child again just for tonight!"—could bring on a sudden attack of homesickness, she told Lizzie. "It makes me want to have you pet me."[9]

Elizabeth had been separated from her family in America for nearly four years. During her absence Earle married Grace Mills in August 1930, and Edward married Susan Wigglesworth in February 1933. Then Lizzie also took a momentous step. She entered a retirement home and rented out the Irwin Avenue house where Elizabeth had grown up from the age of four.

Lizzie urged Elizabeth to come home. She was not only lonely, but uneasy about her daughter living alone. Elizabeth realized that she was fueling that anxiety through her tell-all letters, and she worried about Lizzie. But going home was not an option so long as her sense of call to Japan remained intact. So Elizabeth countered Lizzie's appeals with her own. "Mother, listen," she wrote, "here comes the Macedonian call to you. I do want and need you here."[10]

Elizabeth ticked off the reasons why Lizzie should come to her and not vice versa. First, she argued, Japan needed Christian workers more than America. There was a dire shortage of Christian witnesses and teachers for English Bible classes. Lizzie could help meet these needs while enabling Elizabeth to do so more effectively. Second, the cost of living in Japan was much lower than in the States. Lizzie had complained that she could hardly make ends meet. Third, Elizabeth now had a steady income and could help with Lizzie's travel to Japan and her living expenses after her arrival.

Elizabeth learned that the cheapest way for Lizzie to make the trip was to sail from Boston, a voyage of thirty days. This would save her railroad fare across the continent. She could visit Edward, who lived in Boston, and he could put her on the ship. Her arguments marshalled, Elizabeth pressed her case until Lizzie said yes.

Arriving in March 1934, sixty-eight years old, Lizzie adjusted well. Her room was so tight that she had to climb over the foot of her bed rather than get in it from the side. She entertained visitors with poise despite the language barrier. When anyone came peddling fish or vegetables, she would point to what she wanted, hand out some money, and trust the vendor to make the right change.

Lizzie took care of the house and did all the cooking. Though lacking an oven, she prepared the good Southern dishes Elizabeth had eaten as a child. Most ingredients they could buy locally; others came as gifts. The Bouldins sent sausage, hominy, and popcorn.

Lizzie helped bring Elizabeth closer to her neighbors, Edwin and Mary Ellen Dozier. Earlier, Elizabeth had felt unwelcome when she visited the Doziers. "On each occasion," she told Lizzie, "I felt as if I'd been hugging a block of ice when I left—a painful disappointment."[11] Since Elizabeth had won limited favor with the elder Doziers, the reticence of the younger Doziers to embrace her is not surprising. Edwin and Mary Ellen called her Miss Watkins, even though Elizabeth kept asking to be called by her first name. At length, after hearing Lizzie talk again and again about "Elizabeth this" and "Elizabeth that," Mary Ellen was able to use the name without effort and build a lasting friendship with her Training School sister.[12]

Lizzie further proved her worth as a mission volunteer. She taught several English classes and English Bible classes in the little palace. The young people loved her and called her Grandmother. When Aiko Sano, a university professor's daughter, asked Lizzie to have an

English Bible class especially for her and her friends, Lizzie obliged and gave it her best. As a result, Aiko was baptized, and her friends followed one after another.

When Japanese women called in Elizabeth's absence, Lizzie would hand them a game and have them read the instructions in Japanese while she prepared tea and cakes. Then she would show them pictures of her family and friends, explaining in English while they chattered in Japanese. Afterwards they would play the game. The women often told Elizabeth what a good time they had with her mother.

When serving cookies, Lizzie would say, "Have one, they are delicious." Elizabeth tried to correct her. "You should never say that," she explained. "In Japan you are supposed to talk down anything that belongs to you. You should say, 'These cookies are not fit to eat, but please try to eat one anyway.'"

"I'm not going to tell a lie," Lizzie retorted. "They are good. That's why I'm serving them."[13]

Lizzie learned various culture traits by experience. One was the reluctance of Japanese to blow their noses in the presence of others. An English pupil named Mayashi was an emaciated middle school boy with catarrh. One day he sniffled and sniffled until Lizzie could stand it no longer. She went to her room, returned with a clean handkerchief, and handed it to Mayashi. The boy was puzzled. He looked at her and then at the handkerchief. It occurred to him that she thought his pants were too dirty for her cushions, so he stood up, carefully spread the handkerchief in the chair, and sat down again. Frustrated, Lizzie stamped her foot and shouted, "No, blow your nose!" Mayashi did, but he left the room first.[14]

Repentance and Confession

Lizzie's presence relieved Elizabeth of anxiety over male visitors and harmful gossip. But there was a downside. Elizabeth had been living alone nearly two years, keeping house as she pleased. She knew the ways of Japan as her mother never would. Still, Lizzie was older, wiser, and more experienced in running a home. She acted like a matron. Both women were strong-willed, perhaps a genetic disposition. Inevitably, they sometimes clashed.

Adding to her agitation, Elizabeth was burdened with doubts about her own mental and spiritual health. One day when she dropped a piece of chalk in the classroom, she impatiently made the sound "cht" as she picked it up. Instantly, she heard this "cht" all over the room, the students mimicking her. This little incident obsessed her. She felt that the students perceived her not as a missionary with a wonderful Savior to share, but as "just a redheaded, hot-tempered American woman."[15]

Summer came, and Elizabeth took Lizzie to Gotemba, where they lodged in the home of Southern Methodists John and Victoria Frank. They would have stayed with the Bouldins except that George and Maggie had rented out their house and moved into the club, of which George was manager, and the rates in the club were much higher than in a private home. So Elizabeth and Lizzie had to be content with visiting their beloved friends as neighbors rather than boarders. Lizzie appreciated all that the Bouldins had done for Elizabeth, and she was indebted to George for meeting her own ship at Yokohama.

There were newcomers at Gotemba that summer who would impact Elizabeth's spiritual life. They were ardent members of the Oxford Group Movement, who with bright, joyous faces talked about victorious Christian living. They gave enthusiastic testimonies of how the Lord had changed them from the defeated persons they used to be. Lizzie went to their meeting and was so impressed that she persuaded her reluctant daughter to give them a hearing.

A woman from Denmark told Elizabeth to take a piece of paper and write on it four headings: Absolute Love, Absolute Unselfishness, Absolute Purity, and Absolute Honesty. These were the major emphases of the Oxford Group. Under these four headings Elizabeth was to write down everything she could recall in her life that was not loving, unselfish, pure, and honest—everything from her earliest childhood to the present time. This she did.

That document is lost, but many of Elizabeth's reflections at the time are preserved in a seventeen-page account she wrote of God's guidance in her life. It is a diary-like record of her spiritual pilgrimage from childhood up to that summer of 1934. Following are some excerpts from the last few pages.[16]

Went to Gotemba with a terrible pain in my heart caused by a sense of failure and of broken fellowship with God. Sighing with the consciousness of sin. . . . The 'Spitfire' of childhood days was the same. There were fears terrifying me secretly. . . . Had felt fretted and had pitied myself in conflicts with Mother. We so often differed in ideas. She made me feel impatient.

I wrote out all my sins I could think of, and on my knees alone confessed them to God. . . . The peace in the sense of forgiveness came at once. . . . But my unChristlike speech, short-temperedness, sassiness, etc. caused me grief. I didn't have power over those sins. . . .

On Sunday, Aug. 19, at 4:30 in my room, God gave the victory over my mouth. Christ promising to win the victory in the future and to let my lips honor Him.

Fear had haunted me—a fear of becoming insane. Great desire to take rat poison. . . . Fear of cutting my own throat with a bread knife. Had considered having my brain examined for insanity. . . . After reading [E. Stanley] Jones' *Christ and Human Suffering*, that fear was taken away. . . . Now I can laugh at the knife and that poison, knowing my mind is in the Savior's keeping as well as my body. The dread of insanity during the change of life to come was taken away. Praise His Name! . . .

August 23, 1934. The end of five years in Japan, the first day of the sixth. Spent in my room at the Franks in fasting and prayer. Glorious day, happy day!

The Oxford Group stressed restitution. Being timid and self-conscious, Elizabeth found it hard to apologize to anyone. But she had to do it. The first person she apologized to was her mother. The next was Norman Williamson. She had asked his forgiveness after her Christmas 1932 visit with the Bouldins, when she was first convicted of the hatred in her heart, but the slough of resentment had remained. This time they really forgave each other and became friends.

The next year, sadly, the Foreign Mission Board dismissed the Williamsons from service because Norman had lost favor with his colleagues. Ernest Walne, for one, frowned on him as deficient in the language and unproductive in his work. According to E. O. Mills, Norman "used to be one of our gentlest, most courteous members."[17] But the stress-filled years of trying to fill a need at Seinan Gakuin had made him crotchety in his forties.

Elizabeth further stood before faculty and students in both the college and middle school chapels and apologized for having been such a poor Christian. These painful acts fed suspicions that Elizabeth was cuckoo, or at least "lacks balance in religious matters," as Kelsey Dozier had charged. But they brought her peace and joy. "You look like you are walking on air," the middle school principal told her.[18]

Elizabeth seems to have been freed permanently from suicidal tendencies, but she would never slough off her Spitfire temperament. Two years later she wrote Maggie about outcast villagers who gave promise and then disappointed her. "I have worked myself up into an angry crying fit over the people repeatedly breaking down and tearing up," she wrote. "I've cussed 'em out and then later apologized." She was still handy with the verbal knife.

To America and Back

Missionaries of the Foreign Mission Board normally took a one-year furlough at the end of each six years on the field, but illness often forced them to leave the field before the seventh-year Sabbath arrived. Elizabeth watched the missionaries come and go. In 1936, when she had been in Japan seven years, she still had no plans to leave the country. Japan was her home. It had taken her so long to get there that she was reluctant to leave for fear of not getting back. When asked when she would take a furlough, she would chuckle and say, "When I learn to swim well enough to carry Mother on my back."[19]

At a social gathering one day Elizabeth was passed a long envelope. She opened it after returning home and found it full of money. An anonymous, typewritten note explained that friends had given the money for her furlough expenses. "You may use it for swimming lessons if you prefer," the note read.[20]

Elizabeth conferred with President Mizumachi about taking a one-year leave of absence. He not only granted it but passed the word around as though passing a hat. Donations poured in from the schools and churches and from individuals. A large gift came from the Good Will Center in Tobata, where Elizabeth had worked part-time during Naomi Schell's furlough the previous year. There was sufficient money to buy passage to the States for her and Lizzie both.

They left Japan in April 1937 on the *Chichibu Maru*. The popular liner could accommodate over eight hundred passengers but obviously had fewer on this voyage.[21] Elizabeth and Lizzie, traveling steerage, were the only occupants of a fourteen-bunk cabin. Steerage passengers had no deck privileges, but Lizzie had brought her own games, and she would run up and down the steep narrow steps to enlist players. Elizabeth usually stayed in bed, miserably seasick, subsisting on apples, toast, and tea. When sea water sloshed into the cabin, it was Lizzie who rescued the floating shoes.

After reaching South Carolina, mother and daughter gallivanted around the state visiting relatives. Elizabeth took time in Laurens to have a medical exam:

JOHN GARRETT HART, M. D.
OFFICES AT WATTS MILLS
LAURENS, S. C.

Miss Elizabeth Watkins

c/o Mr. J. E. Watkins

268 South Church Street

Spartanburg, S. C.

TO PROFESSIONAL SERVICES

5-12-37	Physical examination, self	$ 2.00
	Faecal Examination, "	2.00
	Blood Wassermann, "	2.50
	Blood count & Haemoglobin	2.50
	Urinalysis "	1.00
	Faecal examination, mother	2.00
		$12.00

As Elizabeth had expected, the exam showed nothing amiss. During her eight years in Japan, she had missed only one day of school, and that due to a cold. Effie Baker had taken some of her classes during the year she struggled with trachoma, but even then Elizabeth had taught at least a part of each day.

Elizabeth and Lizzie spent the summer at Ridgecrest Baptist Assembly in North Carolina before settling in Spartanburg. Since Lizzie's house was rented out and they did not want to impose on Earle and Grace Watkins, whose home was small, they took room and board with Dr. and Mrs. W. H. K. Hale and his sister Dr. Emma Hale. The brother-sister doctors were osteopaths and fellow members of Southside Baptist Church.

Elizabeth spoke to many churches and other groups, not only to enlighten and challenge people but to raise funds for her return trip to Japan. The offerings and honoraria given her were a pittance. When she would deposit the quarters and half-dollars at the bank where Earle worked, he would say, "Sis, if you hope to return to Japan, you will have to do better than this."[22] By March, however, she had garnered enough cash for two fares on a ship out of Los Angeles.

Elizabeth had given up her teaching jobs in Moji before leaving Japan. Upon her return she learned that Japanese friends had secured her a position at Fukuoka College of Commerce (now Fukuoka University). Elizabeth taught there from April 1938 to March 1941, ever thankful she no longer had to leave Lizzie alone as she had done during the overnight trips to Moji. She continued her previous ministries in Fukuoka, including her teaching at Seinan Gakuin. Several entries in her diary read "Teach, teach, teach" or "Taught, taught, taught."[23]

Lizzie had a bout with pneumonia, and she underwent an operation to remove an unspecified growth that proved to be benign. Elizabeth found it burdensome to take her mother to the doctor or hospital frequently, but she daily thanked God for her mother's presence and asked forgiveness for offending her in any way. She also thanked God for guarding her own health day after day. Thanks to his mercy, her diary reveals, she was "no worse from raw fish," "not hurt worse in accident in bus," and "didn't catch cold from taking off union suits."[24]

No Longer Welcome

Meanwhile, the growing confrontation between the governments of Japan and the United States, aggravated by Japan's full-scale war against China, made relations between the two peoples increasingly awkward and sensitive. Americans came under police surveillance as potential spies. Elizabeth and Lizzie were assigned to a personal detective who had to know where they were at all hours day and night. He was courteous, fortunately, even "like a big brother." Once he told Elizabeth that his baby cried all the night before so that he could not sleep. She suggested he stretch out in the long chair and take a nap, which he did.[25]

When Elizabeth and Lizzie wanted to go to the park to see the cherry blossoms, the detective readily gave his assent and walked between them. When they were trying to make a garden, he pulled off his coat and joined in the work. "I am not supposed to do this," he remarked. "Just a friend." These words he repeated whenever he saw a chance to be of help.[26]

Americans in Japan began receiving letters from their consul advising the evacuation of all women and children and of men whose presence was not deemed essential. Elizabeth dismissed the letters as panicky. Her Japanese friends did not want war, and she did not expect it. But the letters became more demanding, and when Elizabeth learned that the American government was sending an evacuee ship for the women and children, she decided to put Lizzie on it.

On November 19, 1940, Elizabeth Watkins and Maude Dozier sent their mothers off together on the SS *Mariposa*. Lizzie Watkins, seventy-four, had charge of Delia Burke, eighty-four. One can only speculate on the poignant drama of their departure and the emotions it evoked. The two mothers may have looked forward to a time of freedom from their domineering offspring. The daughters probably wondered how their mothers would fare without them. Perhaps they had guilt feelings about shipping them home instead of accompanying them. Perhaps they worried over what their Japanese friends would say. Had they done what filial piety truly demanded?

Without a doubt, Elizabeth and Maude both had a deep, spiritual attachment to Japan. But whether the common experience with their mothers brought them closer to one another is unclear. By a coincidence, Elizabeth and Maude had just become coauthors of a missions study book for children. In reality, *Playmates in Japan* was an editor's compilation of stories obtained from the two women separately.[27]

On November 25, Mary Ellen Dozier sailed for America with her two children, leaving husband Edwin alone. Maude, a widow since 1933, moved in with her son. Elizabeth began to visit there often, staying most nights. With fuel scarce, and restrictions increasingly placed on their movements, the three Americans drew closer together. They observed Christmas with the usual programs and parties, but the darkening war clouds cast a pall over the celebrations.

At New Year's, an army officer called on Elizabeth and wanted to know when she was leaving Japan. "I belong to the Lord Jesus Christ," Elizabeth told him. ". . . I want to get my instructions from Him and as nearly as possible do as He directs. I don't know now what they will be." The officer answered, *"Sō desu ka?"* ("Is that so?"), and excused himself.[28]

When friends asked when she would leave, Elizabeth deftly utilized the Japanese word *saa* ("Well, let me see"). She was asked to teach another year at both Seinan and the College of Commerce, but her instincts told her that her teaching career in Japan would end when the current school year closed in March.

Indeed, since Japan was allied with Hitler, the grounds for optimism were zilch. English signs and names were removed from railway stations and other public places. English terms such as "strike" and "ball" were expunged from baseball. Cigarettes with English names—Golden Bat and Cherry—took Japanese names instead. With English so demeaned as the language of "the enemy," Elizabeth saw her students losing interest and failing. She wrote: "I'm more impressed with the truth that 'tis not so hot to teach folks who don't want to study your subject."[29]

Transportation became a hassle. Bus service was no longer available to the commercial school, forcing Elizabeth to walk an hour each way. She gamely thought of the physical exercise as a bonus to her monthly salary of $16.50.

Beginning the second Sunday in January, Elizabeth attended morning worship at the nearby Seinan Gakuin Church instead of the uptown Fukuoka Church. She grieved when the pastor, who was also a professor, reported having gone with the students to the Shinto shrine. It was a government requirement that school officials take their students on these pilgrimages, but that meant little to Elizabeth. "My heart turns to rock and I want to fly away," she said. "How can we expect people to be saved?"[30]

Food was getting scarce in the markets—and expensive. The price of eggs doubled. By March, meat and fish, even liver and kidney, had disappeared from the shops. Sugar was severely rationed, and milk was getting thinner, obviously skimmed or watered.

Elizabeth ate carrots and turnips raw from her garden. She had an abundance of hominy and cereals, and usually she could get bread. Her cupboard held a can of salmon and a can of tuna—both in reserve—that Maggie had sent her from Yokohama. Maggie was teaching English at Seibi Gakuen, a Methodist girls' school, and George was pastor of Yokohama Union Church.[31] The Bouldins, including Mama-san, would return to the States in July.

Mail between Japan and the States took longer. "I have written every week," Elizabeth wrote Lizzie on March 2, "but you complain of no letters. Everything must be read to try to prove us spies, and the more difficult the writing, the longer the censor takes, I guess. . . . If it were not for certain Mr. Inquisitives between you and me, I'd tell you some thoughts, plans, and ideas. . . . Read between the lines."[32]

Elizabeth resigned her teaching positions effective the end of March. This brought a greater sense of relief than her resignation from Watauga Academy. Teaching was still a means to an end, not a calling in itself. She longed to continue her evangelistic work indefinitely, but in her heart she knew the end was near.

Elizabeth and the Doziers were severely restricted in their movements, virtually under house arrest. Friends who made contact with them were investigated and harassed by the police. Their stubborn presence in Japan, Elizabeth realized, was causing others to suffer. At last she was convinced that God was telling her to leave.

Elizabeth set about disposing of her possessions, as did Edwin and Maude. In her case, though, this was the only way to obtain the necessary travel funds. She turned her house into a store, selling the rugs off the floors, the pictures off the walls, curtains, beds, sheets, cushions, tables, chairs, pots and pans—everything. Although the Japanese feared to buy from a foreigner, they also feared that their yen would plummet in value and were anxious to invest in things they could later turn back into cash. So people came under cover of darkness until all the merchandise was sold.

In April 1941 the three holdouts sailed for the States, the Doziers on the *President Cleveland* and Elizabeth on the gleaming, one-year-old *Yawata Maru*. Many of the three hundred passengers on Elizabeth's ship were Jewish refugees from Europe, some of the forty-six hundred who entered Japan with transit visas in 1940-41.[33] Her cabin mate had waited in France about two years for an American visa. The refugees included many highly educated business and professional people, all alike fleeing Nazi persecution. When the ship reached Hawaii, some of them thankfully kissed the ground.

Elizabeth regretted that she did not get acquainted with more of these people and hear their personal stories. She stayed in her cabin most of the time, seasick as usual. On April 21, someone persuaded her to come to the dining room for supper, and no sooner was she seated than a large birthday cake was placed in front of her. Passengers from all over the dining room came to her table to shake hands and say "Happy birthday."

Three days later the ship docked in San Francisco. Elizabeth paid the fare to Spartanburg—$43.18 including an upper berth on a Santa Fe express. Lizzie had a room fixed up and waiting in the old house at 481 Irwin Avenue, which she had reclaimed from her renters. This childhood home, where her roots were deep, held a unique and cherished place in Elizabeth's heart. But now nestled beside it in her heart was that dollhouse palace overseas.

15

Exile in the Homeland

IN AMERICA, AS IN JAPAN, Elizabeth cast about for ways to do evangelism and social work. Within a month of her return to Spartanburg, she was conducting a "Playhour" for children—games, stories, and supervised play—from three to five o'clock each afternoon except Sunday.[1] This ministry filled a need, but it did not pay the bills. As in Japan, Elizabeth had to earn a living. She worked briefly for Dixie Shirt Company, inspecting shirts made for the Army—the only time in her life to punch a clock. Hoping for something less humdrum, she enrolled in Robinson's Business College on West Main Street for an eight-month course that included Gregg shorthand.

This pursuit displeased her eighty-three-year-old aunt Mamie Montgomery. "Wish I had a million dollars with which to endow you," Mamie wrote.[2] She thought Elizabeth should be promoting missions in the churches, not tying herself down with desultory jobs. The thought was admirable but unrealistic. Elizabeth's return from Japan had coincided with alarmist headlines such as "Senator Pepper Urges That U.S. Planes Bomb City of Tokyo at Once."[3] Spartanburg was a military town once again, Camp Croft replacing Camp Wadsworth of the First World War and swamping the town with its twenty thousand troops. Khaki was common in the churches as well as on the streets.[4]

With jingoism fogging the landscape, there was little demand for a speaker who had anything good to say about the "Japs." Despite her many family connections among South Carolina Baptists, Elizabeth was seldom invited away from Southside Baptist Church, where she and Lizzie, along with Earle Watkins and his wife Grace, regularly filled their pews. By contrast, China missionary Bertha Smith, after repatriation to South Carolina from Japanese internment, was besieged with calls from the churches.[5]

Earlier, Lizzie had heard a four-year-old girl speak of "those bad people." "I was glad to tell her," Lizzie wrote, "of the dear little Japanese children I knew looking like little butterflies in their pretty silk kimono and of their mothers and fathers and brothers and sisters being so good to us."[6]

Genial words like these meant little after the infamous bombing of Pearl Harbor December 7, 1941. Elizabeth and Lizzie lost credibility as surely as they lost contact with those good friends in Japan. The last mail to come through was a package containing a beautifully dressed Japanese doll, an expression of love and gratitude to "Grandmother" from some former members of Lizzie's high school Bible class.

After completing her course at Robinson's Business College, Elizabeth began selling *Compton's Pictured Encyclopedia*, a popular reference work noted for its helpful information to parents on education and family life. She traveled by bus to surrounding communities such as Fairforest and Arcadia and went door to door giving her spiel. The work was appealing because she could set her own schedule, meet new people, and commend faith in Jesus Christ. She distributed evangelistic leaflets from the Tract of the Month Club.

One entry in the spiral notebook Elizabeth carried on her rounds reads: "Mrs. J. L. Flynn, 91 Arcadia St. Both parents work in mornings. Children stay with grandmother. Peggy 10, Janet 8, Sybil 7. Just got a piano - later." These snippets of information could help her make a sale, but they also attest to her interest in people. In another entry she noted that Mrs. W. C. Cox "likes for Jimmy to show off."[7]

Occasionally her religious convictions cost her a sale. Contrary to company policy, for example, she refused to let a wife sign the contract until the husband had given his assent. Had not Paul enjoined, "Wives, submit yourselves unto your own husbands" (Ephesians 5:22)? One of Elizabeth's missionary heros, Mary Slessor, had written in the margin of her Bible next to this verse, "Nay, nay, Paul, Laddie, that will not do." Pearl Buck had declared her hatred for Paul's command because of its damning effect on her mother.[8] But Elizabeth was never one to challenge an apostle. In her view, the man was always the "head of the house."

A husband and wife told Elizabeth that they both wanted the books for their children but lacked the money. "Would you take two goats for the books?" they asked. Unaccustomed to bartering, and being a glutton for anything novel and challenging, Elizabeth went home with a nanny and a billy.[9]

She kept her new pets in a hillside cellar at the edge of her yard. A neighbor taught her how to milk the nanny, but Elizabeth had no more knack for squeezing teats than for pressing piano keys. The nanny would protest the milker's awkwardness by running around the tree to which she was tied. If Elizabeth succeeded in extracting some milk, the contrary goat would put her foot in the pail.

The billy was no less rebellious. When Elizabeth tried to move him from one place to another, the animal would play dead except for rolling his eyes. She had no choice but to drag the limp beast over the ground, an exercise that drained her strength. Her exasperation found no relief until someone mercifully bought the goats.

Elizabeth attended the 1943 summer school at Converse College to study "Tests and Measurements" and, of all things, Spanish. She took the Scofield Bible Correspondence Course from Moody Bible Institute. She also availed herself of the Red Cross training offered in Spartanburg for Volunteer Special Services, completing the prescribed courses for the Nurse' Aide Corps, Staff Assistance, and Home Service Corps.[10]

The Red Cross training was more than academic. A 1944 certificate commends Elizabeth for having completed five hundred hours of nurse's aide work at Spartanburg General Hospital. The training was to prove most valuable in 1945, when a long-awaited opportunity arose to work among persons of Japanese descent.

Issei, Nisei, Sansei

Until passage of the Oriental Exclusion Act in 1923, Japanese immigrants, like Europeans, were admitted to the United States on a quota basis. These immigrants were called issei, a Japanese term meaning first generation. The issei were denied American citizenship except for those who served in the armed forces in World War I. Their children (nisei) and grandchildren (sansei) acquired citizenship by birth.

The outbreak of war between Japan and the United States in 1941 blurred the distinction between citizen and noncitizen. Amid widespread fears of espionage and sabotage, the West Coast was declared a war theater, and about 120,000 persons of Japanese ancestry—77,000 with American citizenship and 43,000 without—were forcibly removed from their homes. They were distributed among ten detention centers built on government land in various parts of the country.[11]

One of these was the Gila River Relocation Center at Rivers, Arizona, forty-seven miles southeast of Phoenix. Covering about 17,000 acres of land leased from the Pima-Maricopa Indian Communities, the site was named "in honor of one Jim Rivers, the first Pima Indian killed in action in World War I." Seemingly endless rows of white barracks on the desert sand—actually 540 barracks, each a hundred feet long—housed up to 13,348 evacuees at any one time and a total of 16,655 during the war. Elementary and high schools were provided for the children, with an attendance of 3,445 in 1942-43 decreasing to 2,665 in 1944-45.[12]

In 1943 Cecile Lancaster obtained employment at Rivers as a high school English teacher—a Civil Service position. The Foreign Mission Board regarded her as on loan to the government. After getting settled in the camp, Cecile brought her widowed mother to live with her as a dependent.[13]

Cecile encouraged Elizabeth to follow her example. At length Elizabeth secured a position at Rivers and persuaded Lizzie to accompany her. In April 1945 the two went by train to Phoenix, then took an Army bus out to the center. They discovered that Rivers was really two camps, each with its own elementary school and high school. Cecile was living and teaching in Canal (Camp No. 1, to the east); Elizabeth was assigned to Butte (Camp No. 2, to the west). The two missionaries were four miles apart.[14]

Each camp was laid out in "blocks" designed to accommodate three hundred people. Canal had seventeen housing blocks, and Butte had thirty-nine. A typical block included fourteen crude barracks (arranged in two rows), a mess hall, a recreation hall (also used for religious services), two latrines, a laundry, and an ironing room. Elizabeth and her mother lived in Block 42, Barracks 10, Apartment C, which was conveniently located between the elementary and high schools. Their sparsely furnished room had a linoleum floor and an evaporation cooler to reduce the desert heat. Their beds were metal army cots.[15]

The mess hall, seating three hundred, offered fresh and sumptuous food at bargain prices. The Rivers community produced forty-two varieties of vegetables and fruits, along with beef, pork, and poultry. Elizabeth and Lizzie savored the daikon and other vegetables they had learned to like in Japan, and they relished their freedom from cooking chores.[16]

The desert with its sagebrush, mesquite, and cacti, its dry air and blowing sand, contrasted sharply with South Carolina and Japan, where rainfall was abundant. Summer temperatures rose to 117 degrees. To Elizabeth, stepping outside into the heat was like opening the door of a blast furnace. She could wash her sheets in the evening, hang them on the line outdoors, and sleep on them that same night.

The cheerful spirit of the Japanese was disarming. They had been uprooted from their homes in California and deprived of their farms and businesses and—worst of all—their freedom. Though the majority were American citizens, they had been herded behind barbed wire as though prisoners of war (the wire was removed from Rivers after six months). Adding to the insult, the people of Arizona had protested the use of their state as a "dumping ground" for these "enemy aliens." One person of Japanese descent, it was said, was "worse than 1,000 rattlesnakes."[17]

Yet the Japanese-Americans had made the best of a raw deal. Elizabeth wrote: "They made toys for the children and furniture for their rough barrack homes out of orange crates, bought pets from the Indians for their little ones, planted fast-growing castor-beans for castor-oil plants for a little shade, and soon had lovely green lawns and beautiful flowers with hollyhocks taller than the roof tops. Huge watermelons and other vegetables they grew right out on the desert sands, all by faithful watering."[18]

Though classified as a secondary teacher, Elizabeth was assigned a third-grade class in Butte Elementary School, which occupied an entire block. On one memorable day she had her class perform a Japanese play—"The Tongue-Cut Sparrow"—before the Parent-Teacher Association in the mess hall. Elizabeth also assisted with a class in "Americanization" for married women. Her salary, paid by the War Relocation Authority, was two thousand dollars per year. By contrast, the Japanese-American teachers earned sixteen dollars per month, in addition to the housing, food, clothing, and medical care provided to all evacuees.[19]

Harder Work and Higher Pay

The summer of 1945 was a time of rapid transition at Gila River. Germany had surrendered on May 7. Japan was obviously doomed, its navy a shambles and its cities an inviting target for incendiary bombs. With the war winding down and Rivers scheduled to close by November 15, the evacuees were being returned to California. Nearly three hundred dogs and cats left behind would be destroyed, the buildings would be disposed of as surplus, and the cultivated land, so fruitful for a time, would revert to desert.[20]

The schools closed permanently in June, their gymnasiums and auditoriums less than one year old. Cecile Lancaster and her mother left for a mission assignment in Hawaii, but Elizabeth stayed on and was transferred to the community hospital as a nurse's aide. The need for medical workers was acute, for every registered nurse except one had departed. Elizabeth was given a crash course and put in charge of the TB patients. Her annual salary was raised to $2,320.[21]

During the process of relocating the West Coast Japanese in 1942, hundreds had been found to have tuberculosis. The infected had been diverted from camps in the colder northern regions to Rivers, whose mild climate and dry desert air were conducive to recovery from the disease. But providing these patients with proper care was never simple. Evacuees who worked in the hospital had a deep-seated fear of tuberculosis—it was the chief cause of death in Japan—and were unwilling to expose themselves for the small salary allowed them. Elizabeth, however, welcomed the assignment. She was confident of immunity, having lived with her tubercular aunt Mary in her teens and having been exposed to patients in Japan. Lizzie was not so sure. While on a visit to Prescott, she wrote to her daughter, "Do be careful when waiting on T.B. patients."[22]

Elizabeth made the rounds with the doctors, admitted and dismissed patients, wrote up the charts, gave medications and insulin shots, fed and bathed those who had none to care for them. The one remaining registered nurse came around once a day to make sure the aide was performing her duties correctly.

Besides her nursing duties, Elizabeth taught school subjects to the young people at their bedsides. Though advised to wear a mask, she declined lest the children think she was afraid of them. Her most memorable assignment was accompanying two young patients to California, one a girl in a wheelchair, the other a boy on a stretcher who had to be put through the train window.

As staff personnel continued to leave, Elizabeth never knew from week to week what day she would have off. The continuing loss of ward aides, diet aides, meal servers, and mess cooks meant added duties. She enlisted the stronger patients to help serve the meals. Often she had to bathe patients at night after the lights had been turned out in the ward.

Some of Elizabeth's patients later sent letters of appreciation. One from Mrs. Fumi Hayashi in Santa Barbara began: "I want to thank you very, very much for the kindness you showed me during my stay in the hospital and also for helping me during my last days in camp." Then came words that the missionary cherished: "I also want you to know I have given my heart to Jesus."[23]

Elizabeth helped with the children's program at Rivers Christian Church, a union Protestant congregation that met in a recreation hall. The worship services, she complained, were "as dry as the desert sands." One Sunday, however, the sermon was a stirring gospel message, just what Elizabeth had craved. The preacher was Reiji Hoshizaki, a recent graduate of Baylor University who had come to Rivers "to see what kind of a situation my folks were placed in."[24] The ardent nisei was later a Southern Baptist missionary in Japan.

Although the Sunday with Hoshizaki was unforgettable, another weekend became the spiritual highlight of Elizabeth's sojourn in Arizona. On Friday, which happened to be her day off, she rode with thirteen companions in a red school truck to Sacaton, seven miles away, for the second annual Indian Bible Institute. The weekend event was directed by J. B. Rounds, superintendent of Southern Baptist Indian work.[25]

After the morning sermon in the adobe-like Pima Indian Baptist Church, the participants went outside for dinner under a brush arbor. On one side stretched wide tables covered with pans of Indian bread, stewed corn, stewed tomatoes, beef stew, and canned peaches. Just outside the arbor a large cooking stove held tins of hot water for washing the dishes. Elizabeth and other guests sat at a reserved table covered with oilcloth and set with glasses instead of the tin cups used at the other tables. Everyone seemed to bubble with joy.

Elizabeth was captivated by China missionary Pearl Todd, an afternoon speaker who told of her internment by the Japanese and her repatriation on the *Gripsholm*. Miss Todd was charming and vivacious, her gestures animated. A WMU secretary in Oklahoma before Elizabeth's stint there, she later taught English in Japan's Seinan Gakuin, as Elizabeth had done before the war.

Elizabeth was also able to attend the Indian Bible Institute Saturday and Sunday, doing night shifts at the hospital. In the climactic service Sunday afternoon, when twenty-six Native Americans were baptized, she stood jubilantly with twenty-two youth she had brought from Butte to witness the rite.

†Elizabeth Bomar Watkins, 1866-1945

When most of the Sunday School teachers at Rivers Christian Church had departed and the church was in rapid decline, Elizabeth saw her chance to evangelize the remaining children without offending the church's leadership. She divided Butte Camp into two parts. Her mother taught Sunday School at one end while she taught at the other end. Both teachers visited the children in their homes.

Summer gave way to autumn, and temperatures began dropping precipitously after dark. Since Elizabeth and Lizzie had brought only summer clothes to the camp, the nighttime walks from their barracks to the bathhouse would leave them chilled. Lizzie fell ill. She endeavored to care for herself, for Elizabeth was needed full time at the hospital and could find no substitute. Professional help was unavailable, the resident physicians permitted to treat only evacuees. A resolute Lizzie continued to teach her Sunday School class and to see the children off at the buses when they left for California.

The first Sunday after the last of the children from her class had left, Lizzie was too ill to get out of bed. Elizabeth persuaded a German doctor to come to their room. "If you want your mother to live," the doctor said, "you will have to put her in a hospital."[26]

At Elizabeth's request, office personnel called around to find an open hospital bed. The closest one was in St. Joseph's Hospital at Chandler, twenty-two miles to the north. A staffer drove Elizabeth and Lizzie over the bumpy desert road, Lizzie lying on the back seat. As Elizabeth was admitting her mother to the hospital, a former Southern Baptist missionary to China appeared at her side. This "angel from heaven" suggested a doctor for Lizzie and invited Elizabeth to stay in her home. Lizzie, they learned, was dehydrated and suffering from pneumonia, which had seriously weakened her heart.

Elizabeth's brother Edward, an Army captain wounded in battle with the Germans and hospitalized in England for "many weeks" earlier in the year, was now stationed in Texas.[27] Notified of his mother's illness, Edward came to Chandler on emergency leave and put up at a hotel. Elizabeth began sleeping in the hall near Lizzie's room. Staying inside the room, she was told, would rob her mother of needed oxygen.

On the night of November 27, a nurse called Elizabeth to Lizzie's side. "Precious Mother" was dying, two months shy of eighty years. Edward was called from his hotel but failed to arrive in time. Sister and brother sat by the lifeless body feeling devastated. A crucifix hanging on the wall looked down on the mournful scene.

Edward had to return immediately to his base in Texas. Elizabeth gathered her mother's and her own belongings and returned to Spartan-burg, riding in the train's baggage car with the corpse. Her brother Earle made arrangements for the funeral at Southside Baptist Church.

Among the mourners at the December 4 service were Earle's tennis buddy, Peyre G. Kennedy, who had won the men's champion-ship in the Carolinas. Also present was Elizabeth's onetime boyfriend, Sam Lawton, now chaplain of the Cedar Spring State School for the Deaf and the Blind in Spartanburg. U.S. Senator Olin D. Johnston sent his condolences.[28] Lizzie was laid to rest beside her husband in Oak-wood Cemetery.

Elizabeth was plagued with a sense of guilt. Lizzie would still be alive, she told herself, if a headstrong daughter had not taken her to the desert, or at least had taken better care of her when she first became ill. Elizabeth came down with the shingles, as though incurring God's wrath.

Almost as painful as the shingles were the feelings of shame that flooded her soul whenever she saw Earle. Devoted to his mother, he had stayed in Spartanburg through the years, always lending a hand when Lizzie needed help. After ten years with the Citizens and South-ern National Bank, Earle had landed a new job as a revenue agent for the U.S. Treasury Department, making his mother all the more proud.[29] Edward remained in Texas, but Elizabeth was painfully aware of his thoughts. He had looked forward to some leisurely days with his mother after the war.

A friend in Plum Branch, South Carolina, invited Elizabeth to come stay with her and get a long rest. She accepted, but there was no escape from grief. "I must go tell Mother that," Elizabeth would think. "She will want to hear it."[30] Lizzie had dedicated her to God at birth, led her to trust Christ as Savior, earnestly and faithfully prayed for her through the years. She had written treasured letters, characteristically beginning with "My precious Girlie" and ending with "God tenderly bless you, my own Darling. Lovingly, Mudder."[31] Elizabeth wondered how she could survive without Lizzie's support.

With Understanding Parents Again

A comforting letter came from Maggie Lee Bouldin, Elizabeth's "Japan mama." She was teaching elementary school at Skyline, Alabama, where she and George had settled because it was only fifteen miles from his childhood home. Maggie could sympathize with Elizabeth as few could, since she had taken her own mother to Japan years before and had recently lost her. "[Your mother] was so happy to be with you," she told Elizabeth, "and to have a part in the work. In every letter to me she expressed her joy in being near you. . . . I am glad that [the Japanese evacuees] could have her to encourage and cheer them in their dark hour."[32]

In February 1946, after returning to Spartanburg from Plum Branch, Elizabeth began cleaning out the attic of the old house and disposing of Lizzie's things. She and the brothers had decided to sell the place. Elizabeth typed out a list of more than a hundred items for sale, from a rolling pin to a seventy-five-year-old New Home sewing machine. She sent a copy of the list to the Bouldins, asking them to choose what they needed for the house they had bought. George finished planting potatoes on his four-acre spread, then came with a truck to pick up some furniture he could use.[33]

Besides the household goods, Lizzie left $10,900 in stocks and $1,200 in cash. The homestead was valued at $7,500. Earle, executor of his mother's will, settled the estate and divided the proceeds among the three children. Each received $6,081.54.[34] Only two years away from a lifetime appointment by the Foreign Mission Board, Elizabeth never again had to pray for money to meet a personal need. Mission needs were another matter.

Earlier Elizabeth had made application to teach high school English in Hawaii, hoping to work with students of Japanese descent. Nothing had come of it. In July she went to Chattanooga to interview for a position at the Baptist Good Will Center. She took her trunk with her, expecting to be employed on the spot. After arriving in Chatta-nooga, however, she felt strangely led to cancel the interview and join the Bouldins at Skyline, about sixty miles away. There was an opening for a seventh-grade teacher, and the motherless single needed the succor of her Japan parents once again.

Skyline lay on a remote section of Cumberland Mountain where the U.S. government had purchased 13,000 acres in the 1930s for a "great social experiment." About two hundred families had been chosen for the new colony. Each had been provided with forty acres of land, a house, a mule, a wagon, and implements needed to develop a successful farm. The pioneers grew mostly potatoes and tomatoes. This ambitious program was phased out after the war, opening the way for the Bouldins to buy a house in the colony with only four—not forty—acres of land.[35]

Elizabeth lived with the Bouldins, two miles from the school, until classes began, when she moved to the teacherage adjacent to the campus. She joined the Skyline Missionary Baptist Church, which met in the school auditorium. George Bouldin was the pastor. In September, when the little congregation reorganized and changed its name to Central Baptist Church, she was elected clerk and treasurer. Elizabeth also taught the Sunday School class for teenagers. George taught the adults, and Maggie, virtually blind, taught the children.[36]

In December the stone office building of the U.S. Department of Agriculture, only a five-minute walk from the school, was put on the market. The Bouldins purchased it as a home for both themselves and the church. The south wing with large windows served as the worship center, and the smaller rooms accommodated Sunday School classes. The congregation would afterwards meet in a log cabin built at the north end of the Bouldin property before moving to its present brick building farther south on County Road 25.[37]

The wooden teacherage where Elizabeth lived during the school year stood at the end of a short walk through the woods, on the site now occupied by the high school gymnasium. It was under the same roof as the janitor's home. The other teachers in residence were young women who returned to their homes on the weekend.

Elizabeth hated taking her turn as housekeeper for the week. She had to plan the meals, shop, cook, and wash the dishes. The facilities were primitive. During the winter the kitchen floor was sometimes covered with a slippery sheet of ice. Once when Elizabeth prepared banana pudding for dessert, she opened the oven door and found the Pyrex dish shattered and the oven splattered with a gooey yellow mess.

Elizabeth's permanent South Carolina teacher's license qualified her for a one-year "Non-Professional Defense Certificate" in Alabama, and her M.A. degree entitled her to "Rank One" and a monthly salary of $212, much more than Maggie's $126.[38] She was required to teach several subjects, although she doubtless could have contributed more by teaching only English to several grades. The experience was a replay of her taxing year as a mountain schoolma'am in Butler, Tennessee.

The students in Skyline seemed more backward than those in Butler. The seventh graders announced on the first day of school, "We ain't goin to study that science book. That science book says the earth is round, and we know it is square. The Bible says it is square, 'the four corners,' and we believe the Bible."

"There are missionaries living right near your school who have sailed around the world," Elizabeth said.

"They haint, neither," was the reply. "They would of drapped off."[39]

The teachers at Skyline often paddled unruly children, a form of discipline that Elizabeth disdained. She refused to keep a paddle in her desk drawer. But the day came when her good intentions crumbled like old-fashioned cornbread. She was keeping some students after school to do homework they had failed to do on time. One of the boys, a son of the school's janitor, kept making cat-calls, and Elizabeth was unable to shut him up. At last she looked in the closet for something to use as a paddle and seized on a piece of a broom handle. Taking the miscreant by the arm, she pulled him up to his feet and gave him two licks with the handle. He sat down, his face ashen white, then jumped up and rushed home.

Elizabeth rued her desperate act. The boy's oldest brother, Jack Martin, recently home from the Army, came running with a gun and threatened to kill her. Other family members joined him, all in a rage. The three-hundred-pound mother waved the broom handle to demonstrate what she would do to Elizabeth as soon as the school buses had left. But the other teachers formed a protective barrier around their threatened colleague until the principal, C. L. Fossitt, could get her in his car and head for the police station in Scottsboro, sixteen miles away.

That evening Jack Martin was arrested at a Scottsboro cafe and released on bond. Elizabeth moved to the Bouldins' home for safety. At the trial, a unique experience in Elizabeth's life, the judge ordered that she and the student have nothing to do with one another and not even speak to one another. Elizabeth moved back to the teacherage, hoping that Jack would obey the order and leave her alone.[40]

"The Lord sent me two understanding friends," Elizabeth recalled. "They were the dogs that belonged to the nearest neighbor. I had never tried to make friends with them, feed them or anything, for I don't like dogs, but after the trouble started, the dogs began sleeping under my bedroom window. If I had to go somewhere in the evening, the dogs would accompany me, wait outside for me, and accompany me back to my room. These understanding dogs were a great comfort to me."[41]

Thanks to her two pairs of guardians—the dogs and the Bouldins— Elizabeth made it through the school year unscathed. Jack frightened her only once, when he tried to run her down with his truck. The summer of 1947 brought joyous prospects as well as a sense of relief. General Douglas MacArthur, Supreme Commander for the Allied Powers in Japan, was allowing missionaries into the land they had been forced to leave six years before, and Elizabeth was raring to go.

16

A Fresh, Jolting Start

Seinan Jo Gakuin
Itozu, Kokura, Japan
August 12, 1948

Dear Dr. and Mrs. Louldin,

I am determined to begin this letter to you tonight, though I am sure that I shall not be able to write much before the "Rock-a-bye Lady from Hush-a-bye Street" will "come stealing ". I have thought about you often and really have a lot to tell you. I wish you could tell me a lot, too. I hope that you stood the cold of the winter better than you did the year that I was there.

August 20, 1948

This is the way my letter writing goes. I still have two boxes of unanswered letters - one from Japanese friends, and one from American friends. And today for the second day in succession I did not have a chance to eat lunch until four or thereabout because of the succession of guests.

Much, very much has happened in this little while we have been back. I do not know where to begin. In January we moved into the new college buildings on the top of a mountain not far from here. If I walk very, very fast (as I often do) I can get there in seven minutes. As yet there are no seats in chapel, the girls standing(teachers, too). The science and home economic rooms for cooking have not been finished But the carpenters are working on them now. They have sewing rooms on the second floor of one wing over the classrooms. They have been having to cook in the halls and in one of the classrooms. Those in the—

ELIZABETH WROTE TO M. THERON RANKIN, executive secretary of the Foreign Mission Board, and asked him to expedite her return to Japan. She was well past thirty-five, the maximum age for missionary appointment, but she hoped for employment as a contract teacher at one of the two Baptist schools related to the Board. To play it safe, she also wrote to the State Department for information about teaching positions with the American occupation forces in Japan.[1]

Theron Rankin instructed Edwin Dozier to inquire whether Japanese Baptists would welcome Elizabeth to serve among them once again. After the postwar Japan Baptist Convention was organized in April 1947, Dozier brought the matter before its nine-member executive council, of which he was vice president. The council issued a formal invitation.[2]

"I am ready to sponsor your return," Rankin wrote Elizabeth, after mulling the invitation several days. "We will provide your traveling expenses and undertake to work out a satisfactory contract for your support."[3] The arrangements he made were generous. The Board would pay Elizabeth the salary of a single missionary for three months, after which Southside Church in Spartanburg would provide a monthly stipend to be transmitted through the Board.

Elizabeth's assignment was to teach at Seinan Jo Gakuin, the Baptist girls' school in Kokura. The school for its part offered free lodging and a native teacher's wage of five thousand yen ($13.88) per month—a pittance by American standards. With Japan's economy in shambles, no other employer could have done much better. Nor did the wage matter, since Elizabeth could rely on the generosity of her home church.[4]

To further hone her skills before going abroad, Elizabeth attended a summer session of the International Child Evangelism Fellowship Institute at Highland Lake, New York. Like the renowned Henrietta Mears, she was a firm believer in religious instruction that could capture and hold the attention of every pupil. The most helpful of her seven courses at the institute was "Visual Teaching." She learned to use flannelgraphs, slides, maps, and other visual aids expertly, gaining a skill that would make Bible stories come alive to the boys and girls of Japan.[5]

Health conditions in Japan had fallen to so dangerous a level that Elizabeth had to be immunized against an array of diseases: small pox, typhoid, typhus, tetanus, and cholera. As a nurse's aide during the war, she had given shots to others. Now she knew how an arm felt that "looked like a pincushion."[6]

The U.S. authorities in occupied Japan required missionaries to bring a ton of food for each member of the family, so as not to be dependent on the scarce Japanese supply. Elizabeth tried to anticipate her needs for two years. Her five-page invoice from a San Francisco grocer lists a wide variety of foods ranging from canned sardines to Kellogg's Pep.[7]

In other shopping, she bought a roll-away bed, a utility table (missionary lingo for a card table), six folding chairs, two rockers, and an electric range. The Foreign Mission Board picked up the tab for crating and shipping 120 cubit feet of freight.[8]

On sailing day Elizabeth checked out of San Francisco's Mark Twain Hotel and boarded the ten-thousand-ton SS *Marine Swallow*, an army transport converted to civilian use. The voyage to Japan reconfirmed her opinion that the Pacific Ocean was misnamed. The ship rolled and lurched day and night, as though at the mercy of a playful, tireless Leviathan. "Suddenly the sea monster would grab her by the legs," Elizabeth wrote, "and shake her so she seemed to double up in the middle and pitch us in all directions at once."[9]

The "sea monster" grew ferocious, disabling the anchor and ripping off a part of the bow. One evening the dining room tables were rudely cleared of everything set out for the meal. In Elizabeth's cabin, where she cocooned herself, it upset the table and chairs and shattered the drinking glasses.

On board the storm-tossed ship were two new missionary couples who had just completed a year of language study in Berkeley, California. A. L. (Pete) and Bee Gillespie had two boys, and Bill and Louise Medling had three boys. Because of the rough seas, Elizabeth scarcely saw any of them till the voyage had come to an end.

When the battered *Marine Swallow* limped into Yokohama port, Elizabeth's old friends Edwin Dozier, Max Garrott, and Floryne Miller were waiting on the dock, their faces aglow. Floryne was accompanied by Frances Talley, a "new missionary who looks like a child tho really 31."[10] Frances too had studied Japanese in Berkeley. Elizabeth called her by the endearing term "Talley-chan" as though she were a child indeed.

Other friends were at the wharf to lend a hand. Captain Bill Carver, a brother-in-law of Max Garrott, and Chaplain David Weaver had come in their army vehicles to help transport the newcomers to Tokyo. Timothy Pietsch, Edwin Dozier's brother-in-law on assignment with Pocket Testament League, had brought his jeep with a trailer for the baggage. "God's policeman" to his biographer, Pietsch was a religious separatist who regarded Dozier and most other Christian leaders as compromisers with error. But in practical matters he was disarmingly helpful toward those he shunned in the spiritual realm.[11]

Elizabeth and the Gillespies were driven to the Kiyoki Yuya residence for a few days' rest before proceeding to Kokura. She was thrilled to see Pastor Yuya again, though sad that he looked like a "living skeleton." During the war he had suffered not only hunger but persecution for his faith, and since the war he had suffered harassment from occupation personnel who mistook him for the infamous General Tōjō. More to his liking, some of the missionaries saw in the bald Yuya a striking resemblance to the comic strip character Henry.[12]

Since the previous autumn, Edwin Dozier had occupied the curtained-off corner of a passageway (rōka) in the Yuya home. Squeezed into this corner was the only bed in the house, one left from Cecile Lancaster's stay with the Yuyas before the war. Elizabeth moved into an upstairs room with Floryne Miller and Frances Talley, while the four Gillespies settled into a downstairs room. Thanks to a kind neighbor's loan of bedding, there were enough futons for all.

Other comforts were scant. Fuel of any kind was scarce and expensive; electricity was on and off. Dirty dishes were washed in cold water without benefit of soap, as were dirty bodies. With no hot water, bathing at the Yuya house lacked the soothing pleasure associated with the Japanese ofuro. But at least there was a place to splash the water about, which was more than Elizabeth could say for her old mountain school in Tennessee.

Food too was hard to come by, but the Yuyas were among the fortunate ones who had received gift boxes from friends in America. They passed around these goodies with the same unselfishness Pastor Yuya had shown in his welcome to Elizabeth in 1929, when he offered to share what he had with her, even if only a few beans and a torn quilt. Chaplain Weaver also was generous, inviting the missionaries to his home for some of their meals and not letting them leave empty-handed.

Life on Mount Zion

After a long weekend in Tokyo, Elizabeth, Frances Talley, and the Gillespies boarded a U.S. Army train for Kokura. Under occupation policy, newly arrived missionaries could use military transportation to get to their first place of assignment. Thereafter, they had to jockey for space on the Japanese trains, which were unheated, dimly lighted, and so crowded that passengers often climbed in and out the broken windows. Elizabeth and her companions were grateful for some comforts on the twenty-six-hour trip to Kokura.

President Matsuta Hara of Seinan Jo Gakuin had arranged a magnificent reception for the missionaries. At Kokura Station, a hundred-voice choir from the school sang "Onward Christian Soldiers." Then as the missionaries rode to the Mount Zion campus in two open jeeps, courtesy of an American Presbyterian chaplain, school girls lined both sides of the road, waving and singing and clapping and shouting. The scene was reminiscent of Jesus' triumphal entry into Jerusalem. When the jeeps had passed, the students would fall in behind, joining the cavalcade. The throng converged on Rowe Chapel, where the six newcomers were feted on stage, the two Gillespie boys the focus of a hundred ogling eyes. That night Elizabeth had her first hot bath in a week.

Cecile Lancaster was still at sea. The American President liner bringing her and her mother from Hawaii was plying a circuitous route by way of Manila, Hong Kong, and Shanghai.[13] As Kokura's senior missionary, Cecile had instructed President Hara in advance on where to house the rookies. The Gillespies were to live in the Mission residence and have exclusive use of two specified bedrooms and the downstairs kitchen. Cecile and her mother would cook and eat separately in an upstairs kitchen near their bedrooms. Elizabeth was to live in the school dormitory and cook on a hot plate.

Elizabeth moved into two adjacent dorm rooms that had been freshly painted and equipped to serve as living room and bedroom. Frances Talley, somehow overlooked in Cecile's instructions, moved in with Elizabeth temporarily and afterwards joined the Gillespies. President Hara had done his best, with meager resources, to ensure the comfort of his foreign staff.

During the war the Japanese army had commandeered the campus and installed an antiaircraft battery on the roof of Rowe Memorial Chapel. The chapel had been painted an ugly black and green as camouflage, and its bronze memorial plaque honoring founder J. H.

Rowe had been removed. Deprived of its facilities, the school had made do with various rented quarters, including a Buddhist temple.[14]

Yet there was cause for profound gratitude. A timely cloud cover had saved Mount Zion and its surroundings from *Fat Man*, the atom bomb that flattened Nagasaki instead. Kokura had also come through the firebomb attacks with less damage than other cities in the region. This is a major reason that the occupation forces, needing houses suitable for requisition, selected Kokura for its North Kyushu headquarters.

Even though Elizabeth and her colleagues now had a place to call home, they were anxious and tense. Their ocean freight, including the ton of food per person, had not been delivered from Yokohama. Even their hold baggage was yet to arrive. The first three days they reluctantly sponged off the Haras, who, like the Yuyas, had received gift packages from America. "Then the kind army people . . . felt sorry for us," Elizabeth wrote to the Bouldins, "and began bringing us food. Don't say a word, for it would get them into trouble."[15]

When at last the missionaries had access to their own food and other supplies, they sometimes felt embarrassed to enjoy such abundance amidst a people so destitute. Most Japanese were thin and undernourished, virtual scarecrows. Their teeth were in poor repair. Few had more than one change of clothes—threadbare clothes. Surrounded by misery, the missionaries began appealing for relief goods to be sent from America on a much larger scale.

At the earliest opportunity Elizabeth paid a nostalgic visit to Fukuoka, going first to the outcast village in Jigyōhama where she had directed the kindergarten started by Maggie Bouldin. A grim scene awaited. The public hall, site of the Garden of Love, lay in ashes, destroyed by firebombs from waves of B-29s. Elizabeth had little time to mourn the loss, for she was quickly surrounded by babbling urchins, the older ones having recognized her after six years of separation. They grabbed hold of her hands and accompanied her as she made the rounds of the homes of Seinan Gakuin faculty members who had been her colleagues. "How surprised the teachers were," Elizabeth wrote, "when they opened their front doors to find their entrance full of dirty children!"[16]

The Seinan campus, a mile farther from the city's center than Jigyōhama, had survived the bombings, though most windows were broken from concussion. Seinan Gakuin Church, unlike the downtown Fukuoka Church, was also intact. The missionary residence Elizabeth had shared with the Bouldins now housed President Mizumachi and his wife Chiyo, who had been her Japanese language teacher. In the Bouldin cabin or "palace" were other esteemed friends, the Fujii family. Both of these houses were later razed to make room for new buildings on campus.

But it was Seinan Jo Gakuin, not the boys' school, that now consumed Elizabeth. One of sixty-five teachers of 1,050 girls, she had twenty hours of classes weekly, ranging from middle school grades to the newly opened junior college. She taught in unheated classrooms, sometimes with snow drifting in through the broken windows. Many of the students were to recall looking up at the foreigner's mouth and trying valiantly to imitate the *f* sound.[17] Elizabeth gave herself without stint, even though teaching was but a means to an end. The religious contacts were what mattered most.

Elizabeth took special pride in the college YWA, which met regularly in her dormitory room. Kiyoko Shimose, her prewar pastor's daughter and now a faculty member, assisted Elizabeth in teaching the life of Christ with materials from the Child Evangelism Fellowship. The YWA girls would go to nearby towns and villages, round up groups of children, and teach the lessons as the lessons had been taught to them. These well-trained students also took leadership roles in YWA conferences and retreats, and in the summer of 1948 they helped with the Baptist encampment that drew three hundred youth to the school.

On Saturdays Elizabeth taught a large English Bible Class in Shimonoseki, across the Kammon Strait. On Sundays she taught classes in three different cities, a tight schedule that excluded attendance at any worship service and left her exhausted at day's end. "With all of this," she wrote, "I do not hear a single sermon! So I turn heathen while I am trying to keep others from being heathens."[18]

Elizabeth discovered that a mouse was sharing her dormitory room. Over a period of three months she borrowed cats and set traps but failed to catch the intruder. Then one evening when she stepped into her bathtub with a kettle of boiling water in one hand, there sat "Nemi-chan" in the tub. "I just gave him the water I had planned to use myself," Elizabeth reported. "Some of the college girls brought me flowers for the funeral."[19]

No Longer a Freelance

In June 1948 Elizabeth received a letter from the Foreign Mission Board that set her to dancing. She could be appointed a regular missionary, the letter said, if she was in "good physical condition."[20] Enclosed was a four-page medical form, two pages to be filled out by the applicant and the other two by a physician. The timing seemed unfavorable, for Elizabeth was worn out from nine months of work without letup. Recalling the exam she had flunked after climbing Mount Fuji, and showing more prudence than usual, she rested for three days before taking the medical form to the American military hospital in Kokura.

"The doctor refused to make an examination for parasites," Elizabeth told the Bouldins, "and did not do a blood count. . . . He found nothing whatever wrong, and gave me a good recommendation."[21] It is ironic that a faulty medical report in 1930 obstructed her appointment, and a contrived report in 1948 enabled it. The new exam was cursory at best.

Soon afterwards Elizabeth fell ill, and the doctor learned belatedly that she had been infected with round worms since before the exam, when her weight had begun to fall. Elizabeth took worm medicine five times over a period of five months to get rid of the parasites. She was undergoing this treatment in September when the Board announced her appointment, retroactive to June 1.

Elizabeth was ecstatic at the news. Her uncle Edward Bomar had assured her, "I may not live to see it, but some day you are going to be appointed by the Foreign Mission Board."[22] This was the uncle who served on the Board's staff when Elizabeth was a child. It was sad that he had died, for she longed to hear him gloat over seeing his prophecy fulfilled. Even more, she yearned for her mother, who had prayed her into missions and joined with her in mission work.

On the same day the American doctor declared Elizabeth physically fit, all but assuring her appointment by the Board, she received a committee from the Woman's Missionary Union of Japan. The visitors asked her to accept a position as superintendent of Rinkōsha ("Neighborhood Lighthouse"), the Good Will Center in the slums of adjacent Tobata. Elizabeth was their third choice for the post. Their second choice, Floryne Miller, had declined to serve. Their first choice, though mere nostalgia, was Rinkōsha's beloved founder, Naomi Schell. Naomi had died in 1946 at the age of fifty-two, after several years of "insidious creeping paralysis."[23]

During the war, Naomi's assistant, Kesako Hikasa, had carried on the work. After her pastor-husband, Shinji, had been drafted into the navy, she had kept Tobata Baptist Church open as well. The city once ordered Rinkōsha's building torn down, and later it tried to buy the property, but Kesako had successfully resisted both moves. In April 1945, when bombs were raining on Japan's defenseless cities, and Rinkōsha's program had ground to a halt, she agreed to lease the property to the city for five years. Tobata's social service department used the facility as a day nursery.[24]

After the war, Baptist leaders were eager to reopen the Good Will Center. In response, the city agreed to cancel the unexpired lease and return the property in September 1948, when a new facility for its day nursery would be ready. The Center's wooden structure had deteriorated so badly during the war that the sky could be seen through the roof. The building had been stripped of its furnishings, the stove sold for scrap iron. "The place was filthy," Elizabeth reported, "and badly in need of repair."[25]

The first postwar WMU convention, held at Seinan Gakuin Church in August 1948, drew fifty-six Japanese women, who brought rice and vegetables for their meals and slept on the church floor under mosquito nets. At this convention Elizabeth was formally elected Rinkōsha's superintendent (*shuji*). Kesako Hikasa held the same title. Two bosses for one institution spelled trouble ahead.[26]

At the time, however, the outlook was rosy. Elizabeth had been initiated into settlement work at the WMU Training School. She had honed her skills among immigrants in Norfolk and had worked successfully among the poor and outcasts of Japan. Now she was confronted with a war-ravaged city where virtually the entire population was desperately poor. It was her greatest challenge yet.

Elizabeth resigned from Seinan Jo Gakuin at once. To ease the impact of her sudden departure, she returned the year's salary—less than two hundred dollars—paid her by the school. Elizabeth could spare the money. Besides her basic salary underwritten by Southside Church, she now enjoyed the financial security and fringe benefits of a Board appointee.

Elizabeth wrote to Secretary Rankin to report her upcoming move to Tobata. Rankin's reply was both congratulatory and disciplinary. Missionaries do not move, he informed her, without the permission of the Board on recommendation of the Mission. "I was so ignorant of how to act as a missionary," said the long-time independent, "and how much freedom I did *not* have anymore."[27]

Elizabeth's faux pas aroused much talk in the Mission, most of it good-natured. At the next mission meeting, held in October 1948 at Fukuoka, her reassignment was the first item on the agenda. It passed without opposition, though not without amusement. Present at the meeting was Baker James Cauthen, the Board's Secretary for the Orient. "Dr. Cauthen has a nice sense of humor," Elizabeth noted with a sigh of relief.[28]

Neighborhood Lighthouse

Elizabeth moved on Thanksgiving Day, when the bedraggled Good Will Center was being renovated and refurbished with funds provided by the Foreign Mission Board. Later Elizabeth could report: "The two-story building, painted a living green, stands out conspicuously in this treeless, flowerless neighborhood."[29] The stodgy houses round about were overflowing with the poor and undernourished, many of them refugees from Korea and other overseas lands that had been a part of the now defunct Japanese empire. Beriberi and tuberculosis were rampant.

Elizabeth reopened the Good Will Center as soon as possible to take advantage of the Christmas season, the most propitious time to gain a friendly response to the Christian message. Assisting her was Kakiwa Tomita, daughter of a veteran pastor in Tokyo. Attractive and vivacious, with previous experience in church and kindergarten work, Kakiwa seemed the ideal associate for Elizabeth. She too was endowed with fortitude and zeal.

Elizabeth and Kakiwa Tomita spent many hours visiting the surrounding homes. They enlisted children and adults for a wide variety of classes spread over six days a week. Tuesday, for example, was girls' day, with GAs meeting in the afternoon and YWAs in the evening—both groups led by Kakiwa. The Mothers' Club met on Wednesday, led by Kesako Hikasa. Monday, the only day of rest, was free of meetings but not of visitors, who often came before Elizabeth was dressed. "*Always* we have someone for lunch on Mondays," she grumbled.[30]

In February 1949 about five hundred persons took part in one or more programs at the Center. As more and more people flowed through its three green gates, a growing number also entered the narrow gate of Christian faith. Elizabeth made that faith attractive. She lived on the level of the people, wearing oft-mended clothes. From morning till night she was helping others. Many of her meals consisted of a baked sweet potato she had purchased while out visiting and brought home hidden under her coat.

A Japanese coworker wrote of Elizabeth: "Hearing that a woman in the mother-child dormitory was ill, she immediately heated a large kettle of water and prepared a meal. She took these to the dorm, wiped the sick woman's face and body with a wet cloth, fed her, used the Bible to tell about God's love, and prayed for her. Often she brought poor children to her own room, bathed them and changed their clothes, fed them and cut their hair."[31]

Elizabeth assembled a staff of teachers for a kindergarten to open in April, the start of Japan's school year. Kakiwa Tomita was to be the head teacher. In preparation for the opening, a large children's room had been added to the facility, and the size of the playground had been nearly doubled by the purchase of an adjacent strip of land, raising the total land area to one-third acre. Entrance fees had been collected from about sixty children. All was ready—or so Elizabeth thought. Suddenly the sky fell in. Under pressure from the board of directors (*kanjikai*), Kakiwa resigned as head teacher. In solidarity with her, her associates also resigned.

Why would the directors force out so qualified a worker at so critical a time? Kakiwa Tomita was a liberated female from progressive Tokyo. She had grown up a tomboy who played with her brothers and taught a boys' Sunday School class in her father's church. "Some of the ladies of our board," Elizabeth was to recall, "were horrified that she sat by the boys in church, and even rode down the street with a boy on a bicycle, and walked with boys to church, laughing and talking along the way."[32]

"This is true, all true," says Kakiwa, now Mrs. Inui. "But there was nothing wrong with it."[33] The problem, she insists, was not that Tobata was more conservative than Tokyo. Nor was it that she was popular with the boys, since she was no less popular with the girls. Indeed, her GA and YWA activities thrived. The real problem, she claims, was Kesako Hikasa. Whether because of jealousy or something else, the older woman disliked her from the beginning and deplored her conduct as scandalous.

One Saturday night Elizabeth told Kakiwa that Mrs. Hikasa was saying, "There are always boys in Miss Tomita's room." That was when Kakiwa exploded and called it quits. On Monday and Tuesday, with help from some of the young people, she packed her things to leave. Elizabeth begged her to stay and "cried like a baby." Floryne Miller and Junko Hara each invited Kakiwa to move in with her. But on Wednesday she boarded the train at Tobata Station and left for Tokyo, while Elizabeth stood on the platform weeping. "I loved Elizabeth," Kakiwa Inui says. "I loved Rinkōsha and everything about it—with one exception."[34]

The task of finding replacements for Kakiwa and the other teachers fell to Elizabeth. "I lost weight," she wrote, "and brown hair was turning gray."[35] But in time she succeeded, and the kindergarten opened on May 10—more than a month late—with sixty-five pupils. The head teacher was Hiroko Watanabe (Hiroko Tsuda after her marriage), who had tried to comfort Elizabeth at the train station when Kakiwa left. Hiroko became to Elizabeth not only a valuable assistant but a lifelong "daughter."

With gifts from LARA (Licensed Agencies for Relief in Asia), the kindergarten was able to serve hot food and milk to the children, supplementing the small lunches they brought from home. Elizabeth asked American friends to send needed supplies: soap, handkerchiefs, combs, washrags, towels, toothpaste, pencils, crayons, color books, tablets, old Christmas cards. The response was overwhelming. Missionary Lenora Hudson was present one day when Elizabeth opened a closet like Fibber McGee's closet in the popular radio series. Supplies from America crashed to the floor in a heap.[36]

Elizabeth pushed for a medical clinic at the Center. "In the summer," she noted, "most of the children break out in awful sores all on their faces and hands. They fill with pus and last until cool weather. Some of the mothers' faces are a sight with them too."[37] These skin lesions were but one of many common afflictions that were treated after the clinic opened in 1950, staffed by a full-time nurse and a visiting doctor.[38]

In the summer of 1951 Rinkōsha was enlarged to 4,700 square feet of floor space. A day nursery was opened, and additional living space was provided for staff members. There were now three Sunday schools and several new clubs and programs, including ministries to blind and deaf persons and to Koreans. The Vacation Bible School enrolled 276 children, with an estimated five hundred persons in attendance at the outdoor commencement. The demands on her time relentless and increasing, Elizabeth grew bone-tired and often dozed at the supper table. Sometimes she slipped away to a missionary home to catch up on her sleep.

Rinkōsha was indeed a beehive of activity, humming night and day with programs and people that taxed the facilities to the limit. It had the trappings of a successful, well-run enterprise. But underneath were festering sores. "It won't work," a Baptist professor in Fukuoka had told Elizabeth early on. "You can't succeed with several Japanese young women on your staff. Without doubt, there will be jealousy and friction."[39]

A Clash of Wills

A workaholic by any measure, and involved in fifty-six meetings a week, Elizabeth demanded too much of not only herself but of her workers. A trusting Christian among Christians, she also gave the workers too little supervision. Not only were jealousy and friction rampant, but one or two staffers were buying at the stores and charging the bills to the Center. Elizabeth was unaware of some of these problems because Kesako Hikasa kept the books. The only financial records open to Elizabeth were the general reports of income and expenditures that Kesako submitted to the board of directors. "Between you and me," Elizabeth wrote cozily to Secretary Cauthen, "if only the money for this work could come some way besides through the W.M.U. of Japan, I feel we could do more efficient work."[40]

Elizabeth clashed with most of the board members and neighboring pastors over religious promotion. They approved of the kindergarten, playground activities, medical work, industrial work, library, and clubs for various age-groups. But they opposed the missionary organizations: WMU, YWA, GAs and RAs. To them, the Center was too much like a church. They objected to the stress on evangelism in a social-work institution. "The report of any Bible teaching or souls saved," Elizabeth complained to Cauthen, "has seemed invariably to arouse jealousy and animosity."[41]

Particularly dissatisfied with Tobata Baptist Church, Elizabeth envisaged a second church in the city that would be closer to the Center both geographically and culturally, a less formal church where worshipers would feel at ease in their everyday clothes. This dream she shared with Kesako, mindlessly it seems, for Kesako naturally told her husband. Nothing was more abhorrent to some Baptist pastors than the proposal of another Baptist church in their city. It sounded like a negative judgment on their work, and even worse, a new church would compete for hard-to-get members and money.

Shortly thereafter, Elizabeth received a letter from Pastor Hikasa and his deacons asking her to leave the Tobata church. Her response was to temporize, for until there was another Baptist church in the city, she felt obligated to attend Hikasa's church with the people she customarily took with her from the Center. This did not prevent her from laboring for the fulfillment of her dream. Elizabeth was one of nine charter members who, in April 1951, formed the Meiji-machi congregation, with youthful Shōzen Kanō as pastor.

Elizabeth's conflict with the Tobata church was more easily resolved than her clash with the Good Will Center's board of directors. The board demanded her resignation as superintendent. Her response was to hunker down, claiming a divine mandate to complete her mission there. Three times the board asked the Japan Baptist Convention's executive committee to intervene. Each time the executive committee declined, noting that full authority for administering the Center lay with its board of directors. Frustrated, the board members resigned en masse. This forced the Convention's executive committee to appoint a special committee to deal with the problem. The special committee likewise failed to persuade Elizabeth to step aside.[42]

News of the turmoil reached the ears of Baker James Cauthen, who, Elizabeth reported in her autobiography, "wrote me that it would have been better if I had never been appointed by the Board."[43] Her recollection is suspect. Cauthen wrote several letters to Elizabeth during her years at the Good Will Center, but the statement attributed to him is not found in the carbon copies of his letters nor in the originals that Elizabeth preserved. Cauthen's extant letters consistently praise Elizabeth for her dedication and service.

"Later," the autobiography continues, "I received a secret letter from one of the leaders of the Japan Baptist Mission, ordering me not to mention the letter to anyone, but to give up the work at the Center and to get out." This probably refers to a forthright but courteous letter from Edwin Dozier. Edwin stressed that the Good Will Center was an institution of the Convention, not the Mission, and that the Mission was pledged to cooperate with the Convention. Whatever the faults and mistakes on both sides, he pointed out, trying to spare her feelings, Elizabeth was clearly at odds with the national leaders. "The Japanese people believe in working out such problems in such a way as to cause individuals as little pain as possible," Edwin wrote. "They feel that if you will accept a field of work and resign that it will help you and them not to make public the causes for dissension."[44] He said nothing about keeping the letter itself secret.

Elizabeth was in a box, and she knew it. It was frustrating enough that the Japanese trustees seemed to quench her missionary spirit. Now she felt rejected by her missionary colleagues. The "secret letter" brought on a passion of sickness. Upset by the noxious brew of blame and rebuke, she began vomiting. Only gradually did queasiness pass, and only gradually was her can-do, must-do attitude softened. In time, a chastened Elizabeth agreed to vacate her post and move on.

Her hard-headedness contrasted sharply with Naomi Schell's pliantness. Schell had worked amicably with Kesako Hikasa; Elizabeth could not. Schell had even served as the Convention's *shuji* in cooperation with Masajirō Kuroda, who bore the same title. Though strongly motivated, Schell was tactful and diplomatic, able to compromise for the sake of good relations. Elizabeth was ever the free-wheeling enthusiast, covetous of untrammeled freedom, impatient to get things done. Her unbridled passion for tangible results precluded any meaningful cooperation with cooler heads.

Elizabeth had much in common with Sir Wilfred Grenfell, for whom she had worked in Newfoundland. Grenfell outraged his mission board repeatedly by his independent streak. So did John Williams in the Pacific Islands, C. T. Studd in Africa, and countless others who won fame and glory in the missionary enterprise. Elizabeth stood in tall company.[45]

Indeed, many were the broken lives she salvaged or enriched. Many were the seekers she led into the Christian fold. It is at least understandable that Elizabeth interpreted the fruitfulness of her ministry as a divine signal to persevere. She felt compelled to "obey God rather than man."

As though a step-up transformer, Elizabeth had raised the voltage at the Neighborhood Lighthouse to a level that made others wince—and made some fear a conflagration. Now the dazzling beam would begin to fade. In the early sixties Rinkōsha's light would be snuffed out and the property sold.

17

Planting Flowers and Churches

536 Minami Machi, 5 Chome
Matsuyama, Shikoku, Japan
March 5, 1955

My dear Twin-in-Kingdom-Work,

Well, yes, we are twins in a way, and in a big way, aren't we, for you are fellow-workers-at-a-distance. You pray and give, we go, and our Lord works through us all to save people.

During my delightful furlough last year, I rejoiced to see some of you, but regretted not being able to meet many more.

Missionary Frances Talley and the members of the Matsuyama Baptist chirch were very gracious in welcoming me back in October, meeting me at different points along the way and accompanying me to the missionary home built for us by our Board in 1952, which Frances and I share.

I rejoiced to hear from our church members how God had blessed this new Baptist work during the second year of its existance, and how zealously the missionary and some of the church members had worked: how our lovely church building had been completed and dedicated; how the Sunday School and most of the church meetings had been moved from rented quarters and the missionary home to the church building; how our church secretary, formerly my co-worker in beginning Baptist work in this Prefecture, had resigned to get married; and how upon the transfer of our pastor to another field, our second pastor had been called and was being awaited. Also how kindly pastors and missionaries had come to preach on Sundays when we were pastorless, or our deacons had ably conducted the services.

IF ELIZABETH LEFT TOBATA UNDER A CLOUD, most of the local people saw it as a nimbus. The mayor and other public officials honored the missionary with lavish citations. Friends showered her with parties and gifts. There was no more need for her to slink out of town unnoticed than for the Neighborhood Lighthouse to darken its beam.

"The kindergarten mothers gave me a very unusual farewell," Elizabeth reported. "They had a professional dresser of brides come in and dress me as a bride—why, I do not know—a Japanese bride, wig and all. So there I sat, a fifty-two-year-old bride, with no thought of getting married, being entertained by those dear friends as they gracefully performed their Japanese dances around me, trying to show their appreciation of what I had tried to do among them."[1]

A host of well-wishers saw Elizabeth off at Tobata Station, and others waited eagerly on the station platforms up the line. At each stop people thrust out flowers and gifts, and hands to be clasped. Their voices broke while singing "God Be With You Till We Meet Again." This on-and-off drama of smiles and tears had its final curtain at Moji Port, where Elizabeth boarded the ferry bound for the city of Matsu-yama on the island of Shikoku.

Shikoku is the smallest of the four main islands of Japan, less than one-fourth the size of Elizabeth's home state of South Carolina. Its climate is hospitable to South Carolinians accustomed to mild winters and long, hot summers. Shikoku has more mountainous terrain, with one peak reaching 6,501 feet, and unlike South Carolina, though in the same latitude, it produces an abundance of citrus fruit, especially mandarin oranges.

The Southern Baptist Mission established a beachhead on the island in 1952 with the sending of Bill and Rebekah Sue Emanuel to Taka-matsu and Elizabeth Watkins to Matsuyama. To complete the mission-ary presence, Frances Talley, with whom Elizabeth had taught at Seinan Jo Gakuin, was to join her on Shikoku after a year's furlough in the States.

Church Number One: Matsuyama

Elizabeth arrived in Matsuyama June 3, 1952. She spent the first night in the home of Mabel Francis, the bike-riding missionary of the Christian and Missionary Alliance who had refused repatriation during and after the war, thus gaining mythic status among her supporters. Miss Francis was to become an honorary citizen of Matsuyama and serve there until the age of eighty-five.[2]

The next day, after Miss Francis had prayed earnestly that God would direct her paths, Elizabeth went hunting for an apartment. A real estate agent took her to the Nomoto home, a sixty-year-old dwell-ing already housing twelve people—four generations of Nomotos and four outsiders. The family patriarch agreed to rent Elizabeth two tatami rooms in the sprawling house, one with three mats and the other with eight, and some storage space across the street. Elizabeth's refrigerator, then a rare luxury in Japan, was placed in the dark, dirt-floor kitchen, to the delight of all the occupants of the house.

Elizabeth slept in the three-mat room (six feet by nine feet), which was barely large enough for the mattress she laid on the floor. The eight-mat room (twelve feet by twelve) was multipurpose: office, dining room, classroom, guest room, and bedroom for her helper, Setsuko Shirabe. Unlike Elizabeth's mattress, Setsuko's futon could be folded and stored by day, opening the space for other uses. Elizabeth's bedroom, usually stifling hot, was separated from Mr. and Mrs. Nomoto's by a paper wall that vibrated with sound waves as though a two-way loudspeaker. "I could hear his drunken breathing with no difficulty," Elizabeth wrote, "and they could almost hear my thoughts."[3]

Elizabeth cooked on her own little charcoal stove. But rather than use it in the dungeon-like kitchen, she would take it out into the yard each time she and Setsuko prepared a meal. Elizabeth remembered all too well that her mother had once fainted from charcoal fumes and that she herself had been nauseated. After cooking their food, she and Setsuko would carry it up the outside stairs to their multipurpose room. The meal would be cold by the time they sat down to it.

In this aging, creaking house there was no place to bathe. The Nomotos, like many other residents of Matsuyama, patronized the mineral springs in Dōgo at the eastern end of the city. Dōgo was accessible by street car, its public bathhouses charged only pennies, and communal tubbing at a hot-springs resort was far more pleasurable than solo bathing in the narrow confines of a bathroom at home.

Elizabeth commuted to Dōgo's spa more out of necessity than desire. In keeping with Japanese etiquette, she washed and rinsed outside the mammoth tub. But unlike the Japanese patrons, who got the most for their yen, she passed up the chance to soak—and be stewed—in water that ranged from 108 to 122 degrees.[4] Nor was she pleased with the stares of fellow bathers, though she learned to ignore them. Since Dōgo's famed alkaline waters drew pilgrims from all over Shikoku and much of Japan, there were always gawkers around.

Her awkward living arrangements in no way deterred Elizabeth from doing evangelism full throttle. The Nomotos allowed her to conduct a Vacation Bible School and frequent English Bible classes in their home. For other meetings, Elizabeth had use of a kindergarten building rentable by the hour when the kindergarten was not in session. Her schedule was so heavy that she would skip meals except to nibble on a raw cucumber.[5]

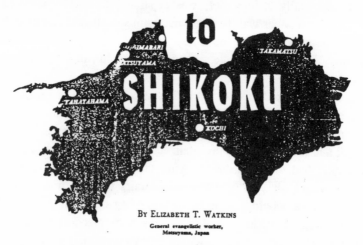

Bringing the Saviour to SHIKOKU

By Elizabeth T. Watkins
General evangelistic worker,
Matsuyama, Japan

Hiroko Tsuda had come with Elizabeth from Tobata as a temporary volunteer. A radiant young women, Hiroko started a Sunday School, a children's Bible club, a girls' club for middle-school students, and a young women's organization. She met with the clubs almost daily to lay an enduring foundation. During her nineteen days in Matsuyama, this ardent evangelist led nineteen people to faith in Christ. Then she returned to the new husband who had consented to the three-week leave after Hiroko's family had forced her to marry him.

After Hiroko's departure, Elizabeth leaned heavily on Haru Takahashi, the only Baptist she had found living in the city. Haru was the seventy-five-year-old widow of Tateo Takahashi, a Seinan Gakuin professor who had graduated from Southern Baptist Seminary with George Bouldin and Kelsey Dozier. She volunteered to be a prayer leader and Sunday School teacher in the nascent Baptist congregation. Elizabeth invited different pastors and missionaries to preach in the worship services each week.[6]

In October, construction was completed on a Mission residence designed for two single women. For the first time since she was four, Elizabeth moved into a house that was new. The Western-style, one-story wooden structure, more plain than pretentious, served also as the church building. Although the residence had a guest room and Setsuko was living with her, Elizabeth always put up the visiting preachers in an inn. She dared not let any gossip arise about a man in the house overnight. The false accusation she had faced at Seinan Gakuin twenty years before was seared in her memory.

The Mission residence stood on land formerly used as a rice paddy, so the yard was a barren waste, with no grass, trees, or flowers. Elizabeth made it a showplace. She sodded a lawn, set out shade trees and fruit trees, and planted a variety of flowers so as to have some in bloom each month. For about an hour after breakfast each day, Sunday excepted, she could be seen working in the yard.

Elizabeth's helper chided her for this practice. Setsuko thought the missionary could better spend that time visiting homes or preparing Bible lessons. Elizabeth wanted to retort, "When I pull up weeds, I don't have to pull out your hair as I feel like doing. And when I hit the ground hard, I don't have to hit *you!*"[7] Yard work for Elizabeth was therapy that helped make her fit to live with.

Elizabeth told some American friends that she let the weeds in her yard represent individuals who caused her trouble. "Yank off this one's head, yank off that one's head," she would say as she pulled the weeds. It was a harmless way to work off frustrations.[8] By growing flowers, moreover, as her mother had done before her, she had something beautiful to share with others.

Sharing was second nature to Elizabeth. She shared her home with the many friends who came and went without letup, beginning with the early morning prayer meetings and continuing into the night. Her gift for charming people and remembering their smallest concerns kept her in demand. "Whenever I go to your missionary house," a young father wrote in English, "I feel my cold heart begins to melt gradually under your warm personality." He said he wanted to go often, but apologized for not bringing his family. "I want to let my wife and children listen to the sermon and love the Christ. But my wife is busy looking after my little rascal."[9]

Elizabeth's hospitality gave rise to humorous anecdotes that circulated among the other missionaries. Bill and Sue Emanuel never forgot their first visit with Elizabeth after she had moved into the Mission residence. She told them there was a bathtub in the guest bathroom, then recoiled in apparent shock at finding only a small shower. "I thought sure I told the contractor to put it in," she said.[10]

When Elizabeth hosted a meeting of the Central Japan Station, she made room assignments that separated men and women—a common practice among the Japanese. After she had gone to bed, the missionary guests regrouped so that couples slept together. Later Elizabeth confessed that she had asked friends in the States to send food for the meeting, not knowing that the Mission would cover all expenses.[11]

Elizabeth never understood Mission policies. For example, a portion of her salary was designated for certain personal expenses considered tax exempt by the Japanese government but not covered by work funds provided under Foreign Mission Board policies. Unable or unwilling to grasp the distinction, Elizabeth gave this money to her church or used it for work expenses covered by other funds.[12]

In March 1953 missionaries Marion Moorhead and Helen Sherer happened to be in Matsuyama at the same time. Helen was accompanied by Jean Falck, a U.S. military dependent. Elizabeth invited all three for what Moorhead later described as "a breakfast never to be forgotten."[13]

While her guests waited in the breakfast nook, Elizabeth and Setsuko prepared the food on a little charcoal stove on the back porch. The window in the breakfast nook was open, and a cold draft made the room uncomfortable. At Jean Falck's request, Marion Moorhead closed the window. When Elizabeth returned to the breakfast nook, she promptly opened the window, exclaiming, "I thought I shut that window. It's so hot in here, we need some fresh air." She repeated this remark several times, for Marion would close the window when she had left, and she would open it upon her return.

The first course was oatmeal, served in large, individual soup plates. The second course was scrambled eggs, a plateful for each person. The third course was toast—a stack of three or four thick slices for each guest. The guests exchanged glances and shook their heads at the huge servings. Elizabeth herself usually ate oatmeal with fruit and two slices of toast. She avoided eggs.[14]

Before the meal was over, Setsuko mopped the breakfast nook, having the guests lift their feet off the cold floor so that she could render it wet and colder. Shortly after, she had them lift their feet for a second mopping.

When Jean Falck was served her oatmeal, she noticed blood on the rim of the soup plate (Elizabeth had cut her hand). "I have a very queasy stomach," she says, "and it was all I could do to keep from regurgitating."[15] Determined not to offend her host, Jean covered the blood with her napkin and ate half the oatmeal. She had never eaten oatmeal before, and she never ate it again. But her admiration for Elizabeth endured. Jean later sent the missionary a wedding dress for loan to Japanese brides and entertained her in the States.

Elizabeth never claimed culinary skills. Her passion was serving the bread of life, and she rejoiced over every taker. Elizabeth had new converts to write out their confessions of faith, as is customary in Japan. These manuscripts she sent across the Inland Sea to Kure Baptist Church, which served as the mother church until the Matsuyama congregation could be formally organized. Only after this church had reviewed the confessions and voted its approval could the converts be baptized. Most were immersed by missionary Curtis Askew, who visited periodically from Hiroshima. Elizabeth took snapshots of each baptismal service. After the sixth of these occasions, Mary Lee Askew laughingly told her, "You have more pictures of my husband than I do."[16]

Rebekah Sue Emanuel came from Takamatsu—seven hours by train—to play her accordion and the congregation's pump organ at a three-day evangelistic meeting. Elizabeth kept her busy playing also at the orphanage, the reformatory, and the home for the aged. Two weeks later Bill Emanuel came as a preacher, bringing their six-year-old Elizabeth with him. The daughter liked to travel with her dad and sing solos with him as accompanist. "At the evening service," Elizabeth Watkins reported, "the little girl was singing 'Jesus Loves Me' when she suddenly stopped, gave a big sleepy yawn, and then went right on with the song, not at all perturbed by everyone's laughter."[17]

There was no lull in Elizabeth's full-organ rendition of planting a church. She kept all the stops out for thirteen months. On July 14, 1953, Matsuyama Baptist Church was organized in her house with forty-two charter members. Gorō Amano became the first pastor. Among those present to sanction the event were the president and the executive secretary of the Japan Baptist Convention. It was much remarked that the first Southern Baptist-related church on the island of Shikoku had taken root in just over one year instead of the several years usually required.

Church Number Two: Imabari

In 1953-54, during her first furlough as an appointed missionary, Elizabeth attended Southwestern Baptist Seminary in Fort Worth and earned a Master of Religious Education degree. Upon her return to Matsuyama, she faced some new adjustments. For one thing, she now had Frances Talley, whom she affectionately called "Talley-chan," as her house mate. The two women were virtual opposites in temperament. A pastor who knew them well compared them to Mary and Martha of Bethany in the New Testament. Frances was the quiet and restrained Mary; Elizabeth was the hustling, short-tempered Martha.[18] Yet they managed to avoid conflict. Elizabeth made the wise suggestion, Frances recalls, "that we each have our own helper and go our different ways, according to our individual schedules. She felt that more could be accomplished that way, and I agreed with her."[19]

During Elizabeth's absence the Matsuyama church had moved its services from the Mission residence into a new building paid for with an appropriation from the Foreign Mission Board. Church membership had grown to seventy. There was a new pastor, Saburō Nakamura, a thin-chested man undergoing treatment for tuberculosis. Frances had won his approval, but to Elizabeth he was "a pharaoh who knew not Joseph." She felt "underfoot."[20]

Elizabeth hacked out a new clearing in which to operate. Her services were welcomed at four institutions: the hospital for persons crippled by a bone disease, the home for sixty juvenile delinquents, the school for the physically handicapped, and the school for the deaf. She also worked in a neighborhood of shacks, among people who had lost their homes and possessions in the air raids or who had been repatriated from other Asian countries. Her only major involvement in the Matsuyama church was to promote a new building project.[21]

Earlier, four of the five children of her uncle Paul Bomar had sent her a gift of five thousand dollars through the Foreign Mission Board. The money was designated for an educational building that was to be a memorial to three women: Nancy Bomar, mother of the donors; Elizabeth's mother Lizzie; and Dru McCollum, the pioneer missionary to Japan who had been dean of women at Judson College.

It was a worthy project, approved by the Board's B. J. Cauthen after consultation with Edwin Dozier and others in Japan.[22] The Matsuyama church building had only four small classrooms for its growing Sunday School. Elizabeth envisioned a two-story addition that would accommodate a kindergarten on the first floor and provide additional Sunday School rooms on the second floor. Unfortunately, a saw mill had been built next door to the church, and the only place on the church property where the new building could be placed was on the side adjacent to the saw mill. "We would be embarrassed," Elizabeth said, "to ask mothers to send their children to such a noisy, dusty place."[23]

On the other side of the church was a corner lot, facing on a major thoroughfare. The original church building might have been erected on that lot had the owner been willing to sell at the time. Now he was willing, belatedly, but the church had to sign a purchase contract by a set date. After that date the property would be offered to the next buyer in line, a man who wanted to build a public bathhouse. Elizabeth coveted that lot as the ideal site for the educational building. Shielded from the saw mill by the church building, it was an excellent location for a kindergarten. The lot had become so valuable, in fact, that the asking price was $31,000.

Although it was against Foreign Mission Board regulations for a missionary to solicit funds for his or her own work, Elizabeth did not scruple to follow her proven two-stage method of getting things done. First, she asked the Lord to provide her needs; and second, she made the needs known to acquaintances in the States. Those two acts sufficed to turn on the spigot and start the flow of funds. Friends in Spartan-burg handed money to Earle to be remitted abroad or put in her bank account. Other friends sent gifts through the Foreign Mission Board. By forwarding the money to Elizabeth, the Board gave priority to its policy of honoring donors' requests over its policy of prohibiting such solicitations.

Desperate for all the money she could raise, Elizabeth asked permission of her generous cousins to apply their $5,000 gift toward the purchase of the $31,000 lot. With the lot secured, she argued, she could raise additional funds for the building. Without the lot, there could be no educational building, and the church would be squeezed between a saw mill and a bathhouse. The cousins said no. Secretary Cauthen had written them that Elizabeth's strategy not only violated Board policy but was fiscally unsound. The price of the lot, he pointed out, was more than the Board usually paid for lot and building com-bined.[24]

Elizabeth worked herself into a lather. Bordering on hysteria, she quoted God's promises to Cauthen, a doctor of theology, as to a Sunday School pupil: "The silver is mine, the gold is mine, saith the Lord"; "Ye have not because ye ask not."[25] To prove her point, she organized prayer meetings in her home and in the church. But all her brashness and well-meant prodding, pushing, and praying failed to raise the $31,000 needed for the corner lot. It became the site of, not a bathhouse, but a gasoline station and a hotel.

After this painful setback, the incurable freelance cast about for a new challenge. She asked permission of the Matsuyama church to start a mission in Imabari, a city of one hundred thousand about ninety minutes by train up the coast. The church sanctioned the venture but could offer no financial aid. The Mission approved funds, though with reluctance, to cover her work expenses including the salary of a teacher-helper who would function as evangelist.

In the summer of 1955 Elizabeth rented a conference room in Imabari and launched the new work. Her search for a teacher-helper ended when missionary Bill Medling introduced Toshio Odori.[26] An employee of the Kagoshima Prefectural Office and a member of Ijūin Baptist Church, Odori was a zealous layman who had taken seminary courses by correspondence. In August, after relentless persuasion on

Elizabeth's part, he gave up the security of his government job and moved to Imabari with his wife and three children. Their small, two-room apartment became the meeting place for the mission. Despite the cramped quarters and the frustrations of pioneer work, Odori proved to be a real trouper. Elizabeth never heard him complain.

The Odoris' six-year-old son Ichirō was a member of Elizabeth's *Kohitsujikai* (Sunbeam Band). "I memorized many Bible verses," Ichirō recalls, "and Miss Watkins gave me U.S. stamps that I showed off to envious friends."[27] Elizabeth later encouraged him to enter the ministry, emphasizing that Christianity was not just another religion but the only way of salvation. Ichirō became the influential pastor of Seinan Gakuin Baptist Church.

Elizabeth now had a new purpose for the funds she had solicited and continued to solicit. She bought a lot in Imabari and put up a two-story building with educational space upstairs and the sanctuary downstairs. Her cousins allowed their contribution, increased to $7,500, to be applied toward this building. To reduce costs, the contractor made use of lumber from an old school that was torn down, and he had the pews and pulpit furniture built in the local prison. Afterwards, Elizabeth gratefully named a hundred individuals who had responded to her fund-raising efforts.[28] Her rule-flouting promotions notwithstanding, she remained on the payroll of the Foreign Mission Board.

Church Number Three: Yawatahama

By 1958, when the Imabari work was well grounded and Toshio Odori had proven himself a capable leader—he was installed as pastor that year—Elizabeth launched a pioneer work in Yawatahama, renting a tatami room in the Labor Hall. A city of sixty thousand, Yawatahama was two hours by train from Matsuyama in the opposite direction from Imabari. Since Elizabeth continued her ministries in both Matsuyama and Imabari, the new work was one more activity in a grueling schedule.

Bertha Smith, veteran missionary to China and Taiwan, and once a prisoner of war under the Japanese, visited Elizabeth at this time. A South Carolinian, she had counted Elizabeth's mother as a friend. The visit to Japan was not unusual, for "Miss Bertha" often took her vacations at Karuizawa, where she owned a summer house. Earlier she had reprimanded Elizabeth, twelve years her junior, for not organizing herself efficiently and not doing her work as Bertha would do it.[29] The two women had much in common as strong-willed, ardent evangelists and personal soul-winners, though Bertha was the more dogmatic and abrasive. She was noted for urging Christians to list their sins one by one, then confess them to God and to others—what Elizabeth had done in the 1930s when influenced by the Oxford Group Movement.

On this occasion, her last year in Taiwan before mandatory retirement, Bertha Smith preached a three-day kickoff campaign in Yawatahama, speaking eight times. Few adults attended the meetings in the Labor Hall, but a group of high school students came with their English teacher to hear English spoken and interpreted. As follow-up, Elizabeth and Odori went to Yawatahama one night a week to conduct a children's evangelistic meeting and a Bible study for adults.[30]

While Elizabeth was on furlough in 1959-60, Pastor Odori strove valiantly to keep the Yawatahama mission alive. Commuting four hours each way once a week, he would return home exhausted at one o'clock in the morning. The small band of believers—only three were committed—would assemble each Sunday morning and go over the lesson Odori had taught them during his visit. The future of the work was bleak.

Elizabeth was living in Auburn, Alabama, with her widowed cousin Harriet Bomar Ellis. The news from Yawatahama was so discouraging, Elizabeth wrote, "that as I hung my clothes out on Harriet's clothesline, my tears dropped to the ground with the water from the dripping clothes."[31] Fortunately, her many speaking engagements kept the furloughee healthily occupied, and her faith sustained an inner peace.

Returning to Matsuyama, Elizabeth continued to assist Pastor Odori at Imabari, teaching an adult Sunday School class and an English Bible class. At the same time she pumped new life into the work at Yawatahama. Elizabeth organized a WMU with RA and GA chapters. She started Sunday evening services with the use of tape recordings of the Sunday morning services at Imabari. With a heavy, cumbersome tape recorder running—cassette recorders were not yet available—the Yawatahama congregation would join in the hymns and responsive readings, then listen to Pastor Odori's sermon of the previous Sunday. The number of baptized believers increased to ten.

For four years Elizabeth commuted to Imabari three times a week and to Yawatahama twice a week. The seasoned traveler made the most of her hours on the rails. Once seated on the "smoky, dusty, germy train," she would untie her furoshiki that contained Bible, hymnal, Japanese language textbook, stationery, visitation notes, and lunchbox. She would study as though alone or write letters to drop into a post box upon alighting from the train. The frequent, repetitive announcements that crackled over the loudspeakers seemed to bounce off her ears.[32]

Even so, Elizabeth grew tired of caroming among three cities. It was a drain on her financial resources as well as her energy. Thus she decided to live in Yawatahama and devote herself to that one congregation. Her able colleague, Frances Talley, had recently returned to the States ill and had been placed on early retirement status. This opened the way to sell the Matsuyama residence and invest the proceeds elsewhere.[33]

The Mission at the time was encouraging missionaries without dependent children to move to outlying towns that had little or no Baptist witness. Those making the move agreed to live in substandard housing, which meant a residence that was smaller, cheaper, and saleable when no longer needed. Elizabeth was one of several missionaries who implemented this new policy. With funds from the Mission and the Japan Convention, supplemented with gifts from her supporters in America, she bought a narrow piece of land in Yawatahama and built a compact house. She moved in November 1962, before the carpenters and painters had finished their work.

Upstairs were a bedroom, storeroom, toilet, and washbasin, all for Elizabeth's exclusive use. This part of the house, she complained, was hot in the summer and cold in the winter. Downstairs were a living room, dining room, guest room, kitchen, and bath. All the rooms were small. The three main rooms downstairs opened up as one, providing space for Sunday School and worship services. The kitchen served the congregation as well as the missionary living there.

The yard featured a baptismal pool where one might expect a fish pond. The pool was put to frequent use as persons of various ages made professions of faith. The inside bathtub served as a baptistry for people who, because of physical conditions, could not be immersed in the outdoor pool.

The Yawatahama mission participated in the New Life Movement of 1963, a five-week evangelistic campaign led by nearly six hundred foreigners, overwhelmingly Texans, at 150 churches and preaching points of the Japan Baptist Convention. Yawatahama's turn came in the fifth week, April 28 to May 5. "I had been suffering for some months with osteo-arthritis," Elizabeth reported, "which seemed to grow steadily worse, making it quite painful to walk, stand, or sit. But as I was prayed for by those observing the Birthday Prayer Calendar, the Lord completely healed me that day [April 21]. I threw away my medicines, said good-bye to the doctor, and feel 20 or 30 years younger. It was a miracle!"[34]

Healed only one week before the start of the eight-day crusade in Yawatahama's Central Public Hall, Elizabeth went into overdrive to make the effort a success. "It was Golden Week, Election Week, Rainy Week, and Obstacle Week," Elizabeth wrote. "We had neither a musician nor an interpreter . . . and our layman [Dean E. Richardson], who pinch-hit for our musician, had a cold and was worn out from the Osaka meeting; and the local teacher who pinch-hit for our interpreter sometimes said just the opposite of what the speaker had in mind, and our visiting preacher [L. D. Ball] turned the invitation part of the service over to my teacher-helper [Masatada Mitsukude] who had no experience in inviting people to come to Jesus for salvation."[35]

In defense of the high school English teacher who was persuaded to interpret, it should be said that he was not a Christian and, as a public employee, was reluctant to express Christian teaching directly.[36] As for the teacher-helper, he had earlier proven his courage and devotion to Christ by opposing emperor worship, a crime for which he had been tortured and permanently scarred.[37]

Despite the negatives of the crusade in Yawatahama, the congregation received a much-needed boost. More than a hundred people attended each night, a total of one hundred signed decision cards, and three persons—two high school girls and a businesswoman—were baptized. The average worship attendance leaped from six to twenty-five, leading to the formation of a choir and other group activities. The Texans who had led the services in Yawatahama donated a piano.

Elizabeth was not content with one crusade in the year. She arranged for three more evangelistic campaigns in the summer and fall, led by two pastors and one missionary. In 1964 she directed seven campaigns of six days each, using four pastors and three missionaries as the evangelists.[38] Most churches had no more than one or two such campaigns in the year. By this criterion, Elizabeth's emphasis on special evangelistic meetings was judged excessive.

Her personal work was no less extensive than the church schedule. She kept in close touch with members and prospects, training them intensively, taking their photos and making notes about them. She visited their houses and places of business. One electrician who sometimes let his work keep him from church recalled how Elizabeth would use humor to rebuke his delinquency. "Has the electrician died?" she would ask. "When is the funeral?"[39]

En route to the States for furlough in 1965, Elizabeth visited the Holy Land and Europe, enjoying the sightseeing of a lifetime. Had she been an average missionary, this exhilarating tour would have marked the end to her career in Japan. Sixty-five was the normal age of retirement from the Foreign Mission Board. With medical clearance and approval by the Mission, however, it was possible for one to continue in service until the age of seventy. Elizabeth chose to continue, to no one's surprise, and managed to gain the assent of the Mission and the Board.

Before leaving Yawatahama the previous year, Elizabeth had in effect installed Masatada Mitsukude as pastor without the Matsuyama church's approval. Pastor Nakamura had exploded, influencing the Convention leaders to transfer Mitsukude to Yamagata in October. From that time the Matsuyama church had sent a deacon or other layman to preach in Yawatahama's Saturday night and Sunday morning services. Now threatened by Elizabeth's return from America, Nakamura and his church petitioned the Mission to remove her from Shikoku on grounds that she hindered the work by her reckless zeal.[40]

It happened to be a time when relations between the Southern Baptist missionaries and Japanese Baptists were at the breaking point. Missionaries were critical of some policies of the Convention and its institutions, and the Japanese were critical of the Mission as uncooperative if not irresponsible. The tension was heightened by the escalating Vietnam War, which made the body-counting Americans seem about as humane as the bayonet-wielding Japanese in the Rape of Nanking. Many Japanese, having seen their own cities leveled by American bombs, identified with the North Vietnamese then going through the same ordeal. Some Baptists were embarrassed and angry that their Convention included in its membership several English-language churches made up of American military personnel, the pariahs of the time.

Elizabeth escaped eviction from Shikoku, however, thanks to skilled mediation by representatives of the Convention and of the Mission. She agreed to be "fluid" and to allow the Matsuyama church more control over the work in Yawatahama. The agreement was put in writing and sealed at a special ceremony, where all rejoiced. The church sent lay preachers two weekends a month, and four local women took turns preaching in the other services. "We made a beautiful new start, . . ." Elizabeth said. "Our relation with the mother church has been delightful, with mutual respect, trust and love."[41] She was nevertheless pleased that Pastor Nakamura moved to another pastorate and was succeeded by Takashi Yoshizu, who had studied at Southeastern Baptist Seminary in North Carolina and related well to missionaries.

Still heedless of Foreign Mission Board restrictions on fundraising, Elizabeth sent out a clarion call for help in buying property. A typical approach: "Please pray the Lord will send me $5,000." She made her pitch to so many individuals and church organizations that money flowed like a fountain. "The brotherhood wants to give 25% of their brotherhood offering to your building fund project," read one letter. "I have inherited a sum of money from my father and I want you and Yawatahama Mission to have $1,000 for whatever use God would have you put it to," read another. One woman, Elizabeth reported, was "doing night nursing and feeding a blind lady to earn money to help us build."[42]

But even though her overwrought appeals brought in hundreds of gifts from individuals and church organizations, including $3,000 from Southside Church, Elizabeth could not afford a lot large enough for a church.[43] She needed not a flowing fountain, but a gushing well. While the cost of wooden house construction in Japan had nearly tripled since 1955, the cost of land in urban areas had increased an average of ten to twelve times.[44] Elizabeth was stymied. Then to her great relief, the Mission decided to transfer its Yawatahama residence to the little congregation on generous terms: a minimal price for the land and no charge for the six-year-old house. The Foreign Mission Board approved the transaction.

So sweet was the deal that Elizabeth had leftover funds with which to double the size of the main meeting room, replace folding chairs with pews made at the prison, and add a platform with pulpit furniture. The enlargement placed the outer walls beyond the outdoor baptismal pool, so that without being moved, the pool became a baptistry inside the auditorium. The residence now looked like a church.

Elizabeth persuaded Masanobu Kubo to come to Yawatahama as pastor. A fingerprint expert with the police department in Takamatsu, Kubo had done evangelistic work with missionary Dewey Mercer, and like Toshio Odori earlier, he was willing to give up job security for full-time Christian ministry. Under Kubo's leadership, Yawatahama was formally organized into a church in 1971.

Kubo worked with Elizabeth only three months before seeing her off to the States for retirement in 1970, but that was long enough for him to catch a measure of her fervent spirit and to be given eight photograph albums she had assembled, with detailed captions that greatly facilitated the work of the new pastor. Kubo appreciated the flowers she had planted at the church, among them pink azaleas beside the entrance, gardenias and pansies on the east side of the building, and lilies of the valley and pink camellias in back. There were colorful blossoms all through the year to gladden the hearts of the church-goers.[45]

Elizabeth's success in Shikoku was due in large measure to the freedom she enjoyed from outside control. She was not accountable to a Japanese board of directors as at Tobata. When she found herself at loggerheads with a pastor or with deacons, she could move on to another city or obtain supportive mediation from missionary colleagues. It was chiefly to the Mission that she was accountable, and the

Mission allowed its members plenty of rope. Its supervision at the time was far looser than in more recent years.

During her 1953-54 furlough in Fort Worth, Elizabeth saw for the first time Southwestern Seminary's rotunda floor with its tiled map of the world. She was shocked to find Japan pictured as three islands, not four. The smallest of the four main islands had been omitted. There lay Japan without Shikoku! Enraged, Elizabeth stomped to the president's office and registered her complaint—in vain.[46]

Had she first seen the map in 1970, after nearly two decades on the island, her hackles would have risen all the more. Elizabeth had discovered in Shikoku the heart of Japan. There she had made church planting—enhanced by flower planting—the crowning work of her career overseas.

18

Retirement on the Run

2119 South 17th East
Salt Lake City, Utah 84106
November 13, 1970

Dear All-of-you,

There you sit in Mission Meeting - the ladies lovely in their latest made or re-made frocks, the men resplendent in hair oil and stylish ties, and the children scrubbed behind their ears. Yes, I can see you sitting there counting the minutes until coffee-break. Have a good Meeting - the best yet!

I miss you truly and love you dearly, but, strange to say, would not change places if I could. No, that is not sour grapes, either. It was grand to work with you, and to be loved and pettied by you, but it is grand to be here, too.

Surely there cannot be a greater Mission Field in the world than is Utah. And the love and fellowship in the Mission Family is as beautiful as it is in Japan. The annual meeting of this Utah-Idaho Southern Baptist Convention was held this week, and I was thrilled beyond words by the spiritual enthusiasm, the evident joy in serving ing a victorious Saviour, and the whole-hearted dedication of those

---

IT WAS THEN A FOREIGN MISSION BOARD POLICY that retiring missionaries depart from the field no later than their seventieth birthday—in Elizabeth's case, April 21, 1970. Yet no one was surprised when the Board made an exception for the singular-minded woman, granting her request for an additional three months on the field.[1] The extension allowed her to join "far-flung friends" at the Baptist World Congress in Tokyo July 12-18 and, escorted by Bee Gillespie and Polly Clark, tour twenty-one of the spectacular pavilions at the Ōsaka world's fair known as Expo '70.

The extension also enabled Elizabeth to attend an event she had not anticipated. Some of her prewar students and friends in Fukuoka decided that she should have a government award for her long years of service to the Japanese. Former governor Katsuji Sugimoto signed the recommendation with five others: the chancellor of Seinan Gakuin, the president of its university, the president of the school's alumni association, the Fukuoka director of the United Nations Association of Japan, and the director of the West Japan Culture Center. They had cleared the matter with Elizabeth's current governor and mayor in Shikoku.

Elizabeth's admirers were tardy in preparing the recommendation, dated July 1. They worried that it could not be processed before her departure July 29. Fortunately, a former vice minister of finance, Kōtarō Murakami, who happened to be in Fukuoka for a lecture, agreed to carry the recommendation to the capital and urge quick government action. "When I read the recommendation during my return flight to Tokyo," Murakami wrote, "I could not restrain my tears." Other officials who read the document were likewise moved by the record of so sacrificial a life.[2]

The recommendation stressed that Elizabeth was different from most other missionaries, who generally retained the living standards of their home country. Elizabeth had humbled herself and identified with the lowly and oppressed. She had denied herself materially in order to help the needy. Miss Watkins, the document said, had served the Japanese people as a "handmaiden."[3]

The Japanese cabinet authorized an imperial decoration, and the award ceremony was set for Saturday, July 25. According to Elizabeth, a cousin of Emperor Shōwa (Hirohito) flew down from Tokyo bringing the tokens. The ceremony was held in Yawatahama, in the mayor's office, and was followed by a formal dinner.

A resplendent Elizabeth stood before whirling cameras and flashing bulbs while Mayor Shinpei Shimizu pinned a large pearl-encircled badge to the formal dress she had designed for the occasion on short notice. The badge was to be worn at special events such as the emperor's birthday party, to which she would be invited each year. She also received a small pin to wear at any time as a sign of the honor conferred upon her, and a parchment scroll to frame and hang on her wall. The chrysanthemum-bordered scroll reads: "The Emperor of Japan confers on Elizabeth Taylor Watkins, an American, the Order of the Precious Crown, with the rank of Fifth Class." It bears the emperor's seal, followed by the name and seal of Prime Minister Eisaku Satō.[4]

清水市長から勲章を胸につけてもらう
ワトキンスさん

Newspaper account of
Elizabeth's decoration.
Ehime Shimbun
July 27, 1970

勲五等宝冠章贈る

米人女性宣教師ワトキンスさんに

約四十年間も日本に滞在し、貧しい人たちの救済につとめた八幡浜市広瀬、米人宣教師、エリザベス・テーラー・ワトキンスさん（七〇）に勲五等宝冠章が贈られ二十五日、清水新平市長から勲章が伝達された。

ワトキンスさんは昭和二年来日、福岡市の西南学院商等部の英語教師をつとめた。戦時中は一時帰国、看護婦の資格を取り、アリゾナ州リバーズの日本人収容所で在米邦人の看護に尽くした。さる二十二年ふたたび来日、西南学院で教べんをとっていた。二十七年以降宣教師として松山、今治、八幡浜で布教に専念、八十六人の信者とともに平和を願いつづけ、このほど定年を迎えたため帰国する。

ワトキンスさんは二十六日「勲章をもらったことはとてもうれしい。しかし故郷のような日本を離れるのは悲しい」となごりを惜しみながら八幡浜をたち、二十九日、羽田から帰国する。帰国後はユタ州で余世を社会福祉にささげる予定。

The next morning, after she spoke in the Sunday School and the worship service at Yawatahama, friends helped her throw her things together, hustled her to the kitchen for a bite, and pushed her into a waiting taxi despite protests that she wanted to fix her hair. At the railway station she was unable to find her tickets. After a frantic and futile search in front of gaping well-wishers, she boarded the train in confusion, just before the pneumatic doors hissed shut. There was no choice but to purchase a new set of tickets from the conductor. The originals lay on the floor of her room.

Elizabeth's route took her through Matsuyama and Imabari, where more friends waited to see her, and across Shikoku to the port of

Takamatsu. After a rousing sendoff there, she crossed the Inland Sea to Uno, where she boarded a train for Yokohama. Elizabeth was never alone on the trip. Many friends rode with her part of the way, and others stuck with her all the way to the ship. Her room in a Yokohama hotel had only a single bed, but two of her travel companions squeezed in beside her.

On Wednesday, July 29, Elizabeth's attendants rushed her aboard the SS *Oriental Jade* minutes before the gangplank went up. "There stood my friends way below," she wrote. "The sun was almost unbearably hot. I found a pasteboard box and put it over my head, grinning foolishly down on them as I held the streamers that they had thrown up to me. At long last the ship began to move, and the tape we held, the last tangible connection with the land that I had loved for forty-one years, was snapped."[5]

Also aboard the Taiwanese liner were missionaries Galen and Arlene Bradford and their daughter Dana. "Later," Elizabeth wrote, "I learned that the Galen Bradfords . . . had been appointed spies to watch me to see that I did not get off and get left in Japan on purpose, for everyone knew that I did not want to leave."[6] The "spies" recall no such assignment, but it would have made sense. Elizabeth was another Bertha Smith, for whom retirement was as welcome as a spiritual drought.

What next? Earlier, Elizabeth had written to Darwin Welsh, executive secretary of the Utah-Idaho Southern Baptist Convention, expressing her desire to work among the five thousand Japanese living in Salt Lake Valley. Welsh had assured her of a welcome. Accordingly, she had told the delegates at the annual WMU convention in Japan that she would plant a new Baptist church in Salt Lake City, and they had given over one hundred dollars toward that end.[7]

The Jack Arakis, good friends, met Elizabeth's ship at San Diego and sent her off by air to Salt Lake City. There she was welcomed by Darwin Welsh, his associate Anita Lemke (later his wife), and Gernice Ward, WMU director for Utah and Idaho. Welsh had painstakingly memorized a greeting in Japanese. Lemke and Ward held out red roses. The hosts had arranged for Elizabeth to live in a red brick bungalow owned by the Home Mission Board, the rent paid by the Utah-Idaho Convention.

The VIP reception befitted Elizabeth. Her résumé was impressive. Her declared hobby—archery—was uncommon. Her imperial decoration gave her an aura above that of other emeritus missionaries. But she would ever be amazed at the kindness of her hosts in the Beehive State. They treated her like a queen.

Still, Elizabeth faced the problems of a commoner. For one thing, she had to manage all her finances, since her banker brother Earle had died in June while she tarried in Japan. The last of his detailed reports on her personal assets in the States had indicated $13,445.01 in securities and funds.[8] Elizabeth received the documents from his widow Grace but never seemed to fathom what they meant. Her main concern was faithful stewardship. "I am expecting Jesus' return to be very soon now," she wrote, "and when He comes, I don't want Him to find any of His money in my hands."[9]

Other problems reared their heads. In her yard were gophers that burrowed indiscriminately, and dandelions with unbelievably long roots. Inside the house were gadgets and appliances she had not known in Japan: central furnace, electric range, water softener, humidifier, refrigerator with a separate door for the freezing compartment. At seventy, she had to learn a bunch of new tricks.

America was truly different. She smacked her lips at giant watermelons, tarried at the long cereal counter in the supermarket, marvelled at the hordes of light-haired people.[10] And though she had traveled around the world and seen a myriad breathtaking scenes, the Salt Lake City area had a fascination all its own. To the west stretched the Great Salt Lake Desert. To the east rose the majestic Uinta Mountains, higher than Mount Fuji.

It is said that when Brigham Young arrived at the Salt Lake Valley in 1847 with 147 Mormon pioneers, he announced, "This is the right place." Elizabeth never had any doubt but that it was the right place for her.

She sorely missed her friends at Yawatahama. She thought of them that Sunday morning when she transferred her membership to the little Highland Baptist Church next door to her house. "Tears were rolling down my cheeks . . . " she wrote to her missionary colleagues in Japan, "but I told myself that I was plain silly and babyish, and must grow up."[11]

Elizabeth set out to make new friends among the local Japanese. The telephone directory listed four places where they worshiped in their own language. Two places were Buddhist, one was Mormon, and one was Protestant—a union church with predominantly Presbyterian influence. Elizabeth visited the union church and liked the warm welcome extended her, not to mention the Japanese food and fellowship. During the next few weeks she taught some classes, visited in homes, and even preached in the pastor's absence.

Then she had to ask herself, "Am I a fly getting into a spider's web?" Her evangelical emphases—sin, the cross, John 3:16—raised hackles in this "social gospel church." Helping senior citizens and promoting the Boy Scouts were praiseworthy deeds; urging the new birth was an affront. Elizabeth asked her friends in Japan to pray for "the salvation of kind Rev. Kato and his attractive American-born wife."[12] He asked Elizabeth to stop confusing his congregation.

Feeling rebuffed and thwarted, Elizabeth explored a different avenue of evangelism. She picked out Japanese names in the telephone directory and began calling them to ask if she might visit. Her assumption was that if she told them she had just come from Japan, they would be interested in meeting her. However, Mormons and Jehovah's Witnesses had often used the same approach, making the Japanese leery of such calls. Almost everyone made excuse.

Taking yet another tack, Elizabeth volunteered to work as a Pink Lady at old St. Mark's Hospital, which enjoyed the patronage of the Japanese community. She visited the Japanese patients and, after their discharge from the hospital, called at their homes. Eventually someone complained about these follow-up visits, whereupon St. Mark's asked her to desist. After a thousand hours of service there, she moved on to the University Hospital and the Veterans Administration Medical Center.

Her initial failures at evangelism in Salt Lake City were discouraging. "I began to wonder why the Lord led me here," she wrote, "and if I would not be a fifth wheel." Then the annual meeting of the Utah-Idaho Southern Baptist Convention rekindled her spark. "I was thrilled beyond words," she testified, "by the spiritual enthusiasm, the evident joy in serving a victorious Savior, and the wholehearted dedication of those serving in difficult places. . . . We were repeatedly carried up to the heights, and felt that our cups were running over."[13]

Several members of local Baptist churches took Elizabeth visiting and offered to help in every way they could. David and Mary Clark of University Baptist Church helped her contact Japanese students in the University of Utah, and they took her to their church each Sunday to teach an English Bible Class for Oriental students.

Elizabeth found a staunch ally in Lavoid Robertson, pastor of Clearfield Baptist Church. This was the church nearest Hill Air Force Base, home to a cluster of Oriental wives. Lou Howard, a base resident and the church's WMU president, helped Elizabeth make some initial contacts in the homes. Then they started an English school in a basement room at Clearfield Church, with Edith Kretzchmar as the school's director.

To upgrade her skills for this new work, Elizabeth attended a Home Mission Board conference at Glorieta Baptist Conference Center in New Mexico. She completed fourteen hours of training in literacy missions techniques, gaining proficiency in using the Laubach Streamlined English Series. Her drive and skills helped the Clearfield school to flourish. Volunteers helped with the teaching, kept the nursery, served refreshments, and provided transportation for those who had none. Pastor Robertson taught citizenship classes that enabled nineteen wives to become Americans.

Robertson was amused at Elizabeth's made-in-Japan habits. She would get new money from the bank for her tithe to the Lord, as Japanese do for their gifts to a bride and groom. The first time Robertson let her out of his car at her home and waited for her to walk inside, she stood there facing him. He rolled down the window and asked, "Is everything O.K.?" He learned that "she was waiting for me to drive off, for as in Japan, she would not turn her back on me until I was out of sight."[14]

In addition to her work at Clearfield, Elizabeth remained active in Highland Church, serving as clerk and tireless promoter of outreach ministries. Among its members was Munemitsu Shioyama, a computer specialist from Tokyo and "the most helpful international that the Lord sent our way."[15] Shioyama assisted the church as song leader and interpreter. He marvelled that Elizabeth wrote so many letters with an evangelistic intent, kept so busy helping others, and sent birthday cards to missionaries throughout the world.[16]

Elizabeth also conducted classes in her home and at First Southern Baptist Church of Salt Lake City. From the outset her little brick house had served as a school of sorts, a place where she taught English and the Christian faith to individuals and groups. Among her pupils were doctors, scientists, the wife of a Buddhist priest, and Chinese cooks descended from laborers brought to Utah in the 1860s to help build the transcontinental railroad.

Still with time to spare, Elizabeth tutored second graders at Rosslyn Heights Elementary School and hosted a "Bible Rap" for students from Highland High School just across the street. She visited in hospitals and homes, conducted a children's Good News Club, and worked in the city's Rescue Mission. She served on the executive board of the Baptist association and on various committees. Her relentless pace kept her younger friends panting and gasping. "I challenge anyone," said Darwin Welsh, "to keep up with her."[17]

Elizabeth's altruism impressed the Salt Lake City Chapter of the Japanese American Citizens League. In 1975 the chapter presented her with a hand-engraved plaque, honoring her "for special meritorious service to the community teaching English to those of foreign extraction and teaching citizenship classes out of the goodness of her heart without any compensation."[18] Although she taught free of charge, grateful pupils—especially those with the Oriental sense of obligation—showered her with dresses and other gifts.

Summers Away from Salt Lake

In 1974 Southside Church in Spartanburg offered to pay Elizabeth's air travel and other expenses if she would come for a Sunday engagement. She balked at first. Writing to Pastor Herbert C. Garrett, she explained:

> A round-trip ticket by air is $297.18. Now for a 30 minute talk should we spend $297.18 when the money is so desperately needed for world missions? I thought I'd go by bus but it is a 3-day trip, taking a week to go and come, and that is $81.55 round trip.

I have osteoarthritis with spurs on my bones and a double curvature, so I sleep on a board. Then I have a touch of gall bladder trouble and diabetes so cannot have sweets or raw lettuce, etc., and cataracts, so eat cabbage daily to keep from going blind. I want to avoid cholesterol so don't eat eggs, etc., or animal fat.[19]

No doubt about it, her health was precarious and her diet was an inconvenience. One of her quirks was to bring a raw cabbage when invited to a meal and cook it as a supplement to what was provided.[20] Yet Elizabeth could not refuse her home church. That summer she headed east by bus, putting frugality above her frailty. She spoke at Southside's morning and evening services on Sunday, July 7, recounting experiences from her fascinating life.

In the morning service Elizabeth contrasted her early years when she was known as Spitfire with her later years in fruitful Christian work. At the close of the service, Pastor Garrett gave her a certificate of appreciation and a check for two hundred dollars. "If God can do that to a Spitfire," he told the congregation, "my, what he can do with some who are more charming."[21] Elizabeth cherished the pastor's gaffe more than the gift.

In 1975 Elizabeth learned that the Iowa Southern Baptist Fellowship wanted a foreign missionary for the summer to promote missions in its churches. She applied for the position and was accepted (hers was the only application). The thousand-mile bus ride to Des Moines brought to mind the thousand-mile train ride to Des Moines when as a college senior in Alabama she attended the life-changing Student Volunteer Conference. Her age had since quadrupled. When the Iowa Fellowship's director, David Bunch, met her bus, Elizabeth heard him mutter, "Usually the summer missionaries are kids just out of college."[22]

The seventy-five-year-old volunteer was housed in Buchanan Hall at Iowa State University in Ames. The hall's other occupants were graduate students, about half of them internationals. Although she spoke in the churches on Sundays and Wednesday nights as requested, Elizabeth saw her greatest challenge among the students from abroad. She encouraged them to attend classes in the nearby Baptist church, and she and her suitemate opened their room for Bible classes twice a week. Students crowded in to learn.

Returning to Salt Lake City at summer's end, Elizabeth continued to pursue this fruitful avenue of service. She found an open door, not at the University of Utah near her home, but at Utah State University in Logan, eighty miles to the north. The Southern Baptist pastor in Logan permitted her to share with the church her vision of evangelizing the students who would return to their own countries and become influential leaders. Convinced by her presentation, the church pledged its full support.

Her travel expenses paid by the church, Elizabeth rode a Greyhound bus to Logan each Saturday and spent the night in the pastor's home. On Sunday mornings she taught a Bible class, and on Sunday evenings she conducted an English class using Laubach's Streamlined English Series. Saturday evenings and Sunday afternoons she spent visiting the homes of internationals and hosting get-togethers. She would arrive back home in Salt Lake City after midnight.

The Logan ministry was so promising that Elizabeth gave it all her time during the summer of 1976. She lodged in the Baptist Student Center, where she conducted classes from nine in the morning until nine at night, every day except Sunday. On Sunday she taught classes at church. By summer's end the Baptist programs with internationals were flourishing, and students from Vietnam, Taiwan, and Columbia had been converted.

The summer of 1978 Elizabeth spent in Tucson, 765 miles south of Salt Lake City, working with students at the University of Arizona. As in Logan, she lived in the Baptist Student Center, teaching English and Bible there. Four days a week she also taught English at the Spanish Baptist Church.[23] Asked to take charge of the Student Center's Saturday night dinners for internationals, Elizabeth made the menus more varied to get more people involved. By summer's end the dinners had included Japanese, Venezuelan, Afghan, Mexican, Chinese, and American cuisine.

In the summer of 1979 Elizabeth was off again, this time to Fillmore, a predominantly Mormon town 140 miles to the south. As a summer missionary under the Home Mission Board's Christian Service Corps, she ministered to refugees from Laos, Cambodia, and Vietnam—the "boat people"—along with migrants from Mexico. She taught in the Summer School for Refugee and Migrant Children, riding the school bus daily and enduring a hot little schoolhouse that buzzed with flies. She also taught English classes for adults. But most of all, she shared her vigorous faith without reserve.

A Heavenly Crown of Life

By 1981 Elizabeth had accumulated a stack of certificates in recognition of her volunteer services. They came from the State of Utah, Division of Family Services; Utah State Library Commission, Division for the Blind and Physically Handicapped; the Retired Senior Volunteer Program; the American Red Cross; the Christian Service Corps of the Home Mission Board; several hospitals.

As Patient Contact under the Red Cross, she wrote letters for those requesting this service, chatted with the lonely, took Red Cross supplies to the nurses' stations. Occasionally she was able to read the Bible and pray with a patient facing a serious operation. At the VA Medical Center, where she was the official birthday greeter, Elizabeth amassed over seventeen hundred hours of service over a period of seven years. Said the director of volunteer services: "Patients are greatly attracted to her."[24]

Elizabeth identified with the patients as almost one herself. She was on medication for arthritis, high blood pressure, and angina. It was her habit to order Christmas cards well in advance each year and then joke about not knowing whether she would be on "planet earth" long enough to use them.[25]

Her sense of humor showed no letup. She still joked about her marital status, expressing the wish to "get married in a bright red velvet dress."[26] Only at eighty did she begin to sound like a confirmed spinster. "I am glad I'm not married yet," she wrote. "I prefer single bliss. And that's not sour grapes."[27]

In August 1981 Elizabeth visited Japan one last time, her expenses paid by Japanese friends, churches, and schools. The frugal missionary addicted to third-class travel now rode about in limousines and the first-class sections of trains and planes. Everywhere she was treated like royalty—at the two Baptist schools where she had taught, at the churches in Shikoku she had established, and at the West Kōbe Church, where Toshio Odori was pastor. Odori was the one Elizabeth had plucked out of the business world and turned into a pastor-evangelist. She invited him to visit her in the United States. "I cannot promise," he said. "Then we'll meet in heaven," Elizabeth replied.[28]

Before leaving Japan, she boasted that her "ten fatal diseases"—diabetes and others—had not slowed her down. But the grandiose, three-week tour took its toll, forcing a switch in her life from "fast-forward" to "pause." "Right after my return to the U.S.," she wrote to the missionaries, "I had a slight stroke. I am not paralyzed but I have a mental blockage and am not normal mentally and am partially blind. Please pray for my recovery."[29]

In December Elizabeth entered the Alpine Chavis Care Center, where she had ministered to patients through the years. Her hands and arms were useless. She could walk only with assistance. Though she recognized old friends and took delight in their visits, the happenings of yesterday were beyond recall. She enjoyed listening to religious broadcasts and having the Bible read to her.[30]

By March 1982 her vision was restored and she was sitting up most of the time. Occasionally she could attend church services.[31] Her thoughts turned increasingly to the higher life ahead. Elizabeth had often mocked the words of a hymn: "I'll shout while flying through the air, 'Farewell, farewell, sweet hour of prayer.'" It was her conviction that praying was not limited to this life but would be one of the blessings of heaven.[32]

Elizabeth departed this life October 15, 1983, dying of "acute heart failure due to arteriosclerotic heart disease."[33] In accordance with her will, the corpse was turned over to the Anatomy Department of the University of Utah School of Medicine for scientific research. "I have about 13 diseases," Elizabeth had written, "so my body should be useful."[34] She wanted to benefit others even in death.

Her good intentions were thwarted. Not only did her body show the ravages of illness and old age, but it had been routinely—and mistakenly—embalmed. It was useless, even her once-sparkling eyes. The School of Medicine had the body cremated and the ashes shipped to Spartanburg.

During the two years Elizabeth was confined to the Alpine Chavis Care Center and then to the Doxey Hatch Medical Center, where she died, the Foreign Mission Board covered more than half of her expenses—all expenses in excess of her Social Security and missionary pension payments combined.[35] She did not have to dip into her savings or otherwise reduce her modest estate.

Except for one thousand dollars designated for her surviving sister-in-law, Grace Watkins, and her clothing offered to Native Americans, Elizabeth left her estate to Baptist organizations in Japan and America. Beneficiaries were Southside Church in Spartanburg, the Utah-Idaho Southern Baptist Convention, Home Mission Board, Foreign Mission Board, Yawatahama Baptist Church, and the Japan Baptist Convention. Darwin Welsh, executor of the will, disposed of undesignated items in a yard sale. The Utah-Idaho Convention retained the Watkins family silverware Elizabeth had inherited, silverware that a slave of her grandparents had buried for protection when Columbia was burned in the Civil War.[36]

Southside Church held a memorial service on Sunday evening, October 23. Marion and Thelma Moorhead, on furlough, represented the Foreign Mission Board and the Japan Mission. Friends in the church shared memories of the deceased. As Elizabeth had requested, the sanctuary choir sang the hymn that best expressed her lifelong faith: "He Will Keep His Promises to Me." One promise she had treasured increasingly was the crown of life reserved for her in heaven.

The memorial service in Salt Lake City was held at Highland Baptist Church October 28. Judy Dawn Barking, who had written a paper on Elizabeth for a "Women in American History" class at the University of Utah, sang in a ladies' trio. Regional Language Missionary John Lee delivered the main address, and Japanese missionary John Kamiyama shared a message of condolence from Yawatahama Church in Japan. Elizabeth's dream of a Japanese Baptist Church in Utah had not been realized, but one would be organized in 1990 that would trace its origin to her groundbreaking work.[37]

In January Elizabeth's cremains were buried in Spartanburg's Oakwood Cemetery alongside the graves of her father Eddie, her mother Lizzie, her aunt Mary, her brother Earle, and Earle's wife

Grace. A matching headstone identifies her as "Missionary in Japan—40 yrs." Adoniram Judson's famous words would also have been fitting: "Missionary for life."

The Reverend O. K. Webb, Elizabeth's pastor at Southside Church during World War II and a eulogist at her memorial service, spoke for a host of friends when he said, "Sometimes we didn't understand her . . . but it wasn't her fault. . . . She was completely dedicated to the work of the Lord. . . . Missions was her mission." Lenora Webb followed her husband with a tribute of her own: "She left an afterglow on us."[38]

The years have come and gone since the sunset of her life, but that afterglow still lingers in many a grateful heart. Elizabeth Taylor Watkins, being human, was not without blemish, but thanks to the push of a precious mother and the pull of a precious crown, there was a splendor about her that will never fade away.

Abbreviations

BYPU	Baptist Young People's Union
EW	Elizabeth Watkins
GA	Girls' Auxiliary
IMB	International Mission Board, SBC, Richmond, Va.
LW	Lizzie Watkins
MK	Missionary kid (son or daughter of missionaries)
NHK	Nippon Hōsō Kyōkai (Japan Broadcasting Corporation).
RA	Royal Ambassador
SBC	Southern Baptist Convention
SBHLA	Southern Baptist Historical Library and Archives, Nashville, Tenn.
SsBC	Southside Baptist Church, Spartanburg, S.C.
WMU	Woman's Missionary Union
YWA	Young Woman's Auxiliary

Notes

Introduction

1. Elizabeth Watkins, address to Central Japan Station, Kōbe, spring 1970; audiotape recorded by Ralph V. Calcote. All quotations in this chapter were taken from this audiotape unless otherwise indicated. Some of the quoted statements were lightly edited by the author.

2. F. Calvin Parker, *The Southern Baptist Mission in Japan, 1889–1989* (Lanham, Md.: University Press of America, 1991), 232.

3. Katsuji Sugimoto in *Nishi Nihon bunka* (West Japan culture) (special issue, 2 April 1971), n.p. This quotation and subsequent quotations from Japanese-language sources were translated by the author.

4. Quoted in Sandra C. Taylor, *Advocate of Understanding: Sidney Gulick and the Search for Peace with Japan* (Kent, Ohio: Kent State University Press, 1984), 52.

5. Thelma Moorhead, conversation with author, Hardin, Ky., 28 October 1994.

6. Louisa Bomar Greene to Winston Crawley, 3 November 1955, Elizabeth Watkins File, Archives of the International Mission Board, SBC (hereafter cited as EW File, IMB Archives).

7. Lois Carter, testimony at memorial service for EW, 23 October 1983, Southside Baptist Church, Spartanburg, S.C. (hereafter cited as SsBC); audiocassette.

8. "Miss Elizabeth Watkins," news release from Office of Press Relations, Foreign Mission Board, SBC, 2 September 1970. The missionary quoted is not identified.

9. *Salt Lake Tribune*, 31 May 1981, B–13.

10. Author's undated memo of a statement he heard from EW.

11. Robert C. and Helen Sherer, letter to author, 16 June 1994.

12. Masatada Mitsukude in Yawatahama Baptist Church, *Megumi ni ikasarete: Dendō 30 shūnen kinen* (Sustained by grace: Commemorating 30 years of evangelism) (Yawatahama, 1988), 16.

13. EW to Baker James Cauthen, 25 September 1953, EW File, IMB Archives.

14. Hiroko Tsuda in *Nishi Nihon bunka* (special issue, 2 April 1971), n.p.

15. EW, morning sermon at SsBC, 7 July 1974, audiocassette. The description borrows from Max Lerner, "A Woman Like My Mother," *Japan Times*, 9 September 1970.

16. George H. Hays to Bob Stanley, 1 May 1978, EW File, IMB Archives.

17. Catherine B. Allen, *The New Lottie Moon Story* (Nashville: Broadman Press, 1980), 223.

18. R. C. and H. Sherer, letter to author.

19. Una Roberts Lawrence, *Lottie Moon* (Nashville: Sunday School Board of the Southern Baptist Convention, 1927), 96.

20. EW, "My Dedication" (1970; mimeographed), Elizabeth Watkins Papers, Southern Baptist Historical Library and Archives, Nashville, Tenn. (hereafter cited as EW Papers).

21. EW, "How God Kept His Promises to a Teenager: The Autobiography of Elizabeth Taylor Watkins" (1980; typescript), IMB Archives (hereafter cited as EW, Autobiography).

22. *Utah-Idaho Southern Baptist Witness*, 26 April 1972.

23. EW, "My Dedication," 1.

24. Katsuji Sugimoto et al., "Recommendation of a Decoration for Miss Elizabeth Taylor Watkins," *Nishi Nihon bunka* (2 April 1971), n.p.

25. EW, Autobiography, 246.

1. Spitfire in Spartanburg

1. J. B. O. Landrum, *History of Spartanburg County* (Atlanta, 1900; reprint, Spartanburg: Reprint Co., 1977), 111; *Encyclopaedia Britannica*, 11th ed. (1910–11), s.v. "South Carolina."

2. Landrum, *History of Spartanburg County*, 360–63; *Minutes of the Baptist State Convention of South Carolina, 1899*, 56–57; F. Calvin Parker, "Ancestors and Relatives of Elizabeth Taylor Watkins," typescript, 1995; Mallie Bomar Johnson to EW, 26 August 1971, EW Papers (unless otherwise indicated, all correspondence cited in this book is found in EW Papers).

3. *Who Was Who in America*, vol. 3, s.v. "Bomar, Edward Earle"; *National Cyclopedia of American Biography*, vol. 23, s.v. "Bomar, Paul Vernon"; *Who Was Who in America*, vol. 1, s.v. "Bomar, Paul Vernon"; *Minutes of the Baptist State Convention of South Carolina, 1939*, 138–39; *Who's Who in South Carolina, 1934–35*, s.v. "Bomar, Horace Leland."

4. Minutes of WMU of First Baptist Church, Spartanburg, 21 January, 12 February 1884, microfilm, Baptist Historical Collection, Furman University, Greenville, S.C.; Mary Collins Green, *First Baptist Church, Spartanburg: A History 1839–1982* (Spartanburg: First Baptist Church, 1983), 146. On the *Heathen Helper*, see Catherine B. Allen, *A Century to Celebrate: History of Woman's Missionary Union* (Birmingham: Woman's Missionary Union, 1987), 32–33, 193; *Encyclopedia of Southern Baptists*, 4:2264.

5. Montague McMillan, *Limestone College: A History, 1845–1970* (Gaffney, S.C.: Limestone College, 1970), 172, 180; Lizzie Watkins diplomas, SsBC.

6. EW, Autobiography, 1.

7. Mary A. Sparkman, *Through a Turnstile into Yesteryear* (Charleston, 1966), 29–32.

8. South Carolina Historical Society, *South Carolina Genealogies*, vol. 4 (Spartanburg: Reprint Co., 1983), 271; Brent Howard Holcomb, *Marriage and Death Notices from Columbia, South Carolina, Newspapers, 1838–1860* (1988), 65; *Camden (S.C.) Chronicle*, 24 November 1889.

9. Wm. Gilmore Simms, *Sack and Destruction of the City of Columbia, S.C.*, ed. A. S. Salley (Columbia, S.C., 1865; Oglethorpe Press, 1937), 104; Lizzie Watkins to EW, 29 May 1925; F. Calvin Parker, "Archelaus Watkins Family of Kershaw County, S.C.," typescript, 1995; inscriptions on Watkins family gravestones in the Quaker Cemetery, Camden, sec. 19, lot 14.

10. Lizzie Bomar, Journal, 30 November 1890, 24 January 1891, EW Papers.

11. Ibid., 17 February 1892.

12. Ibid., 22 June 1892.

13. References to E. F. Watkins in minutes of Bethesda Presbyterian Church, Camden, S.C. (7 October 1886, 10 February 1895), and of the Presbyterian churches at Hickory, N.C. (1 January 1888); Marion, N.C. (13 June 1891); Abbeville, S.C. (17 September 1893). The Abbeville records are in the First Presbyterian Church of that city;

the others are in the Presbyterian Historical Society, Montreat, N.C.

14. Marriage record of E. F. and Lizzie Watkins, EW Papers.

15. Minutes of the Session of Bethesda Presbyterian Church, Camden, S.C., 1887–1907, 88–89; Minutes of the First Baptist Church, Camden, S.C., 8 December 1895, Baptist Historical Collection, Furman University.

16. EW, Autobiography, 5.

17. *Minutes of the Baptist State Convention of South Carolina, 1899*, 56–57.

18. *Camden (S.C.) Chronicle*, 29 September 1899; photograph of Camden Grocery House, Camden Archives and Museum.

19. Minutes of the Session of Bethesda Presbyterian Church, 3 June 1900; EW, Autobiography, 1.

20. Spartanburg Unit of the Writers' Program of the Work Projects Administration in the State of South Carolina, *A History of Spartanburg County* (Spartanburg, 1940; reprint, Spartanburg: Reprint Co., 1976), 210; Landrum, *History of Spartanburg County*, 41–42.

21. The description is based on an old photograph and the author's visit to the home in 1997.

22. EW, Autobiography, 5.

23. Lizzie Bomar, Journal, 19 January 1892.

24. EW to Lizzie Watkins, 11 June 1908 (hereafter cited as EW to LW).

25. EW, Autobiography, 6.

26. EW, "How God Kept His Promise to a Teen-Ager" (typescript, n.d.; EW Papers), 3.

27. Southside Baptist Church, *Golden Jubilee, 1908–1958* (Spartanburg, S.C.), n.p.

28. Ibid.; Green, *First Baptist Church, Spartanburg*, 91.

29. EW, Autobiography, 8.

30. *Spartanburg Herald*, 3 June 1909, 8.

31. EW, Autobiography, 6.

32. Ibid., 8.

33. William R. Estep, *Whole Gospel—Whole World: The Foreign Mission Board of the Southern Baptist Convention: 1845–1995* (Nashville: Broadman & Holman, 1994), 180.

34. Ibid., 7; baptismal records, SsBC.

35. EW, Testimony, 1 January 1930, typescript, G. H. Bouldin Collection, Southern Baptist Historical Library and Archives, Nashville (hereafter cited as Bouldin Collection, SBHLA).

36. EW to LW, 13 May 1923.

37. EW, Autobiography, 8.

38. Ibid., 6.

39. Ibid., 12.

40. Ibid., 9.

41. Ibid.; lease contract, 11 January 1909, EW File, IMB Archives.

42. Vertical file on Broadoaks Sanitorium in Morganton (N.C.) Public Library.

43. LW to Edward Watkins, 5 April 1912.

44. EW, Autobiography, 9. This is the last sentence on p. 9; p. 10 is unaccountably missing.

45. Ibid., 11.

46. EW to LW, 19 February 1920.

47. EW, Autobiography, 9.

2. Coming Out at Judson

1. Robert T. Coleman, Jr., *Providing for Women a Thorough and Liberal Education: Converse College After 100 Years, 1889–1989* (New York: Newcomen Society, 1988), 16–17; Lillian Adele Kibler, *The History of Converse College* (Spartanburg: Converse College, 1973), 465.

2. Julia Murfee Lovelace, *A History of Siloam Baptist Church, Marion, Alabama* (n.p., 1943), 5–6; "Welcome to Marion 'The College City,' Perry County, Alabama," brochure and map, n.d.

3. Certificate of Death, Mary C. Watkins, 4 May 1917, South Carolina File No. 9632.

4. LW to EW, 15, 19 January 1919; Edward Watkins to EW, 15, 19 January 1919; EW to Edward Watkins, 14 January 1919; undated Spartanburg newspaper clipping in posssesion of Don and Judy West.

5. EW to LW, 11 May 1919.

6. EW to LW, 9 February 1919.

7. EW, Autobiography, 15.

8. Willie Hare to EW, n.d., in EW's college scrapbook titled *Stunt Book*, designed and illustrated by Elizabeth Colborne (Chicago: Reilly & Britton Co.), SsBC.

9. EW to Earle Watkins, 15 April 1917.

10. EW's list of 22 resolutions, 28 January 1917, in *Stunt Book*.

11. EW to LW, 27 March 1918.

12. Judson College, *Bulletin, 1917–18*, 14; EW to LW, 4 November [1918].

13. EW to LW, 14 October 1917.

14. Quoted in Frances Dew Hamilton and Elizabeth Crabtree Wells, *Daughters of the Dream: Judson College, 1838–1988* (Marion, Ala., 1989), 136; picture of Uncle Abe in *Stunt Book*.

15. Vertical file on Marion Military Institute, Judson College Library; EW to LW, 16 February 1919.

16. John E. Burks to EW, n.d., in *Stunt Book*.

17. EW to LW, 16 February 1919.

18. Judson College, *Bulletin, 1917–18*, 15; EW to LW, 14 October 1917.

19. EW, Autobiography, 15; EW to Mary Watkins, 27 October 1916.

20. EW to Mary Watkins, 28 January 1917.

21. Calendar item of 2 November 1919 in *Conversationalist, 1919* (Judson College); EW to LW, 17 November 1919.

22. EW to LW, 24 March 1918.

23. EW to Mary Watkins, [3 March], 28 January 1917.

24. Hamilton and Wells, *Daughters of the Dream*, 127.

25. EW to LW, 24 March 1918.

26. EW to Earle Watkins, 15 February 1919.

27. EW to [LW], [January 1918].

28. EW to LW, 17 November 1918.

29. "Senior Regulations and Privileges," mimeograph, in *Stunt Book*.

30. EW to LW, 19 February 1920.

31. Writers' Program, *History of Spartanburg County*, 233–51; Philip N. Racine, *Spartanburg County: A Pictorial History* (Virginia Beach, Va: Donning Co., 1980), 40.

32. Writer's Program, *History of Spartanburg County*, 252–54; Racine, *Spartanburg County*, 40.

33. EW, Autobiography, 16.

34. EW to LW, [October 1918].

35. EW, "The Quarantine at Judson," *Conversationalist, 1918*, 141–42.

36. Paul V. Bomar to R. J. Willingham, 14 March 1903, Franklin and Daisy Ray File, SBHLA.

37. EW, Autobiography, 14; *Conversationalist, 1917*, 159.

38. EW, Journal (1934; microfilm, EW File, IMB Archives), sec. 9.

39. EW to LW, [spring 1919].

40. Blue Ridge Association, "Application for Employment," in *Stunt Book*; W. D. Weatherford to EW, 26 April 1919, in *Stunt Book*.

41. *Southern Student Conference, 1919*, pamphlet, EW Papers.

42. EW, Autobiography, 17–18; EW to LW, 29 March 1920.

43. EW, Testimony, 1 January 1930.

44. EW to LW, [summer 1919].

45. EW, Autobiography, 19.

46. EW to LW, 25 November 1919.

47. Burton St. John, ed., *North American Students and World Advance* (New York: Student Volunteer Movement for Foreign Missions, 1920), 5.

48. EW to LW, 13 January 1920.

49. Donald McGavran, "My Pilgrimage in Mission," *International Bulletin of Missionary Research* 10 (1986): 53.

50. Lou Ellen Combs, "Conference of the Student Volunteers of Alabama," in Judson College, *Yearbook, 1920*, n.p.

51. EW to LW, [1920].

3. Life at House Beautiful

1. EW, Autobiography, 19.

2. *Baptist Woman's Missionary Union Training School for Christian Workers, 1920–21*, 8.

3. Isla May Mullins, *House Beautiful* (Nashville: Sunday School Board of the Southern Baptist Convention, n.d.), 52; Hannah Reynolds, "Mrs. Maud Reynolds McLure: A Brief Biography," in *The New Building of Woman's Missionary Union Training School*, pamphlet [c. 1940–41]; Carrie U. Littlejohn, *History of Carver School of Missions and Social Work* (Nashville: Broadman Press, 1958), 88.

4. "Official Transcript of Miss Elizabeth Watkins," WMU Training School.

5. *Training School for Christian Workers, 1920–21*, 13; EW to LW, 7 October 1920.

6. EW to LW, 4 October 1921.

7. EW to LW, 9 April 1922.

8. EW to LW, 4 October 1921.

9. Baptist W.M.U. Training School, *Students' Hand-Book* (Louisville, Ky., 1920), 3.

10. *Training School for Christian Workers, 1920–21*, 11.

11. EW to LW, 30 December 1920.

12. EW to LW, [December 1920].

13. EW to LW, 19 March 1922.

14. Alma Hunt, *History of Woman's Missionary Union* (Nashville: Convention Press, 1964), 112.

15. EW to LW, 19 March 1922.

16. EW to LW, [20 February 1921].

17. EW to LW, [20 February 1921].

18. EW to LW, 4 October 1921.

19. EW to LW, 20 April 1921.

20. EW to LW, 30 December 1920.

21. Littlejohn, *History of Carver School*, 85; Margaret Rucker and EW, "Case Work," *Royal Service* 15 (March 1921): 30.

22. EW, Journal, sec. 24.

23. EW to LW, [December 1920].

24. EW to LW, 7 October 1920.

25. Ibid.

26. *Report of Baptist Training School Settlement* (pamphlet, n.d.), 7.

27. EW to LW, [7 October 1920].

28. EW to LW, 5 December 1920, 6 February 1921.

29. EW to LW, 21 February 1921.

30. Littlejohn, *History of Carver School*, 86.

31. EW to LW, 17 October 1921.

32. EW to LW, 9 April 1922.

33. EW to LW, 11 December 1921.

34. EW, Autobiography, 17.

35. EW to LW, 16 January 1922.

36. Alice Stockton Lawton, "Biographical Sketch, Samuel Miller Lawton," Baptist Historical Collection, Furman University.

37. T. B. Ray to EW, 3 September 1921, EW File, IMB Archives.

38. Florence Walne to T. B. Ray, 15 February 1923, Walne File, SBHLA.

39. EW, Journal, sec. 16.

4. Among All Nations at Norfolk

1. EW to LW, 12 February 1922.

2. *Fiftieth Annual Meeting of the Woman's Missionary Union Auxiliary to Virginia Portsmouth Baptist Association* (Norfolk, 1950), 11; Blanche Sydnor White, "Highlights in History of Woman's Missionary Union, Auxiliary to the Virginia–Portsmouth Baptist Association, 1885–1949" (Typescript, 1966; WMU of Va. Archives), 13–16; Mrs. E. D. Poe, *From Strength to Strength: History of the Woman's Missionary Union of Virginia, 1874–1949* (Richmond: Woman's Missionary Union of Virginia), 115; Frederick Jarrard Anderson, *Hearts and Hands: Gathering up the Years* (Richmond: Woman's Missionary Union of Virginia, 1990), 54–55.

3. EW to LW, [June 1922].

4. Edward E. Daub, "Death in the Family," *Japan Christian Quarterly* 27 (October 1961): 251–52.

5. EW to LW, 29 October 1922, [spring 1923].

6. EW to LW, [July 1922].

7. Charles E. Ashburner, "Norfolk's Modern Market," *American City Magazine* 28 (March 1923): 261–62; EW to LW, 2 December 1923.

8. EW to LW, 25 March 1923.

9. EW to LW, 6 May 1923.

10. EW to LW and Earle, 23 September 1923; EW to LW, 21 January, 17 February 1923.

11. Earl Lewis, *In Their Own Interests: Race, Class, and Power in Twentieth-Century Norfolk, Virginia* (Berkeley: University of California Press, 1991), 40–42.

12. EW to LW, 4 February 1924.

13. EW, "True Kodak Pictures from the Settlement in Norfolk," *Royal Service* 28 (March 1924): 32.

14. EW to LW, [June 1922].
15. Anderson, *Hearts and Hands*, 87.
16. EW, "True Kodak Pictures," 31.
17. Ibid.
18. EW, Autobiography, 26.
19. EW to LW, 20 May 1923.
20. EW to LW, 24 February [1924].
21. EW, Autobiography, 26.
22. EW to LW, 5 May 1923.
23. EW to LW, 1 October 1922.
24. EW to LW, 22 April 1924.
25. EW to LW, 30 March 1924.
26. EW to Earle Watkins, 27 January 1924.
27. EW to LW, 2 December 1923.
28. EW to LW, 25 March 1923.
29. EW to LW, 7 October 1923.
30. EW to LW, 17 February 1923.
31. EW to LW, 8 April 1923.
32. EW to Earle Watkins, 27 January 1924.
33. EW to LW, 10 February 1924.
34. EW to LW, 4 February 1923.
35. T. B. Ray to EW, 7 March 1923.
36. EW to LW, 10 February 1924.
37. EW to LW, 4 February 1924.
38. Ibid.
39. EW to LW, 17 February 1924; *Virginia Portsmouth Baptist Association, 134th Annual Session* (1924), 23.

5. Mountain Schoolma'am

1. EW to LW, 12 June 1924.
2. T. B. Ray to EW, 29 April 1924, 7 March 1923, 3 September 1921.
3. J. F. Love to EW, 10 June 1924.
4. EW to LW, 12 June 1924.
5. Nonie Gravett, letter of 11 December 1924, *Annual Bulletin, Alumnae Association of the Baptist W.M.U. Training School* (January 1925), 34–35; Woman's Missionary Union of Virginia, *Thy Neighbor — Thyself*, 33; *Newport News Times-Herald*, 21 July 1962.
6. Robert S. Loving, *Double Destiny: The Story of Bristol, Tennessee-Virginia* (Bristol, 1955), 14.
7. EW to LW, [16 November 1924]; *Elizabethton (Tenn.) Star*, 2 December 1983.
8. Mabel Swartz Withoft, *Oak and Laurel: A Study of the Mountain Mission Schools of Southern Baptists* (Nashville: Sunday School Board, 1923), 109–13.
9. EW to LW, 27 September 1924.
10. EW to LW, 27 September 1924.
11. EW to LW, 28 September 1924.
12. EW to LW, [16 November 1924].
13. Dan Crowe, *Old Butler and Watauga Academy* (n.p., 1983), 18.
14. EW to LW, 21 September 1924.
15. J. W. O'Hara, *Signal Fires in the Mountains* (Nashville: Sunday School Board of the Southern Baptist Convention, 1929), 100.

16. EW to LW, 21 September 1924.
17. *Catalogue of Watauga Academy, Announcements 1925–1926*, 10.
18. EW to LW, 4 February 1925.
19. EW, letter of 7 December 1924, *Annual Bulletin, Alumnae Association of the Baptist W.M.U. Training School* (January 1925), 68–69.
20. EW to LW, 12 October 1924; EW, Autobiography, 28.
21. EW, "God Kept His Promise," 8.
22. EW to LW, 21 September 1924.
23. EW, Autobiography, 28–29.
24. George Jenkins, "The History of Watauga Academy of Butler, Tennessee" (MA Ed thesis, Appalachian State Teachers College, 1950), 53.
25. EW to LW, 12 October 1924.
26. EW to LW, 28 September 1924.
27. EW to LW, [October 1924].
28. EW to LW, 18 January 1925.
29. Amy Dugger Medley, quoted in an undated clipping from the *Johnson City (Tenn.) Press-Chronicle*, 1983.
30. EW to LW, 21 September 1924.
31. EW to LW, [October 1924].
32. EW to LW, 27 September 1924.
33. EW, Autobiography, 29.
34. *Minutes of the Fifty-sixth Annual Session of the Watauga Baptist Association, 1924*, 43, 49, back matter.
35. EW to LW, 1 February 1925.
36. *Minutes of the Fifty-seventh Annual Session of the Watauga Baptist Association, 1925*, 18–19.
37. Jenkins, "History of Watauga Academy," 53–54, 72; Crowe, *Old Butler and Watauga Academy*, 21, 53; *Greeneville (Tenn.) Sun*, 12 September 1992, W-2.

6. Wandering the Sooner State

1. EW to LW, 17 May 1925; *Annual of the Southern Baptist Convention, 1925*, 108.
2. EW to LW, 17 May 1925.
3. J. M. Gaskin, *Baptist Women in Oklahoma* (Oklahoma City: Messenger Press, [1985]), 336.
4. *Annual of the Southern Baptist Convention, 1925*, 99.
5. Ibid., 22–23.
6. Allen, *Century to Celebrate*, 129.
7. EW to LW, 19 May 1925.
8. EW to LW, 24 May 1925.
9. EW to LW, 24 May 1925, [May 1925].
10. EW to LW, 4 June 1925.
11. EW to LW, [May 1925].
12. *Annual of the Oklahoma Baptist General Convention, 1925*, 137; EW to LW, 8 May, 1 November 1925.
13. EW to LW, 8 June 1925.
14. EW to LW, [1925].
15. EW to LW, [1925].
16. EW to LW, [1925].

17. EW to LW, 14, 26 July, 11 August 1925.

18. EW to LW, 11 July 1925.

19. EW to LW, 20 July, 2 August 1925.

20. EW to LW, 2 August 1925.

21. EW to LW, 10 September 1925.

22. EW to LW, 2 August, 16 August, 19 September 1925.

23. *Annual of the Oklahoma Baptist General Convention, 1925,* 148.

24. EW, report to WMU convention, in *Annual of the Oklahoma Baptist General Convention, 1925,* 150.

25. EW to LW, [May 1925]; *Encyclopaedia Britannica,* 13th ed. (1926), s.v. "Oklahoma."

26. EW to LW, 10 September, 23 August 1925; David L. Cohn, *The Good Old Days: A History of American Morals and Manners as seen through the Sears, Roebuck Catalogs 1905 to the Present* (New York: Simon and Schuster, 1940), 379.

27. EW to LW, 25 April 1926.

28. EW to LW, 17 January 1926.

29. William Martin, *Prophet with Honor: The Billy Graham Story* (New York: William Morrow and Co., 1991), 63.

30. EW to LW, 31 May 1926; *Baptist Messenger* 14 (2 June 1926), 9.

31. EW, Autobiography, 32.

32. EW to LW, 11 September 1926.

33. Lolita Hannah Bissell, letter to author, 20 May 1992.

34. G. W. Bouldin, "An Effectual Door of Opportunity," *Home and Foreign Fields* 7 (Jan. 1923): 20–21.

35. EW, Autobiography, 33; EW, Testimony, 1 January 1930.

36. EW to LW, 14 September 1926.

37. EW to LW, 14 September 1926.

38. *Baptist Messenger* 14 (29 September 1926), 10; *Annual of the Oklahoma Baptist General Convention, 1926,* 163.

7. Manhattan Mission

1. EW, Journal, sec. 23; EW, Autobiography, 33–34.

2. EW, Journal, sec. 23; EW, Autobiography, 33–34; H. H. Hagemeyer (Secretary on Admissions, Teachers College) to EW, 3 September 1922; *Announcement of Teachers College, School of Education, School of Practical Arts, 1926–1927,* 14–15. 200–201; *Annual Catalogue of the Officers, Teachers and Students of Converse College, 1925–26, Announcements for 1926–27,* 32–33.

3. EW to LW, [September 1926]; *Announcement of Teachers College,* 194.

4. EW to LW, 3 October 1926.

5. EW to LW, 26 September, 25 October 1926

6. Bursar's receipt, Teachers College, 23 September 1926, EW Papers.

7. EW to LW, 21 November 1926.

8. James E. Russell, "Report of the dean for the academic year ending June 30, 1926," *School and Society* 24 (11 December 1926): 735.

9. EW to LW, 21 November 1926.

10. EW to Earle Watkins, 31 October 1926.

11. EW to Earle Watkins, 3 October 1926.

12. EW to LW, 31 October 1926.

13. EW to LW, 10 October 1926.

14. Elizabeth Frazer, "Our Foreign Cities: New York," *Saturday Evening Post* 195 (16 June 1923): 6.

15. Quoted in "New York's Big Foreign Population," *Literary Digest* 73 (29 April 1922): 13.

16. EW to LW, 15 October 1926.

17. EW to LW, 14 November 1926.

18. Ethel Fleming, *New York* (New York: Macmillan Co., 1929), 96.

19. EW to LW, 21 November 1926.

20. EW to LW, 26 September 1926.

21. EW to LW, 18 October, 21 November 1926.

22. EW to LW, 14 November 1926.

23. EW to LW, 21 November 1922.

24. George M. Marsden, *Fundamentalism and American Culture: The Shaping of Twentieth-Century Evangelicalism 1870–1925* (New York: Oxford University Press, 1980), 125–27.

25. EW to LW, 29 January 1927.

26. EW to LW, 14 November [1926].

27. EW to LW, 8 May 1927.

28. J. F. Love to EW, 6 January 1927, EW File, IMB Archives.

29. EW, Autobiography, 35–36.

30. *Announcement of Teachers College*, 110–11.

31. EW to LW, 7 November 1926; EW, Autobiography, 36.

32. EW to LW, 17 January 1927.

33. EW to LW, 27 February 1927.

34. EW to LW, [20 February 1927].

35. EW to LW, 13 February 1927.

36. EW to LW, 13 February 1927.

37. EW to LW, 8 May 1927.

38. *New York Times*, 1 June 1927.

39. EW, Journal, sec. 23.

40. EW to LW, 7 February 1927.

41. Robert P. Pell to EW, 3 August 1927; *Annual Catalogue of the Officers, Teachers and Students of Converse College, 1926–27, Announcements for 1927–28* (Spartanburg, 1927), 67–68.

42. Estep, *Whole Gospel—Whole World*, 208.

43. EW, Journal, sec. 25.

8. "Woppess" at Sops Tickle

1. Logo on the stationery of Newfoundland Hotel, St. John's, EW to LW, 7 June 1928.

2. "Form of Application for Service," International Grenfell Association, EW Papers.

3. Ronald Rompkey, *Grenfell of Labrador: A Biography* (Toronto: University of Toronto Press, 1991), 243–44.

4. Sir Wilfred Grenfell, *Forty Years for Labrador* (Boston: Houghton Mifflin Co., 1932), 325; Rompkey, *Grenfell of Labrador*, 243.

5. EW, Testimony, 4.

6. EW to LW, 12 June 1928.

7. EW to LW, 12 June 1928.

8. EW to LW, 12 June 1928.

9. EW to LW, 12 June 1928.

10. EW to LW, 7 June 1928.

11. EW to LW and Earle Watkins, 12 June 1928.

12. EW, Journal, sec. 27.

13. EW, Autobiography, 40; EW to LW, 12 June 1928.

14. EW to LW, 24 June 1928.

15. Cyril F. Poole and Robert H. Cuff, eds., *Encyclopedia of Newfoundland and Labrador*, vol. 5 (St. John's, Newfoundland: Harry Cuff Publications, 1994), s.v. "Sops Arm."

16. Wilfred Grenfell, *A Labrador Doctor* (Boston: Houghton Mifflin Co., 1919), 94.

17. EW to LW, 30 June 1928.

18. EW to LW, 14 July 1928.

19. EW to LW, 27 July 1928.

20. EW to LW and Earle, 24 June 1928.

21. EW to LW, 14 July 1928.

22. EW to LW, 30 June 1928.

23. EW to LW, 27 July 1928.

24. EW to LW, 30 June 1928.

25. EW, Autobiography, 43.

26. EW, "God Kept His Promise," 14; EW, Autobiography, 42.

27. EW to LW, 9 August 1928.

28. EW, letter of 11 January 1929, *Annual Bulletin, Alumnae Association of the Baptist W.M.U. Training School* (March 1929), 72.

29. EW, Testimony, 5. On Gideon's fleece, see Judges 6:36–40.

30. EW to LW, 15 September 1929.

9. Welcome Mat in Japan

1. EW to LW, 20 August 1929.

2. EW, "My Dedication," 2; G. W. Bouldin to EW, telegraph, 21 August 1929.

3. EW, Autobiography, 45.

4. George W. Bouldin, Autobiography (Bouldin Collection, SBHLA), 163.

5. John Robert Kennamer, Sr., *History of Jackson County, Alabama* (1935; reprint, Scottsboro: Jackson County Historical Association, 1993), 91; *Who Was Who in America*, v. 5, s.v. "Bouldin, Virgil"; Bouldin, Autobiography, 1, 159.

6. EW to LW, 23 August 1929.

7. EW, letter of 7 January 1930, *Annual Bulletin, Alumnae Association of the Baptist W.M.U. Training School* (March 1930), 50.

8. Edward Seidensticker, *Tokyo Rising: The City Since the Great Earthquake* (New York: Alfred A. Knopf, 1990), 40, 55.

9. EW to LW, 23 August 1929.

10. Margaret Bouldin appointment records, Bouldin File, IMB Archives; EW to LW, 20 October 1929.

11. EW to LW, 20 October 1929.

12. Elizabeth Garrott, conversation with author, 28 October 1994, Hardin, Ky.

13. "Ni-No-Oka, Gotemba," typescript, Bouldin Collection, SBHLA.

14. George P. Pierson and Ida G. Pierson, *Forty Happy Years in Japan, 1888–1928* (New York: Fleming H. Revell Co., 1936), 37.

15. Japan mission meeting minutes, 1929, IMB Archives.

16. *Japan Mission Year Book* (1930), 359–60; Seidensticker, *Tokyo Rising*, 48.

17. EW to LW, 9 September 1929.

18. Ibid.

19. EW to LW, 9 September 1929.

20. Publication figures are taken from *Annual of the Southern Baptist Convention, 1930*, 155.

21. EW to LW, 4 March [1930].

22. EW to LW, 19 February 1930.

23. Thomas T. Faucette, telephone conversation with author, 25 June 1995; Maude B. Dozier, "Seinan Gakuin" (typescript, Seinan Gakuin, Fukuoka), 62.

24. EW to LW, 28 October 1929.

25. EW to LW, 17 March 1930.

26. EW to LW, 15 September, 20 October 1929.

27. EW to LW, 8 January, 31 March 1930.

28. EW to LW, 20 October 1929.

29. EW to LW, 25 April 1930.

30. EW to LW, 25 March 1930.

31. EW to LW, 8 April 1930; *Literary Digest*, 9 August 1930, 2–3.

32. EW to LW, 26 January 1931.

33. EW to LW, 3 February 1930.

34. EW to LW, [1929?], 3 February 1930.

35. EW to LW, 20 October 1929; Arimichi Ebizawa, ed., *Nihon Kirisutokyō rekishi daijiten* (Dictionary of Japanese Christian history) (Tokyo: Kyo Bun Kwan, 1988), s.v. "Shimose Kamori," "Yuya Kiyoki."

36. EW to LW, 17 November 1929.

37. EW, Autobiography, 46.

38. Japan mission meeting minutes, 1938, IMB Archives.

39. EW to LW, [September 1929].

Chapter 10. Teacher and Student

1. *Japan Mission Year Book* (1930), foldout.

2. James E. Wood, Jr., "The Teaching of English as a Missionary Method" (Th.D. dissertation, Southern Baptist Theological Seminary, 1957), 161.

3. *Seinan News*, 25 June 1935; Donald Roden, *Schooldays in Imperial Japan: A Study in the Culture of a Student Elite* (Berkeley: University of California Press, 1980), 219.

4. EW to LW, 20 October 1929.

5. EW to LW, [September 1929].

6. EW to LW, 18 April 1930.

7. EW to LW, [September 1929].

8. Shuichi Ozaki in *Nishi Nihon bunka* (special issue, 2 April 1971), n.p.

9. Toraji Murakami, interview with author, 19 November 1994, Fukuoka.

10. EW to LW, 19 September 1930.

11. EW to LW, 27 October 1930.

12. EW to LW, 14 March 1930.

13. EW to LW, 18 April 1930, 14 April 1931.

14. EW to LW, 24 September 1930.

15. *Japan Mission Year Book* (1930), 73.

16. EW to LW, 3 February 1930.

17. EW, Autobiography, 49.

18. EW to LW, 29 June 1930.

19. EW to LW, 14 December, 2 December 1929, 4 March 1930.

20. EW to LW, [September 1929].

21. EW to LW, 19 September 1930.

22. Florence Walne, "Getting Acquainted with Japanese Baptists," *Home and Foreign Fields* 22 (July 1928): 197; *Who's Who in Japan* (1931–32), s.v. "Mizumachi, Yoshio."

23. EW to LW, 6 February 1931, 11 January, 17 March 1930.

24. EW to LW, 27 January 1930.

25. EW to LW, 15 March 1932.

26. EW to LW, 5 March 1932.

27. EW to LW, 20 January 1930, 5 March 1932.

28. EW to LW, 11 July 1930.

29. EW to LW, 8 September 1931.

30. Notebook A, EW Papers.

31. EW to LW, 12 February 1930.

32. EW to LW, 2 January 1931.

33. EW to LW, 12 February 1930.

34. EW to LW, 12 February 1930.

35. EW to LW, 24 February 1930.

36. EW to LW, 1 July 1931.

37. EW to LW, 25 April 1930, 24 May 1931.

Chapter 11. To the Top of Mount Fuji

1. EW to LW, 24 June 1930.

2. EW to LW, 29 June 1930.

3. EW to LW, 29 June 1930.

4. EW to LW, 11 July 1930.

5. *Explanations of Twelve Selected Colour Pictures: Japan, Her Land & Life* (Tokyo: Board of Tourist Industry, Japanese Government Railways, 1936), 2–3.

6. EW to LW, 9 August 1931.

7. EW to LW, 11 July, 26 August 1930.

8. EW to LW, 20 July 1930.

9. EW to LW, 9 August 1931.

10. EW to LW, 26 August 1930.

11. EW to LW, 29 July 1930.

12. EW to LW, 29 July 1930.

13. EW to LW, 20 August 1930.

14. EW to LW, 20 August 1930.

15. EW to LW, 20 August 1930.

16. EW to LW, 20 August 1930; EW, Autobiography, 74–75.

17. EW to LW, 29 August 1931.

Chapter 12. Faith Missionary at Work

1. EW to LW, 19 September 1930.

2. EW to LW, 3 November 1930, 2 January 1931.

3. EW to LW, 6 December 1930.

4. EW to LW, 24 May, 1 July 1931; EW, Autobiography, 46; Allen, *Century to Celebrate*, 187; 1 Kings 17:8–16.

5. David B. Barrett, ed., *World Christian Encyclopedia* (Nairobi: Oxford University Press, 1982), 827.

6. "Miss Elizabeth Watkins," news release from Office of Press Relations, Foreign Mission Board, SBC, 2 September 1970.

7. EW to LW, [1933].

8. EW to LW, 8 September 1931.

9. Shigeaki Ninomiya, "An Inquiry Concerning the Origin, Development, and Present Situation of the *Eta* in Relation to the History of Social Classes in Japan," in *Transactions of the Asiatic Society of Japan*, 2d ser., 10 (1933): 52, 96-100.

10. *Kodansha Encyclopedia of Japan*, s.v. "burakumin."

11. G. W. Bouldin, "Facing 1932 in Japan," *Home and Foreign Fields* 16 (January 1932): 12.

12. Maggie Bouldin to LW, 6 January 1932; Maude Burke Dozier and Elizabeth Watkins, *Playmates in Japan* (Nashville: Broadman Press, 1940), 24.

13. EW to LW, 3 November 1930.

14. EW to LW, 3 November 1930.

15. EW to LW, 14 April 1931; Lolita Hannah, "Ai No So No, or 'Garden of Love,' in an Outcast Village," *Home and Foreign Fields* 16 (May 1932): 9-11.

16. Maggie Bouldin in *Annual of the Southern Baptist Convention, 1932*, 252; EW to LW, 14 April 1931.

17. Bouldin, "Facing 1932 in Japan," 12.

18. EW to LW, 3 June 1932.

19. EW to LW, 2, 26 October 1932.

20. EW, Autobiography, 58.

21. EW to LW, 6 February 1931.

22. EW to LW, 16 February 1931; William Ernest Hocking, *Re-thinking Missions: A Laymen's Inquiry after One Hundred Years* (New York: Harper & Brothers, 1932), ix-xiv.

23. EW to LW, 16 February 1931.

24. EW to LW, 13 July 1932.

25. EW to LW, 13 July 1932.

26. EW to LW, 24 June 1930.

27. EW to LW, 21 August 1932.

Chapter 13. Fire on the Campus

1. EW to LW, 15 March 1932. The following account of the fire is based on this letter.

2. *Home and Foreign Fields* 5 (October 1921): 319.

3. Ruth A. Tucker, *Guardians of the Great Commission: The Story of Women in Modern Missions* (Grand Rapids, Mich.: Academie Books, Zondervan Publishing House, 1988), 52-53.

4. Maude B. Dozier, *Charles Kelsey Dozier of Japan: A Builder of Schools* (Nashville: Broadman Press, 1953), 11.

5. Lolita Hannah, "Rev. and Mrs. E. N. Walne, Senior Missionaries in Japan," *Home and Foreign Fields* 16 (April 1932): 14-15.

6. Confidential source.

7. Confidential source.

8. EW to LW, 3 February 1930, 16 February 1931.

9. Confidential source.

10. Parker, *Southern Baptist Mission in Japan*, 120.

11. EW, "God Kept His Promise," 17.

12. EW to LW, 10 April 1932.

13. EW to LW, 25 April 1932.
14. C. K. Dozier to T. B. Ray, 13 June 1932; Ray to Dozier, 2 July 1932, C. K. Dozier File, IMB Archives.
15. E. O. Mills to Charles A. Maddry, 8 November 1934, E. O. Mills File, SBHLA.
16. Japan mission meeting minutes, 26–28 April 1932, IMB Archives.
17. EW to LW, 13 July 1932.
18. EW to LW, 13 July 1932.
19. EW to LW, 13 July 1932.
20. EW to LW, 13 July 1932.
21. EW to LW, 13 July 1932.
22. Thomas T. Faucette to author, 27 September, 8 October 1993; Faucette, telephone conversation with author, 25 June 1995.
23. EW, Journal, 10; EW, Autobiography, 33.
24. EW to LW, 21 September 1932.
25. Maggie Bouldin to EW, 27 September 1932.
26. EW to LW, 21 September 1932.
27. Edwin B. Dozier, *A Golden Milestone in Japan* (Nashville: Broadman Press, 1940), 99.
28. C. K. Dozier, Diary, 18 July 1928, IMB Archives.
29. EW, Autobiography, 51.
30. John W. Krummel, ed., *A Biographical Dictionary of Methodist Missionaries in Japan: 1873–1993* (Tokyo: Kyo Bun Kwan, 1996), s.v. "Teague, Carolyn Mae."
31. EW to LW, 21 September 1932.
32. EW to LW, 5 December 1932.
33. EW to LW, 10 December 1933.

Chapter 14. Princess in the Palace

1. The figures are given in *Seinan Gakuin nanajūnen shi* (Seventy-year history of Seinan Gakuin) (Fukuoka: Seinan Gakuin, 1986), 1:334.
2. EW to LW, [1933].
3. EW, Autobiography, 72.
4. EW, Autobiography, 67.
5. EW to LW, [September 1933].
6. EW to LW, 28 March 1933.
7. EW, Autobiography, 47; Mary Ellen Dozier, letter to author, 29 November 1993.
8. Masaichi Ono in *Nishi Nihon bunka* (special issue, 2 April 1971), n.p.
9. EW to LW, 2 November 1929, quoting Elizabeth A. Allen, *Rock Me to Sleep.*
10. EW to LW, [1933?].
11. EW to [LW], [1933].
12. Mary Ellen Dozier, letter to author, 29 November 1993.
13. EW, Autobiography, 69.
14. Ibid., 69–70.
15. EW, Autobiography, 77.
16. EW, Journal, sec. 31.
17. E. O. Mills to Charles A. Maddry, 8 November 1934, E. O. Mills File, SBHLA.
18. EW, recorded message at SsBC, 7 July 1974, morning service.
19. EW, Autobiography, 84.
20. Ibid.

21. Arnold Kludas, *Great Passenger Ships of the World*, vol. 3: 1924–35, trans. Charles Hodges (Wellingborough, England: Patrick Stephens, 1976), 132.

22. EW, Autobiography, 85.

23. EW, Diary, 17 June, 10 October 1937, and undated entries.

24. EW, Diary, 17 June, 12 July 1938, 11 March 1939, passim.

25. EW, Autobiography, 88.

26. Ibid., 88–89.

27. EW, Diary, 15 June 1939.

28. EW to LW, 5 January 1941.

29. EW to LW, 2 March 1941.

30. EW to LW, 12 January 1941.

31. Krummel, *Biographical Dictionary of Methodist Missionaries*, s.v. "Bouldin, Margaret Alice."

32. EW to LW, 2 March 1941.

33. Rabbi Marvin Tokayer, "Japan as a Haven for Jewish Refugees in the Nazi Era," lecture summarized in *Bulletin of the Asiatic Society of Japan*, No. 4, April 1976.

15. Exile in the Homeland

1. *Spartanburg Herald*, 16 May 1941; *Journal and Carolina Spartan*, 16 May 1941.

2. Mrs. W. B. Montgomery to EW, 26 September 1941.

3. *Journal and Carolina Spartan*, 6 May 1941.

4. Racine, *Spartanburg County*, 40.

5. Lewis Drummond, *Miss Bertha: Woman of Revival* (Nashville: Broadman & Holman Publishers, 1996), 144.

6. Lizzie to EW, 12 March 1941.

7. Untitled notebook in EW Papers.

8. Tucker, *Guardians of the Great Commission*, 40.

9. EW, Autobiography, 94; EW's check stub, 27 October 1943, EW Papers.

10. Personal notes and four American Red Cross certificates, 1942–45, EW Papers.

11. *Spartanburg Journal*, 19 December 1944; *Japan Times*, 3 August 1988.

12. Milton T. Madden, "A Physical History of the Japanese Relocation Camp at Rivers, Arizona" (master's thesis, University of Arizona, 1969), 27–28, 43; *Kodansha Encyclopedia of Japan*, s.v. "Gila River Relocation Center"; Dorothy Swaine Thomas, *The Salvage: Japanese American Evacuation and Resettlement* (Berkeley: University of California Press, 1952; reprint 1975), 88; Samuel T. Caruso, "After Pearl Harbor: Arizona's Response to the Gila River Relocation Center," *Journal of Arizona History* 14 (1973): 340.

13. Cecile Lancaster, "My Life on the Mission Field, 1920–1960" (typescript, 1967), 113, IMB Archives.

14. Pauline Commack to EW, 27 May 1942; EW, Autobiography, 95.

15. Madden, "Physical History," 38–41; *A Year at Gila* (government document printed by the Records Office, Rivers, Arizona, 1943), n.p.

16. Madden, "Physical History," 42, 106–12;

17. Caruso, "After Pearl Harbor," 336–37.

18. EW, Autobiography, 95–96.

19. Butte Elementary School PTA Program, 8 May 1945, EW File, IMB Archives; Office for Emergency Management, Advice of Personnel Action, 12 July 1945, EW Papers; Anne Keeploeg Fisher, *Exile of a Race* (Seattle: F. and T. Publishers, 1965), 93; Madden, "Physical History," 95–96.

20. Dillon S. Myer, *Uprooted Americans: The Japanese Americans and the Wartime Relocation Authority during World War II* (Tucson: University of Arizona Press, 1971), 203; Madden, "Physical History," 155–57.

21. Office for Emergency Management, Advice of Personnel Action, 12 July 1945, EW Papers.

22. LW to EW, [August 1945]; Michi Weglyn, *Years of Infamy: The Untold Story of American Concentration Camps* (New York: William Morrow and Co., 1976), 89; Madden, "Physical History," 48.

23. Fumi Hayashi to EW, 28 September 1945.

24. EW, Autobiography, 97; Reiji Hoshizaki, letter to author, 25 April 1994; Clifford T. Nakadegawa to EW, 4 August 1945.

25. *Annual of the Southern Baptist Convention, 1945*, 264.

26. EW, Autobiography, 101.

27. Margaret Hamner Bomar to "Miss Sa," 7 April 1945, EW Papers.

28. "Memorial of Elizabeth Bomar Watkins," SsBC; *Spartanburg Herald*, 26 October 1961, 4 December 1945; Olin D. Johnston to Earle Watkins, 4 December 1945, Don and Judy West.

29. Earle Watkins to LW, 29 July [1945].

30. EW, Autobiography, 103.

31. LW to EW, 16 April 1922.

32. Maggie Bouldin to EW, 12 December 1945.

33. Maggie Bouldin to EW, 16 February 1946, 1 March 1946.

34. Elizabeth Bomar Watkins, will and probate records, Spartanburg County Courthouse.

35. Walt Hammer, *A Pictorial Walk Thru Ol' High Jackson. Limited Centennial Edition, Scottsboro, 1868–1968* (Collegedale, Tenn.: College Press, 1967), 102–8; Joyce M. Kennamer, "The Rise and Decline of Skyline Farms: Success or Failure?" (paper submitted to Department of Social Studies, Alabama A & M University, 1978; copy in Skyline High School library), 29.

36. *Minutes of the Tennessee River (Ala.) Missionary Baptist Association* (1946), 10–11; Bouldin, Autobiography, 106; membership records, SsBC.

37. Walter Tidwell, interview with author, Skyline, Ala., 5 December 1995; Roger H. Bedford, Sr. to Eljee Bentley, 13 September 1985, G. W. Bouldin File, Woman's Missionary Union, Birmingham.

38. EW teacher's license, EW Papers; minutes of Jackson County Board of Education, 29 November 1940.

39. EW, Autobiography, 105.

40. EW, Autobiography, 106–9; Lura Duke, telephone interview with author, 5 December 1995.

41. EW, Autobiography, 109.

Chapter 16. A Fresh, Jolting Start

1. M. T. Rankin to EW, 18 December 1945, EW File, IMB Archives; Chester W. Hepler to EW, 16 April 1946.

2. M. T. Rankin to EW, 29 May 1947, EW File, IMB Archives; Edwin Dozier, "A Supplementary Report to the Foreign Mission Board," 10 May 1947, 17.

3. M. T. Rankin to EW, 29 May 1947, EW File, IMB Archives.

4. M. T. Rankin to Rev. Louis H. Wright, 26 July 1948; EW, "My Dedication," 2.

5. International Child Evangelism Institute diploma, 27 August 1947, SsBC; EW, Autobiography, 110; notes in EW Papers.

6. EW, Autobiography, 110.

7. Invoice from Tiedemann & McMorran, San Francisco, 6 October 1947, EW File, IMB Archives.

8. Invoices from Broadway Furniture Mart, Burlingame, and Charles J. McDonald Co., San Mateo, 1947, EW File, IMB Archives.

9. EW to Maggie Bouldin, 23 October 1947.

10. EW to George and Maggie Bouldin, 29 October 1947, Bouldin Collection, SBHLA.

11. Cf. Mary Lou Grunigen, *Timothy Pietsch, God's Policeman* (Menlo Park, Calif., n.d.).

12. Melvin J. Bradshaw, "Samurai for Christ," *Commission* 36 (February 1973): 24–26; Luther Copeland, conversation with author, Greenville, S.C., 4 March 1994.

13. Lancaster, "My Life on the Mission Field," 139.

14. Edwin B. Dozier, "Report to the Foreign Mission Board of the Southern Baptist Convention," 12 December 1946, 3.

15. EW to George and Maggie Bouldin, 29 October 1947, Bouldin Collection.

16. EW, Autobiography, 115.

17. Yoshimi Inoue et al., eds., *Seinan Jo Gakuin rokujūnen no ayumi* (Sixty-year history of Seinan Jo Gakuin) (Kitakyūshū: Seinan Jo Gakuin, 1982), 113.

18. EW to George and Maggie Bouldin, 12 August 1947, Bouldin Collection.

19. EW to George and Maggie Bouldin, 21 August 1948, Bouldin Collection.

20. M. T. Rankin to EW, 3 June 1948.

21. EW to George and Maggie Bouldin, 21 August 1948, Bouldin Collection; cf. EW, Autobiography, 118–19.

22. EW, Autobiography, 118.

23. EW to Mrs. J. K. Drake, 11 August 1948; *Tobata Baputesuto Rinkōsha* (Tobata Baptist Good Will Center), leaflet, c. 1957; Naomi Schell obituary in *Commission* 9 (May 1946): 132.

24. Dozier, "Report to the Foreign Mission Board," 15; Dozier, "Supplementary Report," 11–12.

25. EW, "Naomi Schell Will Live Again," *Commission* 12 (January 1949): 10.

26. EW and Kiyoko Shirabe, "Japan W.M.U. Meets Again," *Royal Service* 42 (November 1948): 6–9; *Nihon Baputesuto Remmei shi (1889-1959)* (History of the Japan Baptist Convention [1889–1959]) (Tokyo: Nihon Baputesuto Remmei, 1959), 553.

27. EW to Maggie Bouldin, 1 November 1948, Bouldin Collection.

28. EW to Maggie Bouldin, 1 November 1948.

29. EW, "Tobata Baptist Good Will Center," *Commission* 13 (March 1950): 70.

30. Frances Talley, "Good Will Center—Japanese Style," *Royal Service* 44 (July 1949): 8.

31. Hiroko Tsuda in *Nishi Nihon bunka*.

32. EW, Autobiography, 121.

33. Kakiwa Inui, letter to author, 14 July 1994.

34. Ibid.

35. EW, "News from the Tobata Baptist Good Will Center," mimeographed, n.d., EW Papers.

36. Lenora Hudson, conversation with author, Hardin, Ky., 28 October 1994.

37. EW to Mrs. Drake, 1 June 1950.

38. *Annual of the Southern Baptist Convention, 1951,* 168.

39. EW, Autobiography, 159.

40. EW to B. J. Cauthen, 8 June 1950, EW File, IMB Archives.

41. EW to Cauthen.

42. Edwin Dozier to EW, 5 June 1951.

43. EW, Autobiography, 160.

44. Ibid.; Edwin Dozier to EW, 5 June 1951.

45. Ruth A. Tucker, *From Jerusalem to Irian Jaya: A Biographical History of Christian Missions* (Grand Rapids: Zondervan Publishing House, Academie Books, 1983), 331, 210–11, 267.

Chapter 17. Planting Flowers and Churches

1. EW, Autobiography, 161–62.

2. Mabel Francis with Gerald B. Smith, *One Shall Chase a Thousand* (Harrisburg: Christian Publications, 1968), 114–21; John W. Krummel, "Mabel R. Francis, 1880–1975," *Japan Christian Quarterly* 42 (Spring 1976): 121–22.

3. EW, Autobiography, 165.

4. *Kodansha Encyclopedia of Japan*, s.v. "Dōgo Hot Spring"; Japan National Tourist Association, comp., *The New Official Guide: Japan* (Tokyo: Japan Travel Bureau, 1975), 804–5.

5. Fusako Tsuda in *Nishi Nihon bunka*.

6. EW, *An Exiting Year: The Beginning of the First Church of the Japan Baptist Convention on the Island of Shikoku, June, 1952—July, 1953* (pamphlet, EW File, IMB Archives), 3–4.

7. EW, Autobiography, 208.

8. Eloise Lovelace, conversation with author, Hardin, Ky., 28 October 1994.

9. Mamoru Hirata to EW, 23 September 1966.

10. Bill Emanuel, conversation with author, Hardin, Ky., 28 October 1993.

11. The author was present at this meeting.

12. Mary Lou Emanuel, conversation with author, Hardin, Ky., 28 October 1994.

13. Marion Moorhead, "A Breakfast Never to Be Forgotten," typescript, 1994.

14. EW, medical report to Board, 10 July 1961, EW Papers.

15. Jean Falck, "Elizabeth Watkins' Wedding Dress," typescript, 23 June 1994.

16. EW, Autobiography, 168; Curtis Askew, telephone conversation with author, 16 July 1994.

17. EW, Autobiography, 171; Bill and Rebekah Sue Emanuel, *A Call Comes Ringing* (n.p., 1955), 41–42.

18. Toshio Odori, "Ai no fujin senkyōshi: Erizabesu Teeraa Watokinsu sensei" (Beloved missionary: Miss Elizabeth Taylor Watkins), *Yo no hikari* (Light of the world), August 1990, 14.

19. Frances Talley, letter to author, 2 August 1996.

20. Judy Dawn Barking, "A Missionary Case Study: Elizabeth Watkins" (paper written for a "Women in American History" class at the University of Utah, 1975), 7.

21. EW newsletter, 5 March 1955.

22. B. J. Cauthen to Frank Connely, 9 November 1954, Frank Connely File, SBHLA.

23. EW to B. J. Cauthen, 8 February 1955, EW File, IMB Archives.

24. Louisa Bomar Greene to Winston Crawley, 3 November 1955; B. J. Cauthen to Harriet B. Ellis; EW to B. J. Cauthen, 27 January 1955; B. J. Cauthen to EW, 31 January 1955; EW File, IMB Archives.

25. EW to B. J. Cauthen, 27 January 1955, EW File, IMB Archives.

26. Toshio Odori, telephone conversation with author, 19 November 1994.

27. Ichirō Odori, telephone conversation with author, 19 November 1994.

28. EW, Autobiography, 191–93.

29. Mary Walker, quoting EW, telephone conversation with author, 30 March 1996.

30. EW, "Bringing the Saviour to Shikoku," *Commission* 25 (August 1962): 17; Toshio Odori in Yawatahama Church, *Megumi ni ikasarete*, 14; Drummond, *Miss Bertha*, 204.

31. EW, Autobiography, 200.

32. EW, medical report to Board, 25 June 1962, EW Papers; Toshio Odori, "Ai no fujin senkyōshi," 14.

33. Cf. Frances Talley to EW, 16 December 1961.

34. EW, "Annual Report," 1963, EW File, IMB Archives.

35. Ibid.

36. Masatada Mitsukude in Yawatahama Church, *Megumi ni ikasarete*, 16.

37. *Baputesuto/Baptist*, no. 497 (December 1996), 8.

38. Yawatahama Church, *Megumi ni ikasarete*, 46.

39. Shigeru Nakamura in ibid., 22.

40. Parker, *Southern Baptist Mission in Japan*, 232; EW, Autobiography, 235; Matsuko (Mrs. Masatada) Mitsukude to EW, 23 October 1965; Yuriko Tamura to EW, 13 April 1966.

41. EW, "Annual Report," 1966; Bob Culpepper to EW, 31 May 1966; Les Watson to EW, 31 May 1966; EW newsletter, 25 October 1969.

42. EW to George and Maggie Bouldin, 19 August 1961, Bouldin Collection; Mrs. Chapman to EW, 1 February 1967; Mrs. R. Earl O'Keefe to EW, 23 May 1969; EW, "Annual Report," 1969, EW File, IMB Archives.

43. Everett L. Deane to W. H. Clapp, 11 February 1966, EW's copy.

44. "Changes in Land Prices and Building Costs," table in *Program Base Design* (Tokyo: Japan Mission, Foreign Mission Board, SBC, 1973), 167.

45. Masanobu Kubo in Yawatahama Church, *Megumi ni ikasarete*, 18.

46. Mary Neal Clarke, conversation with author, Hardin, Ky., 28 October 1994.

Chapter 18. Retirement on the Run

1. Parker, *Southern Baptist Mission in Japan*, 237.

2. Kōtarō Murakami in *Nishi Nihon bunka*.

3. Sugimoto et al., "Recommendation," *Nishi Nihon bunka*.

4. Framed scroll in SsBC.

5. EW, Autobiography, 249.

6. Ibid.

7. "JBM Family Newsletter," 2 June 1970, author's copy.

8. Grace Watkins to EW, 29 August 1970.

9. EW to Marion Moorhead, 1 January 1973, EW File, IMB Archives.

10. "Elizabeth Watkins Arrives, Japanese Work Begins," *Utah-Idaho Southern Baptist Witness*, 26 August 1970.

11. EW to Japan Mission, 13 November 1970, EW File, IMB Archives.

12. EW to Japan Mission, 13 November 1970.

13. EW to Japan Mission, 13 November 1970.

14. Lavoid Robertson, interview with author, Mars Hill, N.C., 13 September 1993.

15. EW, Autobiography, 267.

16. Munemitsu Shioyama, announcement in *Baputesuto* (Baptist), January 1983, 13.

17. Darwin Welsh to George Hays, 1 December 1976, EW File, IMB Archives; undated clipping from *Utah-Idaho Southern Baptist Witness*, 1972.

18. *Utah-Idaho Southern Baptist Witness*, 26 March 1975, 1.

19. EW to Herbert C. Garrett, Jr., 22 February 1974, SsBC.

20. Bea Conrad, interview with author, Sandy, Utah, 12 April 1993.

21. Audiotape recording of morning service, 7 July 1974, SsBC.

22. EW, Autobiography, 257.

23. *Utah-Idaho Southern Baptist Witness*, 28 June 1978, 2.

24. *Deseret News*, 6–7 May 1981.

25. EW to Grace Watkins, 27 October 1980, SsBC.

26. Anita Welsh, letter to author, 14 May 1993.

27. EW to Grace Watkins, 27 October 1980.

28. Toshio Odori, "Ai no fujin senkyōshi," 15.

29. *Jabas News*, October 1981; anonymous letter, 19 November 1981, SsBC; Bill and Rebekah Sue Emanuel to author, 22 April 1996.

30. Margaret and John Morrison, newsletter, Christmas 1981, SsBC.

31. Anita Lemke to Helen B. Davis, 22 March 1982, SsBC.

32. Melvin Bradshaw, letter to author, 8 July 1995.

33. EW certificate of death, file no. 18-3505, Utah Department of Health.

34. EW to Herbert Garrett, 22 November 1979, SsBC.

35. Gary L. Stevens, interoffice memo to George Hays, 6 May 1982, EW File, IMB Archives; Judy Robertson, interoffice memo to Gary Stevens, 21 September 1982, EW File, IMB Archives.

36. EW, "Last Will and Testament," copy in SsBC; DeLyle H. Condie to Beneficiaries, n.d., SsBC; Darwin and Anita Welsh, interview with author, Sandy, Utah, 20 June 1996; "Certificate of Jewelry Evaluation," 29 June 1995, Utah-Idaho Baptist Convention.

37. *Utah-Idaho Southern Baptist Witness*, November 1983, 4; *Baputesuto/Baptist*, no. 496 (November 1996), 9.

38. Audiotape recording of EW memorial service, 23 October 1983, SsBC.

Bibliography

Allen, Catherine B. *A Century to Celebrate: History of Woman's Missionary Union*. Birmingham: Woman's Missionary Union, 1987.

————. *The New Lottie Moon Story*. Nashville: Broadman Press, 1980.

Anderson, Frederick Jarrard. *Hearts and Hands: Gathering up the Years. An Illustrated History of Woman's Missionary Union of Virginia 1874–1988*. Richmond: Woman's Missionary Union of Virginia, 1990.

Announcement of Teachers College, School of Education, School of Practical Arts, 1926–1927.

Annual Bulletin, Alumnae Association of the Baptist W.M.U. Training School, 1922–30.

Annual Catalogue of the Officers, Teachers and Students of Converse College, 1925–28.

Annual of the Oklahoma Baptist General Convention, 1925–26.

Annual of the Southern Baptist Convention, 1925, 1945.

Ashburner, Charles E. "Norfolk's Modern Market." *American City* 28 (March 1923): 261–62.

Baptist Messenger (Oklahoma), 1925–26.

Baptist W.M.U. Training School. *Students' Hand-Book*. Louisville, 1919–22.

Baptist Woman's Missionary Union Training School for Christian Workers. Annual catalogue. Louisville, 1920–22.

Baputesuto (Baptist), 1983.

Baputesuto/Baptist, 1996.

Barking, Judy Dawn. "A Missionary Case Study: Elizabeth Watkins." Paper written for a Women in American History class at the University of Utah, 1975.

Barrett, David B., ed. *World Christian Encyclopedia*. Nairobi: Oxford University Press, 1982.

Bomar, Lizzie (Elizabeth) Journal. 1890–92. EW Papers.

Bouldin, George W. Autobiography. Typescript, [1960?]. George W. Bouldin Collection, SBHLA.

————. "An Effectual Door of Opportunity." *Home and Foreign Fields* 7 (January 1923): 20–21.

————. "Facing 1932 in Japan." *Home and Foreign Fields* 16 (January 1932): 11–12.

Bradshaw, Melvin J. "Samurai for Christ." *Commission* 36 (February 1973): 24–26.

Camden (S.C.) Chronicle, 1889.

Caruso, Samuel T. "After Pearl Harbor: Arizona's Response to the Gila River Relocation Center." *Journal of Arizona History* 14 (1973): 335–46.

Catalogue of Watauga Academy, Announcements, 1925–1926.

Cohn, David L. *The Good Old Days: A History of American Morals and Manners as seen through the Sears, Roebuck Catalogs 1905 to the Present*. New York: Simon and Schuster, 1940.

Commission, 1946.

Conversationalist, 1917–20. Judson College.

Crowe, Dan. *Old Butler and Watauga Academy*. N.p., 1983.

Daub, Edward E. "Death in the Family." *Japan Christian Quarterly* 27 (October 1961): 249–52.

Deseret News, 1981.

Dozier, Charles Kelsey. Diary, 1928. IMB Archives.

Dozier, Edwin B. *A Golden Milestone in Japan*. Nashville: Broadman Press, 1940.

———. "Lantern Lights of Baptist Work in South-western Japan." Fukuoka, 1935. Mimeographed.

———. "Report to the Foreign Mission Board of the Southern Baptist Convention." 12 December 1946. Typescript. IMB Archives.

———. "A Supplementary Report to the Foreign Mission Board." 10 May 1947. Typescript. IMB Archives.

Dozier, Maude B. *Charles Kelsey Dozier of Japan: A Builder of Schools*. Nashville: Broadman Press, 1953.

Dozier, Maude Burke, and Elizabeth Watkins. *Playmates in Japan*. Nashville: Broadman Press, 1940.

Drummond, Lewis. *Miss Bertha: Woman of Revival*. Nashville: Broadman & Holman Publishers, 1996.

Ebizawa Arimichi, ed., *Nihon Kirisutokyō rekishi daijiten* (Dictionary of Japanese Christian history). Tokyo: Kyo Bun Kwan, 1988.

Elizabethton (Tenn.) Star, 1983

Emanuel, Bill and Rebekah Sue. *A Call Comes Ringing*. N.p., 1955.

Estep, William R. *Whole Gospel—Whole World: The Foreign Mission Board of the Southern Baptist Convention: 1845–1995*. Nashville: Broadman & Holman, 1994.

Fiftieth Annual Meeting of the Woman's Missionary Union, Auxiliary to Virginia Portsmouth Baptist Association. Norfolk, 1950.

Fisher, Anne Keeploeg. *Exile of a Race*. Seattle: F. and T. Publishers, 1965.

Fleming, Ethel. *New York*. New York: Macmillan Co., 1929.

Frances, Mabel, with Gerald B. Smith. *One Shall Chase a Thousand*. Harrisburg: Christian Publications, 1968.

Frazer, Elizabeth. "Our Foreign Cities: New York." *Saturday Evening Post*, 16 June 1923.

Gaskin, J. M. *Baptist Women in Oklahoma*. Oklahoma City: Messenger Press, [1985].

Green, Mary Collins. *First Baptist Church, Spartanburg: A History 1839–1982*. Spartanburg: First Baptist Church, 1983.

Greeneville (Tenn.) Sun, 1992.

Grenfell, Wilfred. *Forty Years for Labrador*. Boston: Houghton Mifflin Co., 1932.

———. *A Labrador Doctor*. Boston: Houghton Mifflin Co., 1919.

Hamilton, Frances Dew, and Elizabeth Crabtree Wells. *Daughters of the Dream: Judson College, 1838–1988*. Marion, Ala., 1989.

Hammer, Walt. *A Pictorial Walk Thru Ol' High Jackson. Limited Centennial Edition, Scottsboro, 1868–1968*. Collegedale, Tenn.: College Press, 1967.

Hannah, Lolita. "Ai No So No, or 'Garden of Love,' in an Outcast Village." *Home and Foreign Fields* 16 (May 1932): 9–11.

———. "Rev. and Mrs. E. N. Walne, Senior Missionaries in Japan." *Home and Foreign Fields* 16 (April 1932): 14–15.

Hocking, William Ernest. *Re-thinking Missions: A Laymen's Inquiry after One Hundred Years*. New York: Harper & Brothers, 1932.

Holcomb, Brent Howard. *Marriage and Death Notices from Columbia, South Carolina, Newspapers, 1838-1860*. Columbia, 1988.

Home and Foreign Fields, 1923-36.

Hunt, Alma. *History of Woman's Missionary Union*. Nashville: Convention Press, 1964.

Inoue, Yoshimi, et al., eds. *Seinan Jo Gakuin rokujūnen no ayumi* (Sixty-year history of Seinan Jo Gakuin). Kitakyūshū: Seinan Jo Gakuin, 1982.

Jabas News, 1981.

Japan Christian Year Book, 1932-41.

Japan Mission Year Book, 1929-31.

Japan National Tourist Association, comp., *The New Official Guide: Japan*. Tokyo: Japan Travel Bureau, 1975.

Japan Times, 1970, 1988.

Jenkins, George. "The History of Watauga Academy of Butler, Tennessee." MA Ed thesis, Appalachian State Teachers College, 1950.

Johnson City (Tenn.) Press-Chronicle, 1983.

Journal and Carolina Spartan, 1941.

Judson College. *Bulletin, Judson College, Catalogue Number*. 1916-20.

Kennamer, John Robert, Sr. *History of Jackson County, Alabama*. 1935. Reprint, Scottsboro: Jackson County Historical Association, 1993.

Kennamer, Joyce M. "The Rise and Decline of Skyline Farms: Success or Failure?" Paper submitted to Department of Social Studies, Alabama A & M University, 1978.

Kibler, Lillian Adele. *The History of Converse College*. Spartanburg: Converse College, 1973.

Kludas, Arnold. *Great Passenger Ships of the World*. Vol. 3: 1924-35. Translated by Charles Hodges. Wellingborough, England: Patrick Stephens, 1976.

Kodansha Encyclopedia of Japan. 9 vols. Tokyo: Kodansha, 1983.

Krummel, John W., ed. *A Biographical Dictionary of Methodist Missionaries in Japan: 1873-1993*. Tokyo: Kyo Bun Kwan, 1996.

———. "Mabel R. Francis, 1880-1975." *Japan Christian Quarterly* 42 (spring 1976): 121-22.

Lancaster, Cecile. "My Life on the Mission Field, 1920-1960." Typescript, 1967. IMB Archives.

Landrum, J. B. O. *History of Spartanburg County*. Atlanta, 1900. Reprint; Spartanburg: Reprint Co., 1977.

Lawrence, Una Roberts. *Lottie Moon*. Nashville: Sunday School Board of the Southern Baptist Convention, 1927.

Lawton, Alice Stockton. "Biographical Sketch, Samuel Miller Lawton." Baptist Historical Collection, Furman University.

Lewis, Earl. *In Their Own Interests: Race, Class, and Power in Twentieth-Century Norfolk, Virginia*. Berkeley: University of California Press, 1991.

Literary Digest, 1922, 1930.

Littlejohn, Carrie U. *History of Carver School of Missions and Social Work*. Nashville: Broadman Press, 1958.

Lovelace, Julia Murfee. *A History of Siloam Baptist Church, Marion, Alabama*. N.p., 1943.

Loving, Robert S. *Double Destiny: The Story of Bristol, Tennessee-Virginia*. Bristol, 1955.

Madden, Milton T. "A Physical History of the Japanese Relocation Camp at Rivers, Arizona." Master's thesis, University of Arizona, 1969.

Marsden, George M. *Fundamentalism and American Culture: The Shaping of Twentieth-Century Evangelicalism 1870-1925.* New York: Oxford University Press, 1980.

Martin, William. *Prophet with Honor: The Billy Graham Story.* New York: William Morrow and Co., 1991.

McGavran, Donald. "My Pilgrimage in Mission." *International Bulletin of Missionary Research* 10 (1986): 53-58.

McMillan, Montague. *Limestone College: A History, 1845-1970.* Gaffney, S.C.: Limestone College, 1970.

Minutes, First Presbyterian Church, Abbeville, S.C.

Minutes of the Annual Session of the Watauga (Tenn.) Baptist Association, 1924-25.

Minutes of the Baptist State Convention of South Carolina, 1899, 1937, 1939.

Minutes of the Presbyterian churches at Camden, S.C., Hickory, N.C., and Marion, N.C. Presbyterian Historical Society, Montreat, N.C.

Minutes of the Tennessee River (Ala.) Missionary Baptist Association, 1946.

Mullins, Isla May. *House Beautiful.* Nashville: Sunday School Board of the Southern Baptist Convention, n.d.

Myer, Dillon S. *Uprooted Americans: The Japanese Americans and the Wartime Relocation Authority during World War II.* Tucson: University of Arizona Press, 1971.

Newport News Times-Herald, 1962.

"New York's Big Foreign Population." *Literary Digest* 73 (29 April 1922): 13.

New York Times, 1927.

Nihon Baputesuto Remmei shi (1889-1959) (History of the Japan Baptist Convention [1889-1959]). Tokyo: Nihon Baputesuto Remmei, 1959.

Ninomiya, Shigeaki. "An Inquiry Concerning the Origin, Development, and Present Situation of the *Eta* in Relation to the History of Social Classes in Japan." In *Transactions of the Asiatic Society of Japan.* 2d ser., vol. 10 (1933).

Nishi Nihon bunka (West Japan culture). Special issue, 2 April 1971.

Odori Toshio. "Ai no fujin senkyōshi: Erizabesu Teeraa Watokinsu sensei" (Beloved missionary: Miss Elizabeth Taylor Watkins). *Yo no hikari,* August 1990, 12-15.

O'Hara, J. W. *Signal Fires in the Mountains.* Nashville: Sunday School Board of the Southern Baptist Convention, 1929.

Parker, F. Calvin. *The Southern Baptist Mission in Japan, 1889-1989.* Lanham, Md.: University Press of America, 1991.

Pierson, George P., and Ida G. Pierson. *Forty Happy Years in Japan, 1888-1928.* New York: Fleming H. Revell Co., 1936.

Poe, Mrs. E. D. *From Strength to Strength: History of the Woman's Missionary Union of Virginia, 1874-1949.* Richmond: Woman's Missionary Union of Virginia, n.d.

Poole, Cyril F. and Robert H. Cuff, eds. *Encyclopedia of Newfoundland and Labrador.* 5 vols. St. John's, Newfoundland: Harry Cuff Publications, 1994.

Program Base Design. Tokyo: Japan Mission, Foreign Mission Board, SBC, 1973.

Racine, Philip N. *Spartanburg County: A Pictorial History.* Virginia Beach: Donning Co., 1980.

Report of Baptist Training School Settlement. N.d. Pamphlet.

Reynolds, Hannah. "Mrs. Maud Reynolds McLure: A Brief Biography." In *The New Building of Woman's Missionary Union Training School.* Pamphlet, c. 1940-41.

Roden, Donald. *Schooldays in Imperial Japan: A Study in the Culture of a Student Elite.* Berkeley: University of California Press, 1980.

Rompkey, Ronald. *Grenfell of Labrador: A Biography*. Toronto: University of Toronto Press, 1991.

Rucker, Margaret, and Elizabeth Watkins. "Case Work." *Royal Service* 15 (March 1921): 30.

Russell, James E. "Report of the dean for the academic year ending June 30, 1926." *School and Society* 24 (11 December 1926): 734–37.

St. John, Burton, ed. *North American Students and World Advance*. New York: Student Volunteer Movement for Foreign Missions, 1920.

Salt Lake Tribune, 1981.

Seidensticker, Edward. *Tokyo Rising: The City Since the Great Earthquake*. New York: Alfred A. Knopf, 1990.

Seinan Gakuin nanajūnen shi (Seventy-year history of Seinan Gakuin). 2 vols. Fukuoka: Seinan Gakuin, 1986.

Seinan News. Fukuoka, 1935.

Simms, Wm. Gilmore. *Sack and Destruction of the City of Columbia, S.C.*. Edited by A. S. Salley. Columbia, S.C., 1865; Oglethorpe Press, 1937.

South Carolina Historical Society. *South Carolina Genealogies*. Vol. 4. Spartanburg: Reprint Co., 1983.

Southside Baptist Church. *Golden Jubilee, 1908–1958*. Spartanburg, S.C. Pamphlet.

Sparkman, Mary A. *Through a Turnstile into Yesteryear*. Charleston, S.C., 1966.

Spartanburg Herald, 1909, 1941, 1945, 1961.

Spartanburg Journal, 1944.

Spartanburg Unit of the Writers' Program of the Work Projects Administration in the State of South Carolina. *A History of Spartanburg County*. Spartanburg, 1940; reprint, Spartanburg: Reprint Co., 1976.

Sugimoto, Katsuji, et al. "Recommendation of a Decoration for Miss Elizabeth Taylor Watkins." *Nishi Nihon bunka*, special issue, 2 April 1971.

Talley, Frances. "Good Will Center—Japanese Style." *Royal Service* 44 (July 1949): 8–9.

Taylor, Sandra C. *Advocate of Understanding: Sidney Gulick and the Search for Peace with Japan*. Kent, Ohio: Kent State University Press, 1984.

Thomas, Dorothy Swaine. *The Salvage: Japanese American Evacuation and Resettlement*. Berkeley: University of California Press, 1952. Reprint, 1975.

Tokayar, Rabbi Marvin. "Japan as a Haven for Jewish Refugees in the Nazi Era." Lecture summarized in *Bulletin of the Asiatic Society of Japan*, No. 4, April 1976.

"Training School." Column in *Royal Service*, 1920–22.

Tucker, Ruth A. *From Jerusalem to Irian Jaya: A Biographical History of Christian Missions*. Grand Rapids: Zondervan Publishing House, Academie Books, 1983.

———. *Guardians of the Great Commission: The Story of Women in Modern Missions*. Grand Rapids: Zondervan Publishing House, Academie Books, 1988.

Utah-Idaho Southern Baptist Witness, 1970–83.

Virginia Portsmouth Baptist Association, 134th Annual Session. 1924.

Walne, Florence. "Getting Acquainted with Japanese Baptists." *Home and Foreign Fields* 22 (July 1928): 195–98.

Watkins, Elizabeth Taylor. Autobiography. See below, "How God Kept His Promises to a Teenager."

———. "Bringing the Saviour to Shikoku." *Commission* 25 (August 1962): 198–203.

———. Correspondence. EW Papers.

———. Diary. 21 April 1938 to 31 December 1939. Lavoid Robertson, Taylorsville, Utah.

————. *An Exiting Year: The Beginning of the First Church of the Japan Baptist Convention on the Island of Shikoku, June, 1952–July, 1953.* Pamphlet. EW File, IMB Archives.

————. "God Kept His Promise to a Teen-Ager." Typescript, 19 pp. EW Papers.

————. "How God Kept His Promises to a Teenager: The Autobiography of Elizabeth Taylor Watkins." 1980. Typescript, 292 pp. IMB Archives.

————. Journal. 1934. Microfilm, 16 unnumbered pp. EW File, IMB Archives.

————. "My Dedication." Mimeographed, 4 pp. EW Papers.

————. "Naomi Schell Will Live Again." *Commission* 12 (January 1949): 10–11.

————. Testimony. 1 January 1930. Typescript, 5 pp. Bouldin Collection, SBHLA.

————. "Tobata Baptist Good Will Center." *Commission* 13 (March 1950): 70–72.

————. "True Kodak Pictures from the Settlement in Norfolk." *Royal Service* 18 (March 1924): 31–32.

Watkins, Elizabeth, and Kiyoko Shirabe. "Japan W.M.U. Meets Again." *Royal Service* 42 (November 1948): 6–9, 13.

Watkins, Lizzie (Elizabeth Bomar). Correspondence and papers. EW Papers.

Weglyn, Michi. *Years of Infamy: The Untold Story of American Concentration Camps.* New York: William Morrow and Co., 1976.

White, Blanche Sydnor. "Highlights in History of Woman's Missionary Union, Auxiliary to the Virginia-Portsmouth Baptist Association, 1885–1949." Typescript. 1966.

Withoft, Mabel Swartz. *Oak and Laurel: A Study of the Mountain Mission Schools of Southern Baptists.* Nashville: Sunday School Board, 1923.

Woman's Missionary Union of Virginia, *Thy Neighbor — Thyself.* N.d.

Wood, James E., Jr. "The Teaching of English as a Missionary Method." Th.D. dissertation, Southern Baptist Theological Seminary, 1957.

Yawatahama Baptist Church. *Megumi ni ikasarete: Dendō 30 shūnen kinen* (Sustained by grace: Thirty years of evangelism). Yawatahama, 1989.

A Year at Gila. Government document printed by the Records Office, Rivers, Ariz., 1943.

Index